BRAND REJUVENATION

By the same author

Le Marketing Interactif, Éditions d'Organisation, Paris (1996). Award medal from Académie des Sciences Commerciales 1997

Praximarket, Éditions Jean-Pierre de Monza, Paris (1996). Selection Adetem, Association Nationale du Marketing

Alerte Produit: Quand le produit doit être retiré de la vente ou rappelé…, Éditions d'Organisation, Paris (1998)

La Fidélisation Client, Éditions d'Organisation, Paris (1999)

strategiesdemarque.com, Éditions d'Organisation, Paris (2001)

Lifting de Marque, Éditions d'Organisation, Paris (2002), won the 2002 Prix de la marque honor from Prodimarques

Stratégie de Fidélisation, Éditions d'Organisation, Paris (2003)

L'Encyclopédie du Marketing, Éditions d'Organisation, Paris (2004)

In collaboration with Virginie Barbet, Pierre Breese, Nathalie Guichard, Caroline Lecoquière and Régine Van Heems:

Le Marketing Olfactif, LPM Publishing, Paris (1999)

BRAND REJUVENATION

How to protect, strengthen & add value to your brand to prevent it from ageing

Jean-Marc Lehu

London and Philadelphia

Ouvrage publie avec l'aide du Ministère français charge de la Culture – Centre National du Livre

Publisher's note

Every possible effort has been made to ensure that the information contained in this book is accurate at the time of going to press, and the publishers and author cannot accept responsibility for any errors or omissions, however caused. No responsibility for loss or damage occasioned to any person acting, or refraining from action, as a result of the material in this publication can be accepted by the editor, the publisher or the author.

First published in Great Britain and the United States in 2006 by Kogan Page Limited

120 Pentonville Road
London N1 9JN
United Kingdom
www.kogan-page.co.uk

525 South 4th Street, #241
Philadelphia PA 19147
USA

ISBN 0 7494 4566 1

British Library Cataloguing-in-Publication Data

A CIP record for this book is available from the British Library.

Library of Congress Cataloging-in-Publication Data

Lehu, Jean-Marc.
Brand rejuvenation : how to protect, stregthen and add value to your brand to prevent it from ageing / Jean-Marc Lehu.
p. cm.
Includes bibliographical references and index.
ISBN 0-7494-4566-1
1. Product management. 2. Product life cycle. I. Title.
HF5415.15.L445 2006
658.5'6—dc22
2005033280

Translated by Anglia Translations Ltd, Huntingdon, United Kingdom
Typeset by Digital Publishing Solutions
Printed and bound in Great Britain by Cambrian Printers Ltd, Aberystwyth, Wales

Contents

Acknowledgements

Although just one name appears on the cover, this book owes a considerable debt of gratitude to a number of people. Firstly, my thanks go to all the CEOs, general managers, marketing directors, brand managers and advertisers around the world who generously gave of their valuable time to share with me their experience in brand management. Our discussions yielded many clear and useful insights, which appear as original examples in this book: from these interviews was born the idea of a brand scorecard to identify and evaluate the symptoms of a brand ageing problem. This scorecard is now in use within many of these enterprises. Secondly, I would like to acknowledge the help and advice of Pauline Goodwin, Publishing Director, Business & Management at Kogan Page who always believed in the book, all the more so since the Kogan Page reference list already contains a number of authoritative studies of brand management. Her constant encouragement of the authors she manages should not go unrecorded. Many thanks also to Annie Knight, Development Editor at Kogan Page and my super-efficient direct contact who combined good humour (highly desirable) with day-to-day professionalism (absolutely essential); and to Suzanne Mursell, Project Editor, who succeeded to collect every piece of the puzzle always with true cheerfulness and real efficiency. Marlyne Tolentino, Foreign Rights Manager at Groupe Eyrolles in Paris, made a contribution above and beyond the call of duty to bring this adaptation of the previous French edition before a new public. And finally, sincere thanks to the team at Anglia Translations Ltd for the wonderful translation job they have done and for some helpful suggestions that enrich the content. It only remains for me to express the hope that readers will enjoy the result of this team work, and that it will help them to better manage the most valuable asset an enterprise possesses, its brand.

Foreword

The quest for eternal youth is all-consuming. Women's formidable ally in fighting time is the global beauty industry, a US $160 billion business. The beauty industry grows by roughly 7 per cent a year and encompasses everything from skincare through make-up and fragrance to plastic surgery and diet pills.

The huge amount that women invest in beauty products does not include their time nor the money they spend in other sectors to fend off the effects of time. We take cold showers because they are said to increase circulation and boost hair shine. We trade in our cotton pillow cases for silk or satin to reduce the traction on our delicate facial skin. We endure yoga classes in stifling heat to speed up calorie burning and detoxification. And in extreme cases, we subject ourselves to painful surgical procedures that either add or take away curves based on our own and society's perception of youth.

As those of us in the beauty business know, ageing is a complex process influenced by many internal and external factors. Consequently, preserving youth and beauty certainly requires use of multiple remedies.

Ageing does not only apply to women, or other living creatures for that matter. Everything around us is subject to it. Though the fountain of youth is yet to be found, in many cases proper upkeep can slow the ravages of time. The 12th-century Notre Dame de Paris is as beautiful now as it was 800 years ago, thanks to constant renovations and maintenance that have kept it relevant to so many generations since its creation, while less cared for churches have turned to dust. In *Brand Rejuvenation,* Jean-marc Lehu theorizes that brands are similarly not immune to ageing. He recommends that brand managers actively nurture their brands to keep them young, healthy, and relevant to their target markets.

Brand Rejuvenation begins by carefully exploring the causes and various aspects of brand ageing. If the brand has already started to show signs of ageing, in any of the myriad of potential problem areas, the book proposes a methodology to evaluate the most appropriate next steps, based on the underlying causes of this deterioration. It challenges the brand managers to look honestly at the brand image; not only to uncover and address the emerging 'wrinkles' but also to recognize the positive features that can be built upon and reinforced. A 'wrinkle' should be covered up, while a prominent 'cheekbone' should be highlighted. Once an evaluation of the brand is complete, Lehu proposes specific rejuvenation strategies for each part of the brand such as product offering, target marketing or advertising. These strategies may include retiring previously popular methods of addressing each of these areas.

While tackling today's 'wrinkles', brand managers must also anticipate that their brands' strong points may need a boost in the future. Instead of waiting for a brand element to become obsolete, Lehu encourages brand managers to take pre-emptive measures to fight off any signs of ageing and to avoid quick fixes that can weaken the brand's long term equity.

Brand Rejuvenation does not claim that there is an affirmative solution to brand ageing. Instead, the book provides brand managers with practical tools and lessons from a wide range of real-life case studies that can aid their brands to evolve healthily, successfully and gracefully. The proposed tools go beyond the typical marketing textbook frameworks. Lehu puts forward anti-ageing potions to keep brands young. His approach, just like the perfect moisturizing cream, not only smoothes existing wrinkles but contains the antioxidants and vitamins that help prevent future damage.

Raffaella Pierson
Director of Global Marketing, Jo Malone
A Division of The Estée Lauder Companies

To those marketing knights in shining armour
who have vowed to defend the brand ceaselessly
against the perfidious and constant attacks of time

Introduction

'The wrinkles of age leave their mark more on the spirit than on the face...'
Michel Eyquem, Lord of Montaigne
Essais, III, 2; 1580

Growing old is no fun!

A drastic reduction in the number of neurones, withering of the skin, weakening of the joints, loss of pigment in the hair on the head and around the rest of the body, general slowing down of vital functions, impaired senses, changes in DNA, decrease in the number of glia cells, reduction in the number of synaptic connections in the frontal lobes, atrophy of the brain, reduced physical and associated intellectual performance – to name but a few of the more traditional and common phenomena. It should also be borne in mind that most of these start to occur after the age of 30, or even earlier in some 'privileged' cases! There is no doubt that no changes in life are less welcome than ageing. It is thus easy to understand, as Carrigan (1999) observed, why the elderly are so rarely used in advertising, considering the extent to which the negative stereotypes with which they are associated are perceived as dangerous by agencies and advertisers. This belief is reinforced by another, which holds that the elderly do not enjoy watching commercials depicting people of their own age.

Invisible, ungraspable and disquieting, time has now become a major preoccupation in Western society. Everything possible is now being devised, designed and done to control and conserve some or all of this most precious of commodities. The fact is that in most cases, although humans have been able to adapt to most aspects of their environment and it is plain that much scientific progress has occurred throughout human history – which is nonetheless a tiny fraction of the life span of the entire universe – they still remain powerless when confronted with time itself. There are those who quickly resign themselves to the inevitable. However, it is a fact of human nature to persist in all manner of quests with even greater perspicacity and obstinacy in cases where these tasks would at first glance appear impossible!

In this way, time has become both a sworn enemy and the subject of pure envy; and its mastery, a priceless holy grail. And yet, utterly frustratingly – even though science has allowed us to define, evaluate and (in some cases) even model time – to this day it still remains outside human control. Consider how many stories and extraordinary events the mastery of time has produced thus far. With the help of globalization, it now plays a considerable role in fuelling the already fierce competition between the market's many brands. Some commentators, such as Naomi Klein (2000), have made intricate attempts at slaying the modern giants that own the largest brands, the power of which exceeds that of many nations on our planet. It is true that the final 20 years of the last century saw large groups divesting themselves of their portfolios for reasons of rationalization, and the subsequent growth of the chosen few brands that survived this process. However, although the remaining brands found themselves strengthened as a result, they were then faced with competitors that had also, logically, grown more powerful at the same time.

In its purest – not to say most reductionist – sense, marketing is the branch of management science that aims to meet the consumers' expectations by discovering their needs and modifying the product accordingly. Because time has become a key preoccupation for most consumers, marketing has been obliged to take it seriously as a factor. It can thus fairly be said that all good marketers must, in addition to their many other skills, also become… masters of time! Perhaps it seems paradoxical that such a preoccupation should become increasingly important in an ageing society. However, this is precisely one of the keys to the problem. Western society is indeed ageing; but at the same time it continues to innovate, create and progress. Regardless of what remarkable progress may be made in extending average human life expectancy, it will always seem far too little for us to discover, understand and enjoy the innumerable opportunities for life offered by the modern consumer society.

The phenomenon derives from multiple sources which, when juxtaposed and combined, are gradually inciting *homo sapiens* to rebellion. Without attempting to rank these in any particular order of priority, they include technological progress, medical advances, an explosion in the volume of information of all kinds, reduced working hours, transportation improvements, etc. Each of these components has provided either the impetus, the justification or simply the ability for man to slow down an ageing process characterized by its speed. At present, Europe spends 42 million euros per year on research into ageing. Indeed, from a human point of view, our species is increasingly of the opinion that Nature has made a gross error in allowing us to age at all, and especially at such a rate! Thus convinced that, semi-godlike, they wield more and more scientific power every day, humans are now doing everything possible to correct this 'error'. The first generation to sound the alarm and set themselves to this extraordinary task were the 'baby boomers', who started to reach retirement age at around the turn of this century. Born at the same time as the modern consumer society, they were the first to lay claim, directly or indirectly, to an increased amount of time to give themselves longer to enjoy their consumption. Elated at the ever-increasing rate of scientific progress that continued to offer more and more, and increasingly well informed as to the innumerable opportunities available in both professional and private life, they were the first to become gradually aware that the length of a single human life span on Earth was clearly much too short a time in which to try, sample and take in everything on offer. It was therefore time to mount an attack on the great hourglass of time in order to slow down or even halt the flow of its grains of sand.

However, this observation did not on its own provide any miraculous solution to the problem. Worse still, it gradually transpired that the problem was in fact insoluble from the consumer's point of view. But what humans cannot achieve through their own efforts, they tend to look to others for – and therefore, having understood that the great hourglass could not be turned on its head, and well aware that they were equally unable to divert its grains from their course, our *homo economicus* thus decided to set the entire environment to work compensating for this relative powerlessness. Each grain of sand in this environment therefore needed to be thought out, designed and constructed in such a way as to retard the inevitable flow by the maximum possible amount. A warning was sounded to brands pursuing this objective: the time had come to prepare for battle! Death to old brands that had failed to rejuvenate themselves and had been used, abused, chewed up and spat out by time!

One-fifth incoherency, one-fifth wisdom, three-fifths deception

This new requirement of the modern consumer can be partly explained by the reasons given above, but it clearly has not yet penetrated the genetic code of the species; and many individuals have sought to outdo one another in childishness, deception or plain and simple lies in an attempt to outsmart, conceal or disrupt the inevitable march of time. The battle against the great hourglass is not just a question of the number of years. However – and herein lies the irony of the situation – not all attempts at manipulating time are aimed in the same direction. From childhood to pre-adolescent years, it is amusing to note that the phenomenon is generally entirely absent. As the first mathematical notions gradually start to form in a child's mind, rounded ages are often favoured, and the most recent birthday is used as the simplest point of reference to remember. This is, however, only one piece of the full picture; and indeed, one from which children may desire to distance themselves as far as possible because of its associations with the immaturity and unimportance accompanying their status as children they do not wish to appear to be. Who has never asked one such pre-adolescent his or her age and received the reply, 'I'm ten years and eleven months old!', 'I'm nearly ten!', or even, 'Next week, I'll be over nine years old!'? It is rare, later in life, to find any such semantico-mathematical 'clarifications' in the speech of an adult – especially when that adult is a senior citizen whose acknowledged wisdom will lead him or her to venture no more information than is based on actual fact or perhaps, on the contents of the individual's own memory.

However, as soon as our warrior against time reaches the 'tweenager' stage, the phenomenon switches. At that point, our pre-adolescents are 'between two ages', as indeed the word 'tweenager' implies. They still enjoy their status as children and the blissful comfort of their mother's safe arms, but they are increasingly attracted to those adolescents who seem to have the entire world at their feet. They envy these adolescents' image and status, and therefore unhesitatingly attempt to bring about the artificial acceleration of the sand that appears to flow through the hourglass, and unflinchingly add a few months – or even years – to their own chronological age. This phenomenon continues, for a number of reasons, in more or less embryonic form throughout the teenage years and into the 'young adult' stage. Being older is sometimes advantageous when attempting to circumvent legal restrictions. It suggests maturity, and therefore often increased respect from older generations. It confers a basic status of pseudo-respectability in the eyes of one's peers.

After that, gradually, the aspirations of these 'gluttons of time' become blurred, disappear and reverse their direction. The time of ignorance is over, and the first signs of deception start to appear. Famed as they are for paying attention at an earlier age to their appearances in particular – and their figures in general – sections of the female population are naturally the first to break with their previous pattern of behaviour. However, what often appeared to be a game while the individual was still an adolescent now becomes a genuine preoccupation; a daily struggle; a never-ending war. Time now becomes an enemy to fight by any means necessary. And this is to say nothing of the modern consumer products intended to help this dogged combatant in her fight. In what may be a subconscious throwback to the early years, young adults will generally state their exact chronological age when asked, and without any reluctance, even if they are only a few days away from adding on an extra unit of time. But what will they say when it comes to crossing the divide into an extra decade? Every day, every minute that separates them from this 'great leap' in time should be valued for its role in delaying the inevitable. In the later stages of this aversion to time, our warriors against ageing will be all too willing to subtract a few units from their chronological age, as they are entirely convinced that youth is everything, and that age represents the disappearance of that everything.

Guiot (1996), a French specialist in this phenomenon who has done a great deal of work in the area of subjective age and its effects on marketing, points out that this subjective age is a manifestation of a genuine process of defending one's own self-image. Whether the precise issue at stake is the voice, the face or the body – each of which is a traditional key used to identify the age of an individual – each becomes the focal point of total attention in an attempt to manipulate the signals given out, allowing a more favourable interpretation by others. 'Deception' is practised all the more naturally in cases where it is supported by the firm conviction that our 'real' age is not our chronological age, but rather the cognitive age we feel within ourselves. Using a variety of scientific approaches, a number of researchers have confirmed the fact that many individuals feel younger than their chronological age. As long ago as 1980, Barak and Schiffman noted the non-chronological nature of this cognitive age. In 1987, Barak advanced the notion of cognitive age as a more precise measurement of the identity concept of age. In 1991, Stephens studied the value of the cognitive age concept in advertising. In 1999, Carrigan and Szmigin argued scientifically for the greater use of older characters in advertising in order to reflect the products' target market more accurately.

The rejection of age is characterized by many aspects, the meaning of which must be taken into consideration as much as possible by marketing so that it can continue to adapt to the characteristics of the surrounding environment. In particular, we should note the innumerable references, both conscious and subconscious, to childhood that persist in many adults' environments. These might include a refrigerator covered in toys (magnets, stickers, drawings, etc): souvenirs from a more or less distant past in which the warmth of childhood intermingled with blissful ignorance. And the presence of children in the home in question is not sufficient to explain why such a phenomenon is tolerated, because it's not a matter of tolerance, but merely an adult's wish. Also included are the teddy bears and other friendly soft toys that hark back to peaceful, comfortable and safe times and have become welcome additions to the everyday personal and/or professional environment. Another example is the computer workstation and/or the office desk covered in toys, gadgets and other reminders of childhood, adolescence or simply a past now remembered with a tender, pleasant nostalgia. It can also be the choice of sporting and/or leisure activities that are generally associated with younger audiences, but provoke positive memories and experiences from the past. Not all video game consoles are being bought by teenagers, after all! No doubt a number of socio-psychologists will be quick to sum up all of those behaviours in a single word: regression. However, let us be clear about our interpretation. If this is indeed regression, it is not only temporary, but also entirely controlled in such a way as to derive the maximum benefit, yet without becoming its captive. Because it provides well-being, a more pleasant and often more flattering self-image, and a quality of life more closely reflecting the aspirations of a youthful, dynamic identity, let us leave the analysts to their analyses while we instead try to understand the main marketing impact this will have on the brand.

The fight against ageing: a major and pressing need

Not all sectors are affected in the same way. However, almost paradoxically, the markets where the rate of concentration has increased are those in which awareness has become strongest. A novice observer may be forgiven for thinking that since the economic concentration of recent years has led to the disappearance of a number of brands, the situation would have eased off. This is far from the case: the brand has become a factor of total importance, given the consumers' increasing difficulty in distinguishing the characteristics that could potentially allow them to spot the difference between the products of one brand and those of its direct competitor.

Although advertising budgets are generally on the rise – despite the fact that reductions in advertisers' brand portfolios may have suggested the opposite – this is in part because strategic reallocations have now been settled. From this point, it becomes essential that the brand be given its own individual identity capable of creating value if it is to contribute to the clear differentiation of the brand's product range from those of its competitors. Docters (1999) confirmed the power of the brand as a component used by consumers when evaluating the goods and services on offer and making their choice. Brand managers are well aware of this fact, and the most canny of them exploit this lever of differentiation. At 3M, the Scotch and Highland brands convey different meanings to the consumer, even though they are both basically adhesive tape. The actual quality of the product is even set at different levels in order to provide practical justification for the difference between the two brands.

Amid this competitive nightmare, the brand should naturally be not only remembered by the consumer, but – more importantly – appreciated, and if possible, to the detriment of its competitors. The problem, however, is that consumers are now better informed and more demanding; and today, more than ever before, they are thirsty for life and even for eternity. The old age that naturally awaits at the symbolic opposite end of this life is not only rejected, but also avoided in all its manifestations. Its stereotyped symbolism associated with low productivity, senility, illness, slowing down, sluggish vital systems (and sometimes even ugliness) give it a negative image overall, while it is clear that the brand must also remain young if it is to win the custom of the largest possible number of consumers in search of an environment commensurate with their own aspirations.

The brand's potential power is phenomenal; and yet it remains intangible. The aim of this book will therefore be to assist the brand manager in protecting, strengthening and adding value to this intangible in its battle against the ravages of time. This is why we will study the causes of ageing in part 1; then, in part 2, their remedies, detailing the various factors of rejuvenation. In the third and final part, we will construct the foundation of a preventative strategy for combating ageing: not for the purpose of rejuvenating the brand, but instead to prevent it from ageing in the first place.

PART 1

The causes of ageing

'The talent of most men is limited by a flaw which becomes increasingly evident with age'

Charles-Augustin Sainte-Beuve

Les Causeries du Lundi, 1851–1862

The UK drinks brand Robinsons (Britvic) completed its rejuvenation in the early 2000s. Several years later, Jaguar was considering a similar strategy, while the French footwear brand DD and the UK firm Calgon were also initiating rejuvenation remedies. Oil of Olay, the anti-ageing cream, had established a strategy focusing on the promise of product satisfaction. Each of these very different brands constituted a specific case requiring a specific approach tailored to the precise reasons for the ageing of that particular brand.

Niall FitzGerald, Unilever PLC Chairman and CEO, at the annual congress of the Marketing Society in London, 18 June 2001

How can arrogance kill a brand? In plain and simple terms, you forget the fundamental truth about brands: ultimately, they belong to the consumer. You delude yourself that brands belong to brand managers and you forget what initially helped to make the brand useful for the consumer. You lose sight of the fact that a brand derives its value from its consumers [...] Inevitably, brands begin to lose their coherency – and there is nothing more harmful to a brand than a lack of coherency. Consumers like brands for their consistency. Remove this consistency and the consumers disappear in droves [...] What is important is to remain connected to the consumers as individuals, then to innovate to fulfil their developing needs, rather than to confuse them with unnecessary complexity. We want our brands to be favourites – to be in first place in the market, sometimes second, but not fifth, sixth or seventh – because strong brands can innovate and develop with their consumers.

Certain brands are doomed to die because their target market has totally disappeared, because their products have totally disappeared, because their profits have fallen too far or simply because they have been allowed to age and the cost of rejuvenating them does not seem viable compared to the cost of introducing a replacement brand. In 1999, NEC, the computer giant, decided to kill off the Packard-Bell brand on the US market, resulting in the laying-off of 88 per cent of its workforce, despite the fact that the brand had been the leading PC manufacturer in the eyes of the general public in the United States. The brand's margins had become far too slim for it to continue on the international stage.

Unilever's brand portfolio reduction programme at the turn of the century is a model of good management: the Anglo-Dutch group implemented the Brand Focus plan, which amounted to a strategic decision to cut 1,600 brands down to just 400. Only the strongest 'core brands' – or more specifically, those with the greatest potential – were kept. In its dairy ice-cream business, for example, two of its products, Titan and Magnum, were in direct competition with each other. Once the equity of the two brands had been strategically analysed, only Magnum would be retained. This allowed Magnum to be systematically strengthened: its range was extended and its brand status was enhanced to that of an umbrella brand.

While it is true that we have witnessed a veritable explosion in media channels, the average cost of communication has significantly increased. Combine this with the traditional overcrowding in the more profitable media, and it is not hard to appreciate the difficulties facing a group managing many brands. In simple terms, if the company wishes to maintain a sufficiently large market share to safeguard its image and protect its brands from ageing, it has to focus its investments on its strong brands, as its global budget can certainly not be stretched infinitely. To take one example, Unilever reduced its French washing powder portfolio from seven to four (Skip, Omo, Persil and Coral), which meant that the budget for each of the remaining core brands could be almost doubled.

The example of Cadbury

In 1996, the UK company Cadbury audited one of its chocolate selection box brands: Biarritz. The brand had clearly aged. However, a detailed brand study showed that over and above Biarritz's other problems, the selection box sector itself was in decline, as most of the target customers were over 65 years old and they were not being replaced. Furthermore, the competition, and in particular Nestlé's Black Magic, was very much alive. An attempt to relaunch the product had been made in 1995, but it was not successful as merchandising gaps provided too little shelf space to allow the brand to fight its corner. Cadbury therefore opted to abandon this brand and launch a new one, Darkness, which would then claim a new, more profitable positioning. Interestingly enough, 10 years earlier, Biarritz had been in a similar situation, effectively replacing the Bournville Selection brand, which had been accused of the same premature ageing.

Some people have the misfortune to be affected by Werner's syndrome, commonly known as premature ageing. But although it is to be hoped that one day, in the not too distant future, geneticists will manage to rectify the mutation of the gene located on chromosome 8 that is responsible for this syndrome, brand managers already have a considerable advantage when a similar affliction hits their brand; there is no reason why the brand's genetics must inevitably be affected by ageing. Therefore, when brand managers decide to analyse the causes of a brand's ageing, it is mainly with the intention of saving it with the utmost urgency. And if they have such intentions, it is primarily because they are aware of the potential that the brand represents and, therefore, the return on investment that can be expected at the end of the rejuvenation process. The preliminary stage of the brand audit must therefore clearly and objectively identify whether there is sufficient justification for saving the brand from its dismal fate. In other words, is it profitable to rejuvenate the brand? To find out, it is sufficient to establish the proposed strategic targets that are to be assigned to the brand once the rejuvenation process has been completed. If, after a meticulous market study including an analysis of the environment, the competition and, in certain cases, a complementary study of the motivations of the elements making up the target market, it appears that the brand has a future provided that an *ad hoc* marketing strategy can enable it to survive and re-establish its reputation and its image; then at that point, a detailed audit of the causes of its ageing becomes essential. The objective is then to be able to address in an appropriate way the problems that brand ageing has generated. Not only is the audit essential in determining the appropriate rejuvenation programme, but it must also be able to identify all possible causes of ageing; because if a single one of them were to be omitted from the rejuvenation factors the company is ready to deploy, the entire rejuvenating strategy would be potentially jeopardized.

Although examples of brand rejuvenation have proliferated since the end of the last century and are today a major issue, it is not because brands have been ageing more quickly at the dawn of the new century, or as the result of any paranormal phenomena. The reality is much simpler. Many companies have allowed their brands to age, failing to recognize that such ageing would by its very nature change their capital and eventually harm their business. This is not to suggest that these companies did not do any marketing. Most of them observed the behaviour of the market in an attempt to understand consumers' explicit or potential expectations. They could then adapt and react in the most appropriate fashion. Using this traditional approach, some obtained excellent results, even becoming leaders in their sector. Unfortunately, what the 'Teach yourself marketing' manual omitted to mention is that the work was a long way from being complete. The simple fact is that the work is never done. This led to proposed new models and new approaches that are more interactive and better suited to an environment that would from now on be changing in real time.

The OCARA principle (Observation – Comprehension – Adaptation – Reaction – Attention) features two advantages designed to protect the brand manager from the ever-present danger of falling asleep on the job. First, it is based on total interactivity, where the objective is not just to listen to the consumer, but to establish a genuinely two-way dialogue. In other words, there has to be feedback from the consumer in order to constantly nurture the brand strategy and to allow it to react more effectively. But considering that consumers themselves have radically changed over the last few years, creating meaningful dialogue is no easy matter. In an interview with *Stratégies* magazine in 2001, Jean-Pierre Villaret, co-CEO of the Devarrieuxvillaret agency, stated: 'Consumers are informed, critical and mature, but we continue to speak to them as if they were children. One-way communication continues to be the norm. The task of challenging the edifice that marketing has constructed over the past seventy years through the mass media, given today's educated and critical population, poses huge difficulties.' The second advantage is that it links the reaction phase – the last phase in the model used before OCARA – to an attention phase, allowing the brand to remain vigilant in the face of the changes that its environment (competitors, consumers, legislation, suppliers, social trends, cultural movements, etc) will be sure to experience. That is why this attention phase itself is naturally linked to a new observation phase. The latter link has the advantage of relaunching the whole process and thus allows the brand not only to be more reactive but also, gradually, more proactive.

We can therefore conclude that, today, if any brand is falling prey to the problem of ageing, it is to a large extent because it has not been vigilant about itself, and has not provided itself with the means of perceiving the effects of ageing. We can only hope that once rejuvenated, it will, as a result, become more aware of the risks and will consider pursuing a preventative anti-ageing strategy. But we are not there yet. Most brands will need to compile a balance sheet showing the ravages of time – and draw up an audit of their perceived age.

Alain Rouchaud, Brands Director, Piper & Charles Heidsieck Champagnes

Clearly, a brand has a life span that will inevitably cause it to age, and probably to die. It is just a question of time.

The youth of a brand derives from the quality of its 'genes' which are expressed in its positioning and rootedness in a composite set of key values where the consumer is found. Strong brands, which do not age or are no longer ageing, are those whose native soil consists of creativity, mixed with continuity/patience/coherency and nurtured by the appropriate financial resources.

To ensure good management of the brand equity, we need to be extremely specific about the positioning and distinctive features of the brand which enable it to be differentiated from its principal competitors. Similarly, we need to check regularly with our target audience that this positioning is relevant, and develop it whilst retaining the same fundamental principles: to be uncompromising at all times in ensuring the coherency of all marketing tools connected with positioning, whilst fostering creativity to encourage its development (advertising, promotion, public relations). We must invest sufficient quantities; but more importantly, we must invest regularly over time. We must be determined and patient.

Miracles are rare: only a valid strategy wins in the long term.

1 Auditing an 'old' brand

With regard to human ageing, research laboratories working on skin ageing for the major cosmetic groups worldwide are now focusing on two main areas. Firstly, there is chronological ageing: ageing naturally linked to the age of the individual's skin. Secondly, there is photo-ageing: ageing linked to UVA rays and considered as premature ageing. In the first case, the challenge thrown down to the gods of time seems slightly presumptuous, although considerable progress has already been made in the area of life expectancy and the quality of that life. For example, it is estimated that over half of girls born today in developed countries such as the UK or France are likely to live to over 100 years old. In the second case, the fight against oxidative stress on cells is already underway. Whether using enzymes, vitamins, hormones or other agents, it is possible to fight (with varying degrees of effectiveness) against the ravages of ageing. In fact, the problem lies in a range of factors that, taken together, cause people to age, some more rapidly than others. Although biological factors are naturally the most commonly cited, we should not overlook others: psychological, social, genetic, geographical and, in the widest sense of the term, environmental factors.

It is easy to make an analogy with the brand, with respect to not only age itself (and therefore ageing), but also the factors contributing to whether a brand ages, and if so how quickly. When we talk about brand ageing, there are several traps to be avoided to ensure that a correct analysis is reached. The first of these involves taking only the chronological age of the brand into account. In such a case, at the whim of the analyst's own judgment, a brand can be deemed 'old' after it has existed for a certain number of years; the precise period varies according to the sectors, the benchmarks and the criteria used. It is therefore preferable to talk about the 'vintage' brand. Not because 'old' is necessarily pejorative; but given that it is the condition that we wish to tackle, a distinction needs to be made with the 'vintage' qualifier, which may actually be a strong asset. As can be seen from the numerous examples below, certain brands whose chronological age can be counted in decades, or even centuries, seem much younger than other brands that have been officially launched over the past 10 years.

The second classic error is to cling to the brand's reputation rather than its image. Admittedly, a brand that progressively sinks into oblivion would also logically be affected by the ageing of its image. Yet except for very young brands that are not correctly managed, the progress towards oblivion is a slow one. On the other hand, the brand image can appear to be ageing, even though its reputation remains the same or even continues to grow. As younger brands managed to innovate and bounce back on the fashion trampoline, Playtex observed in the 1990s that its brand was ageing, although brand awareness studies still indicated that the brand was in a leading position. Playtex then reacted by developing more 'trendy' products.

The third trap it is easy to fall into relates to the target market of the brand and/or of its products. Is a brand for the elderly an old brand? In other words, should a brand whose consumers are exclusively elderly be classified as an old brand? Not necessarily. Admittedly, a brand will naturally be classified automatically as young if its target is mainly made up of individuals belonging to the younger segments of the population. However, the brand should not be systematically and stereotypically classified with respect to the age of its target. Pokemon is of course a much more recent brand than Burberry. The chronological age of the former is of a different order of magnitude to that of the latter, and the Pokemon target is mainly much younger than Burberry's. However, if, today, one of the two brands had to be classified as 'young' and the other as 'old', or if we simply needed to establish the younger of the two, Burberry would now undoubtedly appear to be younger than Pokemon. Pokemon was the victim of the classic phenomenon of premature ageing because of a short-lived fashion. Burberry has had the advantage of benefiting from an effective rejuvenation remedy that has granted it a new youthfulness.

Some people still rely on the simple stock market value of a brand or of the group that owns it as the basis for assessing the brand. The information may well have been relevant in certain cases in the past, but it would be a major error to make do with this today. It is common knowledge that certain quoted companies are greatly undervalued, while others are clearly overvalued. The reason is 'simple'. While some analysts still use only the financial results of a company, coupled with their most objective opinions, to establish whether shares should be sold, held or bought, there are many others who no longer believe this is adequate. Nowadays, share price has more to do with the life of the company and its global image than simply with its economic performance. Crisis management case studies are full of 'healthy' companies that have looked on as their share price crashed, not as the result of any possible financial impact of the crisis as such, but simply as a result of their bad management of the human, ecological and/or ethical aspects of the crisis. And yet, in today's world of interconnected stock markets, day traders and the constantly increasing speed at which information is circulated, such managerial errors may have a far-reaching impact on the share price, literally moments after they occur.

Aware of this phenomenon and the associated difficulty of evaluating the brand in economic terms, some market research companies regularly publish estimates. Numerous and varied criteria can be used, which explains the sometimes considerable variations from one institute to another and the completely different rankings produced. This also applies to this type of ranking based on brand image. It is therefore understandable that it is very difficult to ensure an objective approach if we are too closely attached to economic value. Even though some countries such as Australia or the UK already require such a brand evaluation to appear on the balance sheet of the owner companies, defining the criteria and the calculation methods is not without great difficulties if the aim is to obtain an objective value. As Paul B W Miller, Professor of Accounting at the University of Colorado and a specialist in this area, points out, the major problem lies in the fact that at any given moment the valuation is likely to appeal to subjective judgments, which are alien to standard accountancy models.

However, a joint study produced by the Interbrand market research company (a subsidiary of Omnicom Inc.), the Citigroup financial group and *BusinessWeek* magazine is now undeniably the benchmark in this field, thanks to the reliability of the methodology employed and to the criteria used (see the excerpt in Table 1.1). Not only is it based on the economic results of the specific brands; but, in addition, it combines this information with market research studies and surveys carried out by professional analysts. Finally, the third phase involves an Interbrand model using seven variables applied to determine the potential risk to the future earnings of the brand. However, such an approach requires access to information, which has excluded companies such as Mars: its legendary secretiveness has prevented its inclusion. We should conclude by emphasizing the fact that the study examined the brands and not the companies themselves, which makes the ranking even more interesting for our purposes.

Table 1.1 Analysis of the economic value of the top brands in 2005

Rank	Brand	Origin	2005 value in US $ billion	2005 vs 2004 fluctuation
1	COCA-COLA	United States	67.52	↗
2	MICROSOFT	United States	59.94	↘
3	IBM	United States	53.37	↘
4	GE	United States	46.99	↗
5	INTEL	United States	35.58	↗
6	NOKIA	Finland	26.45	↗
7	DISNEY	United States	26.44	↘
8	McDONALD'S	United States	26.01	↗
9	TOYOTA	Japan	24.83	↗
10	MARLBORO	United States	21.18	↘

Based on: Berner, R and Kiley, D (with Mara Der Hovanesian in New York, Ian Rowley in Tokyo, Michael Arndt in Chicago), *Global Brands* (2005); bureau reports and *BusinessWeek*. *BusinessWeek*, European edition, September 5/12, 2005, pp 54–61.

Keller believes that the brand audit has to be 'a comprehensive examination of the health of a brand in terms of its sources of brand equity from the perspective of the firm and the consumer' (1998: 373). Thus, the canned fruit brand Del Monte discovered that the reason for the brand's decline throughout the 1970s and 1980s was that its target was ageing and was not being replaced by a younger segment. Younger consumers began to see the products as being old-fashioned and not 'natural' enough (having too many additives and preservatives) as the fashion for natural and organic products became more established. As regards the audit under discussion, the economic value of the brand is therefore just one indicator among many. However, from the point of view of, say, its competitive position, the decline or rise of this value is very interesting. In fact, taking into account the extremely meticulous analysis by Interbrand/Citigroup/*BusinessWeek*, and despite the authors' insistence that this information has no official value, we consider that a brand judged by this calculation to have a declining economic value is a brand showing clear signs of ageing. The case of Ford, which experienced a number of quality problems, as well as the Firestone tyres crisis, reveals the impact the brand's global image has on its value. The authors of the study reveal that with a market valuation of US$30.09 billion, the car manufacturer was down US$6.3 billion in 2001 on the previous year (value of the brand was US$13.5 billion in 2005).

The standard life cycle of a brand

A brand ages in the eyes of its customers and/or its consumers because it loses its appeal, its relevance and, usually, all or part of its identity. Admittedly, this is simply the result of the phenomenon of ageing, and we will be attempting to isolate the causes in order to propose a suitable remedy. Yet if we believe that a brand can age, we can apply the concept of a life cycle to the brand (see Figure 1.1), which is similar to the one commonly applied by marketers to their products. Thus, the brand is born at the end of a natural process – for example when the name of the founder gradually becomes to be considered as a brand; or initiated – for example when a specialist firm is asked to come up with a name. Then, in the best case, its reputation and image grow. Once the high point of these two indicators is reached, it enters the mature stage. Then, at the end of this stage a period of decline begins, during which the brand starts to become obsolete and ages either gradually or dramatically. Finally, the brand dies. Its products and/or services disappear and its name is only remembered by people nostalgically looking back at the past or when something triggers a flash in the depths of a person's mind. It is for this reason that brand life cycle management is essential.

The analogy may be an interesting one in that, at the end of the audit, the position of the brand on its own life curve can be identified. But one thing should be clarified. It is a standard life cycle, which means that the possible different phases are included, but that, in any case, these phases are neither inevitable nor anchored in an inevitable sequence. On the other hand, since it is a standard life cycle, it has the merit of attracting the attention of the brand manager to the logical sequence that the brand may follow if care is taken. The only real reason for taking this cycle into consideration is therefore to draw the manager's attention to the possible dramatic end facing the brand. In other words, and in short, the brand's

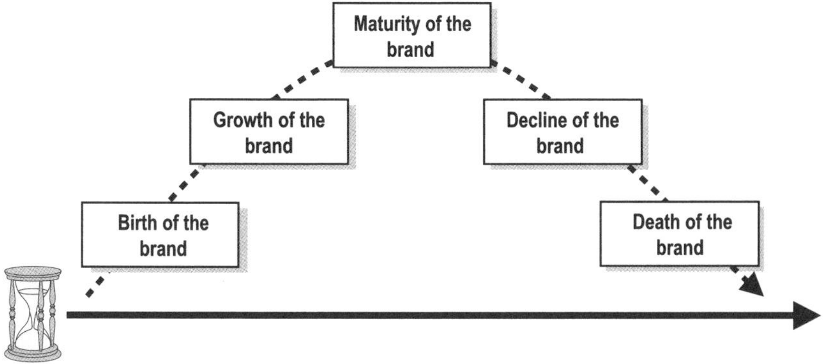

Figure 1.1 Standard brand life cycle

death is never a certainty, but it is always a possibility. Admittedly, some people will say that a brand can always be resuscitated, and this is often true. But the approach is far from being straightforward. It can be costly under certain circumstances, or even as expensive as simply launching a new product. And however much enthusiasm is put into it, the outcome is never guaranteed. The audit may produce a recommendation involving four possible approaches as shown in Figure 1.2.

First, sufficient potential will have been detected in the brand to justify implementing a rejuvenation plan. Assuming that the audit has been carried out with due diligence, this is logically the most common conclusion reached; after all, it is unusual for the brand to be completely lifeless at the point when a decision is taken to carry out an audit. The plan begins with a brand awareness study to establish whether people still remember the brand and if so, under what circumstances. Georges Lewi, the brand specialist at the Bec Institute, estimates that if the assisted residual awareness is 10 per cent 'we can say that the brand is not totally dead; and at over 30 per cent, it is truly alive.' When, in 1999, Swatch Group bought the Breguet watch brand from the investment fund company Investcorp, and then proceeded to invest 20 million Swiss francs to increase Breguet's production capacities in Switzerland, it was not done merely to add yet another prestigious name to Nicolas Hayek's collection (Rado, Longines, Blancpain,

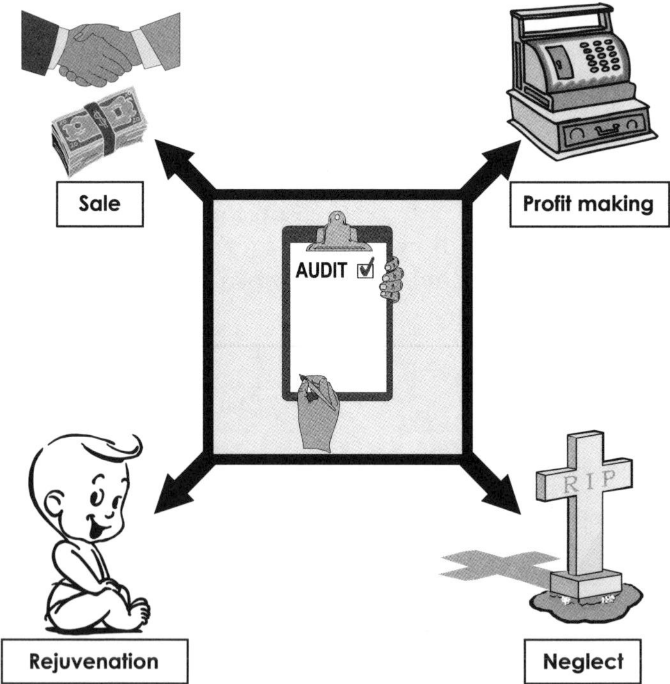

Figure 1.2 Possible approaches to the audit

Glashütte Original, Jacquet-Droz, Omega, Tissot, Pierre Balmain, CK Watch, Hamilton, Certina, Flik Flak, Swatch, etc), or because of the company's long list of illustrious clients ranging from Napoléon to Churchill and including Pushkin and Stendhal, but purely and simply because the Swiss watchmaker's perspicacity had enabled him to recognize the potential of this renowned brand. In the case of some brands that have truly become ghosts, the rejuvenation plan may be long and difficult, but it is all a question of assessing the investment compared to the expected final return. In the United States, Altoids sweets have already effectively benefited from such a rejuvenation plan and the confectionery brand has now been completely relaunched. De Chernatony and McDonald (1994) stress that when a brand is being rejuvenated, a manager can justify taking such a step as it is often less expensive to revitalize an established brand than it is to develop and launch a new one. However, the authors go on to point out that it is desirable in such a case to protect the essential values. This point of view is shared by Aaker (1991) who also stresses that a launch results in far more failures than successes.

Florence Courtheoux Gratiot, Marketing Director, Shiseido France

Just like any living being or inanimate object, a brand ages. The many reasons for this include:

- the products' unsuitability in light of changing consumer trends;
- the excessive rigidity of the brand image 'content', which no longer meets consumers' evolving expectations;
- failure to anticipate fading products;
- lack of consideration for the evolution of the contents of the brand image...

The Shiseido brand is young because its contents are in line with the main market trends:

- non-ostentatious luxury;
- refined sophistication;
- going beyond the basic fact of how the product is used;
- well-being and relaxation (constantly important in Japan).

First and foremost, the brand has to have a content in order to express its uniqueness, its differences and its anchor points. Today in the world

> of luxury goods, the brands that 'suffer' the most are those with little or no brand content. In order to survive, this brand equity has to be based on constant values if it is to overcome the vicissitudes of fashion and short-lived sociological fads. It has to be able to put down European and international roots to guarantee its development. It has to be able to communicate its differences and its uniqueness to its public in order to create a sense of 'belonging'.

The second approach is when it is observed that it is too late and/or that the effects of ageing are too significant to be able to be defined, offset and overcome, and the brand is left to its sad fate, which usually occurs in a very short period of time. General Motors recently reached this conclusion for one of its divisions, Oldsmobile, and announced that the brand would be progressively phased out. The case is interesting as it is partly the key result of an audit that was not totally objective. Halfway through the 1990s, Oldsmobile managers convinced GM directors that the brand could be rejuvenated and tens of millions of dollars were subsequently invested. Admittedly, the new models did succeed in reducing the average age of Oldsmobile drivers from 60 to 51 years, but the brand's overall image did not fundamentally improve as a result. Worse still, the main problem of this inadequately researched attempt at rejuvenation was that it was carried out at the expense of another of the group's brands, Saturn, which, during the 1990s, was only assigned a bare minimum share of GM investment. At the end of the 1990s, a more objective assessment was made: Oldsmobile was left to its fate and Saturn was resuscitated. Between these two opposite approaches, there are two possible intermediary recommendations that constitute the third and fourth approaches.

The third approach is where the company is prompted to sell the brand. This solution is interesting insofar as it allows several sources of income to be generated which could be used to develop other brands. However, the vendor is exposed to the risk that the purchaser is more competent and manages to breathe new life into the brand, which then starts to compete with the brands of its former owner. Petrole Hahn, sold by Procter & Gamble in 1998 to Eugène Perma laboratories, now competes against some of the products of the Cincinnati-based group.

Hence the fourth and last approach, in which the brand resources are exploited to the bitter end, without any precautions being taken to protect its capital. This triggers a process focused on achieving total profitability, which is nearly always performed at a brisk pace, the result of which is naturally to accelerate the ageing of the brand still further. The process logically ends with the death of the brand, once its last resources have been totally exhausted. In this last scenario, the consequence is not an inevitable outcome but a strategic decision.

The potential danger threatening the brand is comparable to the one that threatens a product, in which an analysis of the life cycle demonstrates a period of decline. Entry into that period of decline is, above all, the signal indicating one or more strategic errors that have brought the product and/or brand to this stage; or worse, one or more cases of neglect with the same outcome. Two main scenarios are then possible. The first consists in reacting to and, at the end of the audit, understanding the reasons for this ageing in order to determine which *ad hoc* marketing factors will be used in the rejuvenation remedy. This approach will undoubtedly result in money having to be spent; or, more precisely, invested in rejuvenating the brand. And that is unfortunately the nub of the problem. The second option, which is the most common one to be proposed following the assessment, is to reduce the amount spent on marketing a product or a brand whose scheduled death has already been announced. Once again, the death of a brand is never scheduled – unless this is built in intentionally from the start, for example for a specific event, and/or a product with a life span of a set period. Gadgets are a typical example of this. However, it is not the authors' intention that the reader should sign up for some form of 'WWbF' ('Worldwide Life Brand Foundation') to save all the brands in the market from a certain death – not all brands are worth saving. The audit has to provide the information to establish fairly which brands should live and which should be left to their fate.

Perception and evaluation criteria in brand ageing

It is a very tall order to manage a brand with such devotion that it becomes a 'passion brand' that consumers constantly care about. Edwards and Day (2005) explain the importance of a rigorous analysis in the early stages to provide an understanding of the consumer and the environment on the one hand (external factors) and, on the other hand, the value system of the brand and its ability to act (internal factors). With respect to ageing, two given brands perceived as old are not necessarily so for the same reasons. It is therefore important in the first instance to list the different criteria allowing the ageing of the brand to be perceived. This is because the brand image is often a very complex combination of highly disparate components, and scrupulous auditing is needed. Rolls-Royce enjoys an upmarket image of indisputable quality. However, Bentley outsells Rolls-Royce by three cars to one. The brand audit is therefore fundamental in explaining why this is so. Andrew warns in Hart and Murphy (1998): 'A brand cannot be revitalized without a clear understanding of the soul of the brand, the DNA of the brand and the values that it represents [...] The original revitalization of a brand therefore requires the creation of a new 'reality' with which its consumers can identify and which they will be able to share.'

Numerous interviews with professionals who manage one or more brands reveal that the criteria can be divided into three groups: offer, target and communication (see Table 1.2). The first can generally be based on secondary external and/or internal sources of information. The second usually require the help of primary external sources of information; in other words, specific studies that allow the phenomenon of perceived ageing of the analysed brand to be accurately assessed. For the analyst, one of the traps to avoid is that of making do with the explanation of the first variable to be identified. It is unusual for the ageing of a brand to be attributable to any one single cause. In other words, it is rare for ageing to alter only one criterion. An audit is conducted in order to identify the raft of criteria that have been affected by time, otherwise the risk is that the efforts at rejuvenation will only focus on a single criterion, while others, equally relevant, could continue to damage the image of the brand.

It is fundamentally important to recognize and monitor these systems and the signs that herald ageing if an idea is to be obtained of the value of the brand image and the capital it represents in the eyes and minds of its targeted consumers. Activating these indicators will allow the brand to deal with the problem of ageing sooner. Great importance should be given to these indicators, as we know that, in more than 9 out of 10 cases, the ageing of the image of a brand heralds a decline in its business activity. All of these criteria contribute to the image of the brand. Although quantitative marketing studies are often preferred, for reasons of precise data or even for the fact that they reveal a more direct correlation between the variables, it is important not to overlook a qualitative approach which may provide valuable information. The brand image is based on a complex matrix of data, in terms of positioning, mental imagery, emotional imagination, status, values, behaviour, etc, that will progressively build up the nature of the brand identity. Qualitative studies can be of great help here in sounding out the brand's consumers, in order to define their perception of the brand compared to the value of each aspect of its image. When differences are noted, the marketer will need to use *ad hoc* information sources to check whether this difference has a positive effect on the brand image, or whether it is instead a negative factor contributing to its ageing.

Table 1.2 Brand scorecard to identify and evaluate the symptoms of a brand ageing problem

Criteria	Symptoms and advance signs of ageing	Brand perception indexes				Manager's strategic decision
		Danger index	Easiness index	Cost index	Time index	
Offer	• Research & development					
	➢ Slow down of new product launches					
	➢ Outdated technological generation					
	➢ Multiple successive strategic moves in a short period of time					
	➢ Absence of marketing validated innovations					
	➢ Decreasing number of registered patents					
	➢ Obsolete development/ production process (upon standard criteria)					
	➢ Unperceived new uses of the product category					
	➢ Product disappearing from consumers' ranking or other contests					
	• Product characteristics					
	➢ Current old promise of satisfaction					
	➢ Non-conformity to technological standards					
	➢ Growing number of products sold under licence without control					
	➢ Multiplication of not-relevant line extensions					

Table 1.2 continued

Criteria	Symptoms and advance signs of ageing	Brand perception indexes				Manager's strategic decision
		Danger index	Easiness index	Cost index	Time index	
	➢ Obsolete materials compared to category competitors' products					
	➢ Out-of-fashion colours					
	➢ Outdated design and/or product ergonomics not adapted					
	• Competitive position					
	➢ Constant lowering market share					
	➢ Altered positioning and/or new positioning attempts without effect					
	➢ New entrants growing power on the market					
	➢ Objective quality index lower compared to competitors'					
	➢ Reducing of the economic valuation of the brand					
	➢ Crawling increasing level of stocks					
	➢ Decreasing share price					
	• Consumers					
Target	➢ Studies show a tendency for non-renewal of the target					
	➢ Studies show mean age of the target is getting older					
	➢ Loyalty is evaporating regularly					

Table 1.2 continued

Criteria	Symptoms and advance signs of ageing	Brand perception indexes				Manager's strategic decision
		Danger index	Easiness index	Cost index	Time index	
	➢ Number of contacts (letters, calls, claims, etc) are reducing					
	➢ New products are repeatedly not welcomed					
	• Customers					
	➢ Declining listing rate from usual distribution partners					
	➢ Brand is becoming listed essentially by downmarket shops					
	➢ Deteriorated merchandising plan in volume (reduced orders)					
	➢ Deteriorated merchandising plan in value (penalizing localization)					
	➢ Ageing sales force (back and front office)					
	• Opinion leaders					
	➢ Obvious and natural opinion leaders are difficult to identify					
	➢ Opinion leaders begin to ignore the brand/the products					
	➢ Increasing difficulties to find an in vogue opinion leader/ spokesperson for the brand					

Table 1.2 continued

Criteria	Symptoms and advance signs of ageing	Brand perception indexes				Manager's strategic decision
		Danger index	Easiness index	Cost index	Time index	
Communication	• Advertising					
	➢ Constant decreasing investments in communication					
	➢ Permanently declining brand share of voice					
	➢ Media plan appearing not to be relevant to reach the target					
	➢ Global creativity contested and/or jeered					
	➢ Communication style appearing to be out-of-date					
	➢ Fashion effects sized by competitors but ignored by the brand					
	➢ Brand spokesperson(s) – if any – irrelevant and/or out of date					
	➢ Studies show that the packaging is perceived as old fashioned					
	➢ Frequent changes of ad agency and advertising copy strategy					
	➢ Ad campaigns not (well) ranked in ad festivals and contests					
	• Brand corporate communication					
	➢ Vague and doubtful categorization of the brand					

Table 1.2 continued

Criteria	Symptoms and advance signs of ageing	Brand perception indexes				Manager's strategic decision
		Danger index	Easiness index	Cost index	Time index	
	➢ Increasingly negative perception with the chronological brand age					
	➢ Completely different communication positioning than competitors					
	➢ Brand name does not appear anymore in the evoked set					
	➢ Decreasing opportunities for television and/or movie brand placements					
	• Public relations					
	➢ Declining press coverage about brand events or product launches					
	➢ More systematic association with aged or disappeared brands					
	➢ Parasite communication or bad jokes about the brand/the products					
	➢ Overreactions to a crisis situation compared to similar competitor's case					

KEY

Danger index: Indicates the potential danger of the symptom – (1) no danger/not relevant (2) dangerous (3) requires immediate action

Easiness index: Indicates how easy the problem is to solve – (1) easy to solve (2) difficult to solve (3) could be very difficult to solve

Cost index: Indicates the potential cost of solving the problem – (1) not expensive (2) expensive (3) could be very expensive

Time index: Indicates the possible time needed to solve the problem – (1) short time (2) medium time (3) long time

Manager's strategic decision: Indicates the resulting choice – (1) ignore (2) monitor (3) take corrective action

Note: A fuller version is presented in: Lehu, J-M (2004): Back to Life! *Journal of Marketing Communications*, **10** (2), June.

Deploying ad hoc information systems to detect the first signs of ageing

Some people can be critical of an audit because of its cost. Information is not a cost, it is an investment. A lack of information can become an extravagant or even fatal cost. If you do not know that your brand is ageing, you may have to urgently implement a plan to save it via a rejuvenation remedy or an ill-considered relaunch. In the most frustrating of cases, this audit will take place too late, and the most logical and most economical conclusion will be to abandon the brand to its fate. The most common outcome is a promotional campaign to run down stocks, which will reduce the company's income even further. What a way to go!

The main opportunity now available to the company involves technology. Information storage capacity (data warehousing) is now almost limitless. The techniques and means to manage and analyse (data mining) this information are increasingly sophisticated, and provide results that are not only more refined but also more reliable. In more picturesque terms, the crystal ball exists and a mass of information can already be gleaned by gazing into it, although interpreting it might be something of a black art. The most forward thinking of these companies therefore already have information systems in near real time, allowing them to react more effectively to the hazards of the environment, as well as to changes in demand, without losing sight of the main strategic process. In the present case, it means that the brand audit procedure should not be considered as an isolated operation, possibly to be repeated at a frequency specified by the brand manager. Right from the very start, the audit must be part of the ongoing monitoring process, allowing the symptoms of brand ageing to be detected, even anticipated, as soon as they start to be noticeable. In the past, such an approach was unwieldy and costly. Nowadays, information technologies can be used to schedule constant monitoring of this kind – automatically in most cases – and, moreover, at a cost that, thanks to automation, is usually absurdly low.

Even though it has been around for some time now, there is great interest in the use of such monitoring software today, as it is now possible to program it with masses of information from indicators that could not previously have been linked together for technological reasons. Such information can of course come from studying demand (analysis of client portfolios, growth in turnover, average basket, type of purchases, frequency, etc), but also feedback from the sales force (comparative studies, type of product stocking, changes to merchandising, customer comments, etc), reports from customer service (nature and frequency of calls, changes, etc), together with external environmental data such as reports on how trends are evolving, reports on the economic situation in the various locations of the company, studies on related sectors, forecasts from different market research companies, consumer analyses for the product category, reports on competitors' product innovation, advertising, packaging.

The considerable progress made in the field of artificial intelligence over recent years has resulted in systems not only capable of running various models at the same time, to get the best out of each one, but also to enrich the heart of the system with their own results (including their failures) on an ongoing basis. Obviously, the objective is not only to reduce the physical volume of the mass of information, but also to avoid simply accumulating tables and graphs and to dispense with the voluminous piles of reports – and of course the painstaking task of producing an overall analysis of this information. The ageing process of a brand often results from a complex alchemy of many variables. Taken independently, these variables do not raise any suspicions as to the metamorphosis underway in the brand. However, when intelligently correlated against each other, these variables can contribute to a coherent and significant information chain that will necessarily force the brand manager into immediate action. Errors will always occur; but obviously, they are becoming increasingly difficult to forgive!

Fast-moving consumer goods (FMCG): possible traps that can be avoided

Logically, brand ageing is no respecter of sector or company. However, from an auditing point of view, a distinction needs to be made between fast-moving consumer goods (FMCG) and less common consumer goods, in order to alert the brand manager.

We can now refer to one of the many classifications by product lines that are available to the marketer. The system defined by Melvin T Copeland and used by the American Marketing Association since 1948 is a simple one that suits our purposes well. This classification is divided into three main categories of goods which include the vast majority of all consumer goods. Firstly, there are convenience goods; in other words, commodity goods with generally low prices. These goods include the vast majority of FMCG that are frequently bought and where the period of time for selecting and considering the purchase is short. Secondly, there are speciality goods. The purchase of these goods is often decided on the basis of their own image and/or the image they are likely to confer on the purchaser. They are generally relatively expensive and are often highly sought after by the consumer. Copeland places the third category, shopping goods, between these two categories. The purchase of these goods is generally preceded by a period of reflection and comparison of product features.

Apart from their prices and their intrinsic features, the average consumer cycle makes a clear distinction between these various types of products right through the classification. In the case of FMCG, the cycle is naturally short, while the cycle for speciality goods is generally long. Consequently, an analogy can be made with the people with whom we rub shoulders in everyday life. The symptoms of ageing are always a great deal less noticeable in the case of a person we see each day, or even live with, compared with a person that we meet, say, every 5 or 10 years. The phenomenon is an entirely understandable one, since for an ageing process to be noticeable in its early stages, points of reference are needed that allow comparisons to be made. This is clearly very difficult in the case of a person we see every day, as these references become blurred by such regular contact. However, in the case of a person who does not live nearby, and where contact is sporadic, the reference points are then anchored in the memory at a specific time (t). The comparison with the same elements recorded at instant t + n is fuelled by the distance in time, making the comparison easier or simply possible. The potential ageing factors are therefore more easily discernible.

For similar reasons, there is therefore a tendency to assert that the most representative examples of ageing are those affecting speciality goods, or even certain shopping goods, rather than convenience goods that are permanently present in our consumer world. Furthermore, FMCG, which are often less well developed and less sophisticated, can be less susceptible to ageing than, say, fashion garments, or even a car or a computer. Even though these explanations can often be verified, the analysis does not always present itself in quite these terms. It is a fact of life that all manufactured goods, together with the majority of services, are exposed to ageing factors. In the same way, it is accepted that the rate and extent of this ageing can vary from one product to another. Believing that a product is immune to ageing because it is in almost permanent contact with the consumer would be an error, the consequences of which may be difficult and costly to manage after the fact. Admittedly, the permanent nature of this contact often makes ageing less perceptible to the consumer, but time continues to do its devilish work. It means that the perception of this ageing could raise a problem for a brand audit; consumers could, in all good faith, answer that they are not aware that the brand has aged. In reality, with time being equal, what distinguishes most products across the entire classification scale is the suddenness with which the impression of ageing appears.

In the case of speciality goods, ageing factors are often easier to perceive as they are usually more gradual. In the case of FMCG, this may simply be the launch of a new product by the competition that suddenly shows consumers that the brand they have been buying so far, out of habit or by conviction, is totally out of date and it is high time for them to change. The consequences of this statement are important but simple. They encourage the FMCG brands to be much more vigilant in clearly perceiving ageing factors, even though the consumers are still not aware of them. This does not mean that speciality goods brands have more time to react, but simply that, for them, the appearance of the ageing signs is often more obvious – and far more progressive. This applies even more to certain brands belonging to this category and influenced by fashion. Although often said to be cyclic, fashion is perpetually evolving, and the more talented brands in this area have now identified the signs that herald such change. The flexibility currently provided by information systems and modern production techniques then allows the most perceptive of them to adapt and evolve while permanently defying the attacks of time.

Luxury products: an increasingly frequent potential pitfall

What is a luxury brand? It is difficult to state in clear and objective terms. However, it is certainly a brand renowned for the quality of its product; a brand where an above-average price is applied to the product, which helps to position the goods. Its production is limited for reasons of quality and exclusivity; this is highlighted by a top-of-the-range positioning and message. The key word in the above statement is 'exclusivity'. For the reasons stated above, a luxury brand is a brand whose products are rare and mostly beyond the easy financial reach of the average consumer. Nowadays, companies in this sector are obliged to turn in a profit, as far as possible, or else risk upsetting their shareholders. This is precisely their Achilles heel. In simple terms, there are two main ways in which to increase profits. Either retail prices can be raised while maintaining or lowering costs, or volumes can be increased while keeping costs relatively stable. Both of these methods can be applied at the same time, but it is rather uncommon for volume to increase at the same time as prices (except for the special case of Giffen-style goods[1]). Priority is therefore usually given to the tactic of increasing volume.

And yet, although all luxury brands legitimately aspire to conserving, protecting and constantly improving their image, since it lies at the very heart of their existence and of their competitive differentiation, they aspire even more to improve their profits. Selling one or two more pairs of shoes

[1] A Giffen good is when the price of a good (such as a staple food, ie: bread or potatoes) increases, the consumer may be pushed to buy *more* of the good because his buying power decreases. Thus he has to limit the consumption of other, more expensive, products (ie: meat or fruit). This is a typical case of positive price elasticity of demand.

may be no bad thing, the odd additional litre of perfume here and there is welcome enough, and a few extra garments quite acceptable. Yet, when these increases run into the thousands, or even tens of thousands of units, what happens to the legitimacy of the brand, its proclaimed image and its desired positioning? A good number of these brands now post turnovers exceeding US $1 billion, and not just because they sell US $5,000 dresses, US $800 perfumes or US $1,500 pairs of shoes. All the analysts in the sector agree that this is undoubtedly one of the most controversial 'trick questions' to be answered by the profession as a whole.

The example of Prada

Founded in 1913 by Mario Prada, the brand that today bears his name has grown from the modest leather shop in Milan to become a worldwide fashion icon, easily on a par with Hermes or Gucci. The brand's famous design is the work of Miuccia Prada. Yet the dilemma facing a brand such as Prada is to know how to tread the fine line between increasing volume and keeping its image as a luxury brand. A brand can rapidly age if it loses this status and quality with its roots in rarity.

Prada has therefore already opted for brand diversification. Its Miu Miu brand has prices lower than Prada's, but still not within the reach of the general public. This has increased the company's volume without entirely dragging the brand down to mass-market levels. Furthermore, Prada owns or is the majority stakeholder or partnership of other brands, such as Superga, Church, Fendi (with LVMH), Helmut Lang, Jil Sander, etc. Unlike a large number of luxury brands, including some French brands, Prada completely oversees its own production. It carries a cost, but this cost may be equally perceived as a sound investment, as it guarantees the quality of the products that bear the Prada label.

The main factor that has allowed this Italian brand to become Prada – which is still a very recent arrival by luxury brand standards, and can to a certain extent be subject to replication – is its total control of the entire production chain. This ranges from the design stage supervised by Miuccia to the presentation of the products in an appropriate merchandising environment in the shop, and includes absolute quality control over the production process. This control of each link of the chain has allowed the brand gradually to construct its own distinctive image: positioning coherence with its prices, image

coherence with its communication policies, and produc' ence with customer expectations and the latest trends.

Numerous designers from the sector agree that luxury is a selfish pleasure that must allow the smallest, most discreet detail to create an overall expression of total sophistication. And yet, such luxury refinement has much to fear from mass production and large-scale distribution. From 2001 onwards, Bally, the footwear manufacturer, has therefore been restructuring and closing down some of its retail outlets with locations and/or aesthetics that did not tally with the brand's desire to become more upmarket. Such a strategy of opting for fewer retail outlets is indeed a rarity; and some may consider it to be a risky venture. Others will see it as a coherent approach if the aim is to project a luxury brand image and to help to protect the brand against ageing.

Retaining or killing off the brand: the ultimate test

Auditing a brand is a very important action, since it should enable the manager to make a number of equally important choices regarding the brand. The decision to let a brand die is often a very difficult one for any manager aware of the strength of its capital and potential power. This sometimes results in rose-tinted audits that actually only delay the fatal outcome and make it a little more expensive. It is therefore very important that the brand being examined should be put to the ultimate test. Admittedly, the level of brand awareness, together with an image score, constitutes important information. Yet it is not enough. We have to investigate the heart of the brand. Blind tests (tests where the name of the brand is not revealed) are therefore systematically applied to its products. The goal is simply to establish that even in the absence of the brand name itself, the promise of product satisfaction is still confirmed by the product's target consumers. If blind tests are negative, it will then be necessary to rethink the product features before any decision regarding the brand is taken. The declared goal here is not to rejuvenate the brand in order to hide a product that no longer lives up to the target market's expectations. No brand – not even the most powerful – is a smokescreen for concealing faults. Even if it were, it would not survive for long, and time and human and financial resources would have been wasted. The brand is there to serve its products, which will serve it in return.

Auditing an ageing brand is akin to mining exploration. The auditor will need to delve deeply into the brand's capital to establish the reasons for its weaknesses and the nature of its enduring assets. Like any modern miner, the auditor now has access to a large amount of useful information which enables him or her to direct explorations efficiently. Yet this does not mean that the auditor will always be guaranteed of finding an exploitable seam quickly. It may happen, but it is never guaranteed. That is partly the reason why he or she should, as far as possible, establish the perceived age of the brand.

2 The perceived age of a brand

In order to determine the age of a brand, it may be useful to identify its key components. But in Franzen *et al* (1999) Franzen points out that, regardless of its direct or indirect tangible indications, in reality the brand only truly exists in the minds of people who know it and who come to form value judgments about it. For this reason, he also uses the concept of a network of associations between the various components stored in the memory:

> [...] these associations are the result of a simultaneous and collective process in the time and space of interconnecting sensory stimuli and thoughts of different phenomena. Overall, it means that all elements in this network are interconnected: the direct and the indirect, the strong and the weak. In psychology, the term used to describe this network of associations is 'cognitive structure'.

Age is a very interesting notion, because it has a richness that often goes unrecognized. It could be supposed to represent the number of years since the birth of a person, an asset, a service, a company, an organization or an idea. Yet age, the true marker of time, is often completely devalued in everyday language. However, as Netchine (1994) reminds us:

> [...] age has only gradually begun to comprise an essential part of personal identity, and for a long period of time the data was imprecise: in France, the date of birth was not taken into account until during the reign of François

I, and started to appear in parish records only from the eighteenth century onwards. From the Middle Ages to the 'Modern Era' (17th and 18th centuries), the 'Ages of Life' referred to roughly-divided periods of time (childhood, youth, old age): the course of existence was marked by these broad biological and social divisions, which defined roles and behaviour, ways of dressing, and so on.

The age of the brand that will fundamentally occupy our attention here is the age perceived by other people; or in other words, the age that an observer will, spontaneously or after careful thought, attribute to a brand. It is irrelevant whether or not the brand is an 'old' one (that is, a brand whose chronological age is advanced), as we will see that, far from being a handicap, advanced chronological age can even be transformed into a firm marketing asset if it is developed judiciously. Using the concept of perceived age means accepting the idea that brands do not belong to companies, but to their consumers. Figure 2.1 helps us to understand properly why it is that the age perceived by other people is one of the most difficult to calculate. If we trace the time line, only two objective facts can be placed directly on the line. Firstly, there is the date of birth of the brand, which therefore represents the starting point of the time continuum for the brand. Secondly, there is the date of its chronological age. Between the two lies the exact number of days, months or years that have passed since the birth of the brand. If the biological age of the brand is plotted on the graph shown, it can be seen to be located in a time interval on either side of its chronological age. In fact, the biological age of the brand cannot be determined as accurately as its chronological age, since, if the brand's 'state of health' is taken into account, we allow a measure of subjectivity that derives from the criteria used to evaluate it. The assessment that it engenders may vary to a greater or lesser extent compared to the chronological age. Let us now plot on the graph the factor of cognitive age; in other words, the age that the brand believes itself to have. As the reference system used naturally varies from one brand to another, from one company to another, and as a function of the criteria used, the time interval is stretched somewhat compared to the interval obtained for the biological age.

Considering that the subjective age introduces the additional criterion of the reference point for one or more groups, its graphical representation stretches the time interval a little further, although this is still located around the time line represented by the chronological age, in which this new brand age is located. However, it will be seen that it is not perfectly balanced; and if it stretches slightly beyond the chronological age line, it then stretches well beyond this same age. When, finally, we place the age as perceived by others on the graph, we notice that two things happen. The first is that the chronological age is always located inside an interval that is

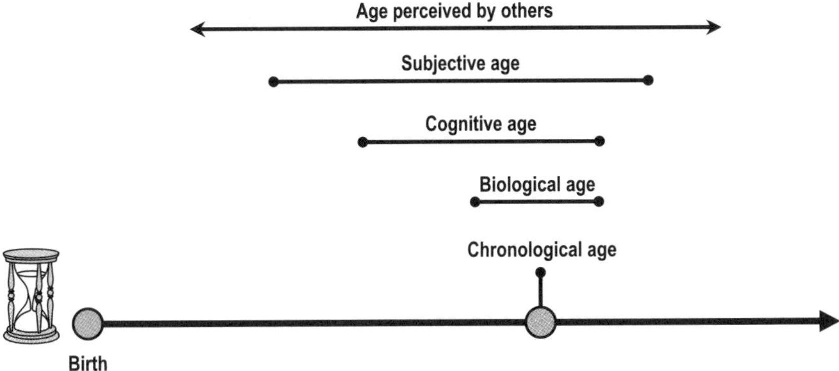

Figure 2.1 Time graph comparison of the main different ages

still extended. The second is that the limits of this interval are open; in other words, there appear to be no limits.

For the brand manager, this lesson is an important one because it indicates that this age is subject to all manner of possible and imaginable assessments. On the one hand, it means that an average individual may believe the brand to be far older than it is in reality and that over and above any longevity it may have, the individual perceives it primarily as being old. But it also indicates that a non-average individual may consider the brand to be much younger than it is in reality; and in addition, he or she perceives it primarily as being up to date. On the other hand – and this is undoubtedly the most important point – it means that because this perceived age is not (solely) based on objective grounds, it may be possible to influence it using an *ad hoc* marketing strategy. This may not offer the brand manager much consolation, but it does at least enable him or her to take steps to achieve some control over the age of the brand as perceived by consumers, or at least to give him or her hope of rectifying it in cases where the brand is being damaged by ageing.

This perceived age of the brand is unquestionably the most important of all. Why? As we have said, any of the traditional sources of competitive advantage (product features, pricing policy, choice of distribution channel, promotional assets, etc) can potentially evaporate overnight if a competitor adapts one of them to its benefit. However, we should avoid simplistically considering the brand as some kind of invincible white knight. Admittedly, the brand is essential, if only because it is the determining factor providing justification for the true loyalty of a customer. But we have to be careful here not to treat it simply as a superficial public face. Its name, logo, emblem, signature and product packaging – constituting its own distinctive public face – are certainly very important. Yet, when all is said and done, they are no more than the expression of the brand. Simply trusting that they will be able to represent the brand on their own is a woefully inadequate approach. Put another way, it would be very simplistic, and indeed risky, from a strategic perspective to attempt to answer the question, 'What is the brand?' using these building blocks. The brand is above all represented by the image it evokes in the mind of these consumers. Admittedly, each of the aspects mentioned above makes its own contribution to this image, and should even be considered as vital for the brand. Yet, as our analysis will show, these aspects in no way constitute the entire identity of the brand. Consequently, we are interested not in the hard facts of the brand's chronological age and the other factors above; but rather, in its perceived age – the age that grows, develops and becomes rooted in the minds of the individuals who constitute the brand's target market. Envisaging how to obtain a strong brand therefore involves thinking beyond marketing alone.

The brand must be considered as the absolute basis on which the marketing strategy will be created, executed and continually improved. This prerequisite is essential if we are to achieve a truly coherent approach that, above all else, respects the brand in all its forms. Without this, it is inevitable that certain actions will be perceived as illogical and contradictory when viewed against the image the brand is seeking to convey. Regardless of whether this is a matter of cognitive or affective dissonance, the outcome is that the brand is precariously balanced and the whole of its image is weakened. Let us reiterate that the brand that concerns us is the one perceived by its target market in its wider sense. Disturb this perception, and the brand is naturally and logically jeopardized. The consumer's own experiences, beliefs and attitudes will describe, position and potentially strengthen the brand in his or her mind. The brand's equity is therefore created not on the bottom line of the balance sheet, but rather in the minds of those at whom it is directed. This demonstrates the brand's fragility, the constant vigilance needed to protect it, and the fact that we are dealing more with perception than with hard facts. Under these circumstances, with most brands keen to appear in a positive light in the minds of their target audience, their concerns about ageing will be focused on its perceived age rather than its ordinary (and uncontrollable) chronological age. And for this perceived age to be seen in positive terms, the brand will naturally have to fulfil the promise of satisfaction spelled out in part by the marketing message.

Most authors agree that three indicators can be isolated that allow the age of an individual to be guessed at. These three elements are: voice, body and face. In fact, when people age, their voices, bodies and faces appear changed by the ravages of time to varying degrees. A child's voice bears no comparison with an adult's. The face changes during a lifetime, if only because certain cells no longer regenerate themselves. Finally, the body also changes; primarily in terms of size, but also in terms of muscular mass, weight, suppleness, vitality, etc. Figure 2.2 shows this in terms of analogy

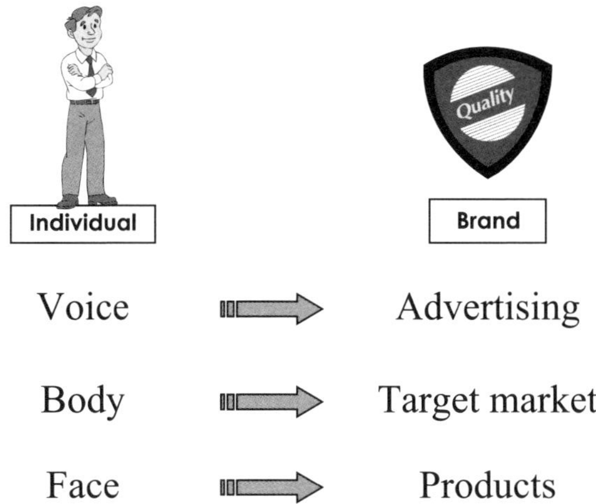

Figure 2.2 Analogies of the signs of ageing between the individual and the brand

to the brand. The voice represents the brand's advertising; the body is the factor that enables the brand to exist; that is to say, the consumers in its target market; and the face represents what the brand stands for; in other words, the products and/or services that bear its name.

The perceived age of the brand is an important strategic factor that can either destroy it or, conversely, protect it. However, we are not suggesting that old age in a brand is inevitably a negative factor. We are dealing here with the perceived age of the brand, and not its chronological age. Several European brands that are several centuries old are still perceived as being very young, particularly in the luxury sector. In the event of ageing, this perceived age *may* become a negative factor.

The example of Lego

Building a brand 'brick by brick' seems to have been the ambition of Ole Kirk Christiansen. The Danish words *leg godt* mean 'play well'. It was in 1932 that Ole Kirk Christiansen came up with the idea of a little plastic brick for his son, Godtfred, that could be put together in many different ways. But in an era of video consoles, electronic games and virtual internet gaming, the little brick has really aged. Its theme parks are no longer crowd pullers now that its competitors have begun striving to outdo each other in terms of raw thrills. The weight of the years hangs heavy; so much so that amusing 21st-century children seem to require more than a little coloured plastic brick: they have become totally informed, demanding and capricious consumers. Thus, over the years, Lego has ended up by becoming an old brand.

The little brick is a timeless product that relies more on the imagination of the child using them than the technical specifications of the latest electronic gizmo. Admittedly, it is endowed with a major asset: the Lego brand. Yet it is precisely this asset that has aged it; it is no longer the stuff of the dreams and imaginations of young experimenters with a passion for the brand's 1001 multi-coloured bricks. Its ageing has had an adverse affect on all of the company's products, damaging the brand still further in the process.

Lego began to fight its way back in the late 1990s on several different fronts. One of these was to rejuvenate the product range, with a tentative step towards electronics. In 1997, Mindstorms, a robot, brought a breath of youthful air into the company and in 2001, Bionicle repeated the process. Naturally, such a rejuvenation plan involved a restructuring of the company in order to find a way of reducing costs. Production was relocated and the supply chain dramatically rationalized. Today, the often costly licensing policy has been reviewed and there has been a renewed focus on Lego's core business. It was high time some sort of action was taken; other brands now offer little bricks that are 'legally' compatible with Lego's.

The case of products that constantly suffer the slings and arrows of outrageous fashion is even more interesting, as the perceived age of the brand can be hit brutally hard by the effects of time.

The example of Nike

The Swoosh to rejuvenate? It is probable that if a teenager were to be asked about brands of sports shoes and accessories, both in Europe and the United States, Nike would almost certainly be a guaranteed top-five entry. In the same way, the majority of adolescents would be likely to recognize the US brand as a market leader – and yet the brand with the iconic 'swoosh' had been stagnating since the end of the 1990s.

Caution is always advisable when attempting to provide an explanation and/or analysis of the good or bad financial results of a company, as they are often the outcome of a rather larger set of factors than is generally highlighted in the analysis. Nonetheless, several financial analysts, mainly US-based, are in agreement that relative ageing of the Nike brand lies behind these results, in which growth seems to have ground to a halt after several years. Its core original target has naturally aged, and Nike has not always been able to stay with them on the journey, chiefly by failing to recognize early enough and clearly enough the growth in the 'outdoor' niche, or the development of traditional sports footwear into more urban styles, a phenomenon described by specialists as 'the move from white to brown'.

The success of Philip Knight, the company's founder, is undeniable, and no-one would question that Nike has continually innovated to the benefit of this performance. Yet this technological innovation has come at a price – one which has sometimes had the effect of distancing the brand from a potentially wider market. Building a veritable technological fortress around the brand runs the risk of cutting it off from the world. By attributing too much importance to technological performance for the athlete, Nike had left the field open for its competitors to target consumers in terms of fashion and price. Corrective action was thus taken at the start of 2000 and today, with an extended portfolio of complementary brands (Converse, Hurley International, Cole Haan, Bauer, etc), the brand has once again become a symbol of sports fashion. It has achieved this by intensifying its sports partnerships (particularly in football), but also by developing more fashionable new ranges, improving its supply chain (with US $500 million invested), and so on, causing revenues to sprint to over US $12 billion in 2004.

3 Brand advertising

Apart from the product itself, advertising is without doubt the variable of the marketing mix that changes the most over time. The basic advertising areas, the themes covered, the tone adopted, the preferred colours and music, the media and formats used all make advertising a potential source of perpetual youth to anyone who can find the fountain. Conversely, however, if care is not taken, advertising can easily become a cause of ageing, in both quantitative and qualitative terms.

The quantitative aspect manifests itself through a decrease in the brand's investment on advertising, in all its forms, or perhaps even a complete cessation. Most companies evaluate their advertising budget according to revenues, assigning a larger or smaller percentage depending on the goals being pursued. This method may appear satisfactory from an accounting point of view, despite the fact that, at the time of the product's launch, the scrupulous use of this method requires the calculation of predicted future revenues. However, it runs into a strategic obstacle once the product and/or brand involved have reached the so-called maturity phase. This is the point at which revenues are at their highest; and so, therefore, are advertising resources. However, advertising needs are naturally lower than they were at the time of launch. But this incoherent method collapses under the weight of its own paradox when, 'unfortunately', the brand enters the decline phase. Logic dictates that advertising investment must then increase to rectify the situation. However, because of the decrease in revenues, the opposite happens, when the company does not take the more radical decision of cancelling all advertising investment.

Although no intelligent business person would deny the value of advertising, many question its real effectiveness. However, marketing research has changed considerably in this respect over the last 50 years. More rigorous, precise and scientific than previously, it now supplies corroborated information that is of enormous use to the brand manager. However, the fact is that doubt remains – and, in some cases, will continue to remain – as to whether such-and-such a gain in market share, or even simply the retention of this share, or the fact that it has declined more slowly than before the advertising campaign, is attributable to advertising or not. The consumer's behaviour is the result of a complex alchemy incorporating so many variables that not even the most scrupulous of researchers, armed with the most sophisticated of models, would reliably be able to identify the nature and value of the sought-after causal link with absolute precision.

In such circumstances, it should be no great surprise that when a brand enters a decline phase, one of the most common reactions is to reduce advertising expenditure. Such a decision, if taken without any real brand audit, will generally only have the effect of sounding the brand's death knell a little sooner and a little more loudly.

Using TV and film stars to assist the brand

Just like the stars themselves, the shadowy figure referred to as 'the average housewife' – although no-one has ever really met her to be able to know for sure – has changed considerably over the course of the 20th century, as have consumers in general. If marketing and advertising have enjoyed something of a boom during the second half of the last century, to the detriment of sales and poster campaigns, it is first and foremost because the consumer is no fool. Well accustomed to sales techniques, the machinery of advertising and the subtleties of seller-speak, consumers are now much more mature and have a far better understanding of the content of such talk over and above its mere form, regardless of how beautiful this may be. Consumers are better informed and more independent, and now aspire to receive more attention and a more honest, increasingly specific sales proposition that will allow them to feel that they have been listened to and taken into account. For very many products and services, mass marketing is now giving way to an increasingly personalized approach. Comparisons may be drawn with the world of TV and film stars. Stars may have been the stuff of dreams for the general public back in the early glory days of the cinema; but nowadays they are being gradually supplanted by the emergence of 'personalities', some of whom are undeniably famous, but enjoy much closer links with their fans. From inaccessible gods and goddesses, they have gradually become more... human. The reason for this lies mainly in their gradually increasing independence from the production studios. The studio originally exercised total control, and could manage and organize the lives, both professional and private, of the star in order to create mystery, adoration, and even passion, allowing the legend to take shape unhindered. Today, the vast majority of stars still need the studios; but it is apparent that this need is now mutual. Furthermore, where the cinema formerly created a distance between the star and his or her audience, television has played an enormous part, in one way or another, of bringing them closer together.

The example of Lux

Lux used to be the world's best-selling soap – but not any more.

It was in 1927 that Helen Lansdowne Resort, a creative director at the US advertising agency J Walter Thompson, devised a new strategy that consisted of using stars from the still-evolving world of the cinema to advertise the qualities of Lux soap. Back in the late 1920s, the concept of a 'star system' hardly existed. Actors' and actresses' names, hitherto unknown, were just starting to appear for the first time on movie credits. A mere year later, there were already more than 700 advertising endorsements for Lux, which had become 'the soap of the stars'. Today, even at Unilever (the manufacturer of Lux) the precise number of stars who have advertised Lux worldwide is not known, but it can be confidently stated that the figure is in excess of 2,000.

Starting in the last quarter of the 20th century, in Western countries in general and the United States and Europe in particular, the brand has slowly but very surely aged. As is most commonly the case, there are numerous reasons underlying this ageing. Foremost among these is a product that has for too long been offered in its traditional soap-bar form alone, while at the same time its competitors were promoting bubble baths and shower gels. Another reason is a lack of change in advertising.

A timely attempt at rejuvenation was made in 1995. Newer products were developed, and a new advert hit the screen. The first break with tradition was the star. Not a female star; but male this time, in the form of the actor Paul Newman. The second break was the fact that the star was no longer the user of the product. An anonymous woman was seen attracting admiring glances from the actor because of her radiant appearance.

However, the product change was not sufficient and the advertising change arrived too late; Lux's clientèle had already switched to other brands. Unilever then turned its attention to another brand, Dove, with a positioning and message that suited the modern Western female consumer perfectly. It should be pointed out, though, that Lux is still a strong brand in certain Asian and developing countries.

4 The brand's target market

Never let it be said that if a new company were to be founded to offer services manifestly aimed at a target market consisting of senior citizens, its brand could be criticized for being old! A brand's target market is, without doubt, potentially an ageing factor. However, this ageing cannot be assessed simply by calculating the average age of the target population. The target market ages because it is not renewed over time. Independent of the fact that a company can make changes to its product range as well as its advertising, its target market may itself also change – or not. Many different cases can be identified to show at what point it becomes meaningful to talk of ageing.

Over time, four main general facts relating to customers can be pinpointed, as shown in Figure 4.1: first, customers do not change, and they age with the brand; second, the target market is renewed, and new consumers are on average older than the brand's existing consumers; third, the target market is renewed, and the average age of its individual consumers as a whole remains stable; and fourth, the target market is renewed, and its new consumers are on average younger than the brand's existing consumers.

Regardless of the market sector in which it operates, the company must take the greatest possible care to scrutinize changes in its brand's target market over time: consumers' behavioural characteristics over time, beliefs and attitudes regarding the brand, and, of course, changes in the traditional psycho-socio-demographic variables that describe the brand. A product without consumers cannot survive for long. However, a brand that fails to

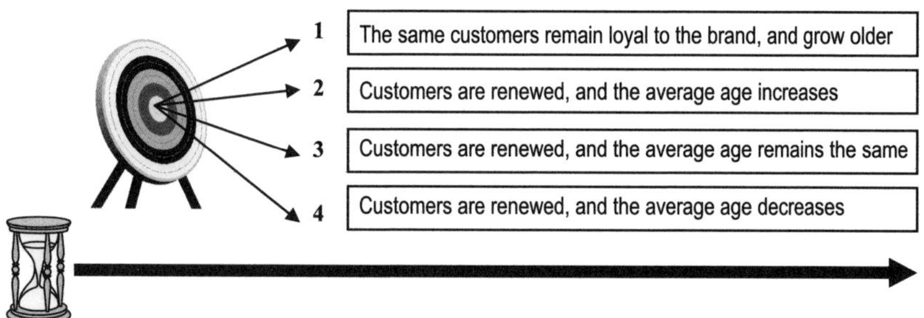

Figure 4.1 Possible consumer changes for a brand over time

notice that the target market for the same product is not being renewed is also, sooner or later, unwittingly digging its own grave. When such renewal occurs, it is very rare that the change in the target market is a sudden, drastic one. This naturally means that the phenomenon is likely to slip in 'under the radar' of any company failing to monitor the situation closely. When the name of Chanel is mentioned in association with perfume, one is naturally tempted to think of the famous No.5: a legendary product that has captured an international clientèle. However, Chanel understood that the positioning, image and heritage of the scent would never be enough to make it a young perfume, even if its use of Estella Warren, directed by Jean-Paul Goude and then Luc Besson, followed by the sublime magic of Nicole Kidman under the direction of Baz Luhrmann, suggested a more up-to-date, contemporary form of advertising. However, although there was a real desire for rejuvenation, the idea was to re-examine the entire marketing strategy to avoid cutting the brand off from its existing target market. By devising Allure, Chanel gained a perfume with market positioning very different from that of No.5, having a younger target market but an image that continued to benefit from Chanel's core identity. With such strategic operations, Chanel has remained in people's minds and in fashion, and is attracting a rejuvenated target market.

Every brand must remain in contact with the young sectors of the population, because, for a variety of reasons, to cut itself off from them is to run the risk of rapid ageing. Three different scenarios are possible. In the first, the target market consists of senior citizens, and the aim is therefore to publicize the brand among younger generations in a dynamic way in order to prevent them from avoiding it – consciously or subconsciously – when they themselves reach retirement age. The second possible scenario is that the brand's target market consists of young people; a failure to renew this target market would sooner or later result in the death of the brand. In the final scenario, the brand is aimed at a multi-age target market, and it must renew each of the segments that form this market; a failure to do so would imply a gradual change in its own image and positioning, with the associated risk of ageing this represents. Of course, the most interesting of these scenarios – because it is also probably the most difficult to achieve – is the first, in which the brand must remain in contact with the younger sectors of the population even though they are not its target market. They reinforce the target market aspects with a cognitive age younger than their chronological age. The solution operates mainly through advertising. Two main types of advertising are possible. The first of these is based on the brand's renown alone, and the aim is to imprint it in the consumer's memory – naturally, in the most positive manner possible. To do this, a suitable media plan will make it possible to select media and advertising types that will also provide exposure to these young segments. The second type demonstrates the brand's ambition in terms of image. In this case, it is the basic advertising that needs to be adapted, energized and rejuvenated.

Balancing the client portfolio: a daily fight against Pareto

Electronics is probably one of the most rapidly changing sectors of all, and also one of the most sensitive to the randomness of demand. It is a sector in which producers are not only faced with intense competition, but are also often confronted with the choice of whether to specialize in specific components or specific user sectors, allowing them to focus their research and development efforts, or whether instead to diversify in order to spread the risk, albeit at the price of increased associated engineering and research costs.

The danger that a brand will age as a result of the ageing of its target market is even greater in cases where this segmenation is concentrated on a narrow segment of the population. The Pareto principle, also known as the 80–20 rule, stipulates that 20 per cent of a company's clients contribute 80 per cent of its business; or, in terms of the product portfolio, that 80 per cent of the various products manufactured are bought by only 20 per cent of the company's consumers. If the Pareto principle is correct, the company's business is centred on a small number of customers. In an environment in which consumer volatility is a fluctuating but constant variable, it is easy to appreciate the potential danger this can entail. Our aim in this case is not to criticize specialization while eulogizing the virtues of diversification. However, although extreme specialization is likely to increase the company's skill in its chosen field and enable it to benefit from optimal economies of scale, it is also – inevitably – a source of potential fragility, as it is particularly susceptible to downturns in market trends that affect the company's product. Some companies have been able to master the art of combining both approaches without placing themselves in a situation of contradiction.

The example of L'Oréal

Critics often attempt to explain away the group's positive financial results during economic downturns by pointing out that the cosmetics market is traditionally less sensitive to the vagaries of macroeconomics, and that the group is renowned for the 'regularity' of its performance. This is a very simplistic analysis, since the group's success is first and foremost attributable to a strategy as relevant in the long term as it is responsive in the short term.

L'Oréal has created a product mix with judicious diversification and good balance between high-end and entry-level products. Furthermore, the group is constantly innovating, not only in terms of consumer expectations but also with regard to the variations in these expectations that may exist from one segment to another, one ethnic group to another, and so on. L'Oréal's great innovation in terms of ethnic products is also a successful illustration of the total adaptability of the group's marketing strategy to the underlying needs of its consumers.

The product balance is almost ideally complemented by another area of equilibrium, this time from the perspective of geographical strategy. In particular, L'Oréal has developed a 'growth base' in most emerging countries with a real strategic vision in the medium to long term.

Taken together, these components give the group and its brands a young image that is very effective among its target market. However, this image is not the product of chance, nor of natural evolution, but rather of persistent hard work on each product in each country.

5 The brand's products

When attributing the ageing of the brand to its products, we actually need to be more precise and analyse whether this ageing is solely attributable to the company's products, or whether in reality the product category to which the brand's products belong has aged. In fact, the result is the same for the brand in either case: ageing. However, from the perspective of deploying a rejuvenation strategy, the consequences are entirely different. In the first case – an ageing product category, and thus a market entering its decline phase – all efforts undertaken by the brand are likely to be in vain in situations where consumption of the product category is gradually (or rapidly) drying up. For example, only 20 years ago, the cost of a black and white television was significantly lower than that of a colour unit. For this reason, a market existed that operated mainly on the basis of price differentiation. Today, not only is that difference no longer significant, but most manufacturers have ceased production because the black and white market has gradually disappeared in favour of colour televisions. In the second case, the brand's products appear to have aged, while those of their competitors have been able to overcome the potential effects of ageing. The Levi's jeans brand suffered from just this problem until the early 21st century, when it reacted in dramatic fashion with new shapes, new cuts, new ranges, 'vintage' series and an additional entry-level range (Signature) for the mass retail market. The rejuvenation was a difficult process, but the brand was ultimately able to reinvent itself without denying its basic essence.

Ageing because of a declining range

The decline of a range of products is very often associated with the decline of the category itself, except in specific, and fortunately very rare, cases in which the company in question naïvely allows the whole of one of its ranges to fall into utter neglect. In every case, the cause of ageing has its roots in a characteristic (constituent part, method of sale, type of advertising, etc) which is common to all of the products in question, even though the products themselves remain different. It may be the result of a dramatic shift in fashion that renders the range and/or category of products entirely outdated and outmoded. Consider, for example, the case of Caps and Pogs, the little coloured discs that were all the rage in playgrounds in the early 1990s and the names of which are scarcely even recognizable today. Gadget products, by their very nature, usually belong to this category. Ageing may also be attributable to a simple technological development. Who would now be interested in buying a computer fitted with an Intel 8086 microprocessor clocked at 4.77 megahertz, when the clock rates at the time of writing are into the multiple gigahertz region? It is also instructive to note that manufacturers or assemblers no longer base their promises on the attribute of speed. For the average user, a few extra megahertz does not constitute a competitive advantage.

A design too heavily rooted in forms that are out of date or already overused can have the result of creating the same appearance of ageing across the whole range. In such cases, safety considerations may prompt ageing at a more or less rapid rate. Imagine, for example, a situation where one of the constituent components of the range's products starts to be thought of as toxic. A case in point is the range of insulating products using asbestos; formerly praised for their efficiency, these products are now condemned for their harmfulness.

Regardless of the exact nature of this cause, it creates an additional difficulty for the brand manager. Ultimately, the brand ages chiefly because the range and/or the category has aged. This means that, regardless of the proposed treatment, the brand manager must be aware of the fact that such treatment has to be applied from one end of the range and/or category of the brand's affected products right through to the other. It may be that the selected rejuvenation factors will act simultaneously on both sides in certain cases, but the anti-ageing treatment **must** be clearly applied individually to each side. Naturally, this makes the task a more difficult one.

The example of Tampax

TSS stands for Toxic Shock Syndrome. It is the name of a possible infection caused through the use of tampons for some women. However, the infection is not specific to tampons, and the exact link between their use and the infection has never been entirely clear. TSS can, for example, also affect people who have suffered burns or insect bites (including children and men). The *Staphylococcus aureus* bacteria that produces the toxin in question can prove fatal in some rare cases. It was mainly in the United States, in the early 1980s, that cases relating to women's use of tampons were identified and monitored by the Center for Disease Control and Prevention – (see Figure 5.1, which records cases examined between 1979 and 1998). These cases coincided with the market launch of a far more absorbent type of tampon, and in particular polyester-based products, offering added comfort to users. However, various studies subsequently showed that prolonged use of the same tampon could create a situation that was more likely to induce TSS.

When these cases were first identified, tampon sales fell dramatically in favour of sanitary towels. For the entire range of Tampax products, and – via a classic contamination effect, for the entire category – a real crisis seemed to have occurred, particularly since competitors (whose tampon ranges had also been affected) were hastily introducing innovations to their sanitary towel ranges. Studies

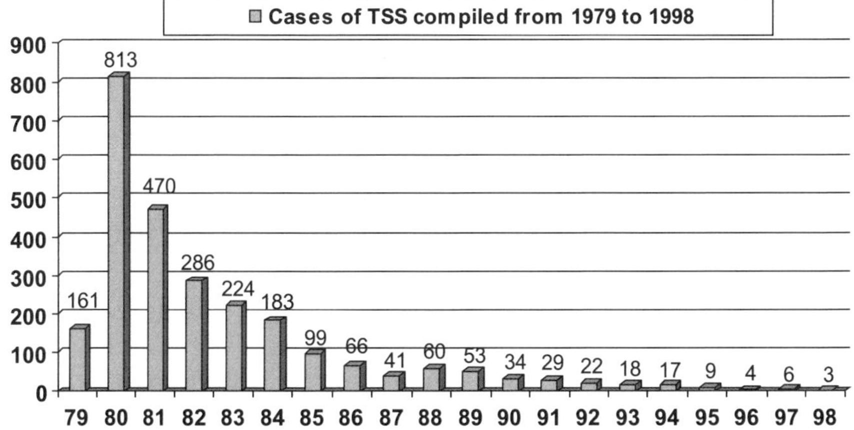

Figure 5.1 Cases of Toxic Shock Syndrome compiled in the United States by the CDCP

conducted by Tambrands, the manufacturer of Tampax tampons at that time, showed that certain segments of the target market were starting to believe that the product had aged, that it was no longer as safe as it had been and that it was a better idea to switch to a different sort of protection – one that seemed as if it would be safer, and featured a series of innovations (related to size, comfort, absorbency, etc) trumpeted daily in advertisements. This is a clear example of a paradox showing that the causes of ageing do not necessarily have to be real and demonstrable to affect the brand.

The response had to take the form not only of a change in the product, but also a suitable advertising campaign, to put an end to the premature ageing process affecting the product range, and thus the brand, that had started to take effect. To start with, the problem was a result of the fact that a tampon is not considered to be an ordinary product. Its advertising adhered to a precise structure, and the media strategy had to follow precise rules regarding broadcasting timetables. This rigidity is still found today in most countries, even though it is now a little more relaxed. Many press articles, produced from information supplied by Tambrands, detailed the characteristics of TSS. These articles, now appearing in the teenage press, were also a means of recruiting new users by reassuring them over the TSS problem. Today, the product category still exists. However, 20 years on, the brand belongs to Procter & Gamble, and the advertising situation has changed considerably. It is true that the risk of TSS related to tampon use still exists, but identified cases are now few and far between. Clear user information accompanies the product, and even the brand's website offers direct access to a host of detailed information on its home page (see Figure 5.2). So, now that the product can boast potential users across the entire globe, the information it offers consequently also has a global reach.

Ageing as a result of a product in decline

When considering a product in decline, the product should be examined in its wider marketing sense; that is to say, the product may be a type of physical goods, a service, an idea, a concept or even an organization which, because it has not been protected against ageing, ends up dragging the brand down with it. The Planet Hollywood brand, for example, would not automatically be considered as being old. However, the original concept of

Figure 5.2 Home page for www.tampax.com website (2005)

a restaurant themed around the concept of the cinema has aged, for want of careful observation and sufficient upkeep – and caused the brand to age too. Indeed, in the late 1990s, the brand was forced to close a number of its units, the concept and positioning of which were no longer deemed to be relevant. Other brands, aware of this potential decline as a result of product ageing, have conducted meticulous research into their relevance, image and residual potential. Their aim was to discover whether, instead of getting rid of the old and clearing the way for brand rejuvenation work, it was instead possible to promote it as it was.

The example of TAG Heuer

The approach adopted by the jeweller TAG Heuer (LVMH group) is an instructive one. The TAG Heuer range of watches includes old models that play no positive part in increasing the brand's contemporary, sporting image. A traditional reaction would have been gradually to abandon these models, replacing them with newer versions. In this case, however, the product is a high-end one which, in addition, still occasionally makes references to the date of the brand's creation, despite the fact that this is now a century or two removed from the watches being sold today. These old TAG Heuer models, described by the brand as 'classics', account for an average of 20 per cent of revenues and from time to time the brand enthusiastically runs advertising campaigns to promote the watches' enduring character. This is a case in which the product is not in decline. Some models have become such classics that they appear simply to have stepped out of time. If the original Monaco model were to be rejuvenated and redesigned, it would no longer be the Monaco model; the identity that now makes this watch an ageless product would have been erased. However, there was no reason not to produce modified versions of it, such as the Monaco V4. TAG Heuer's power derives in part from its ability to preserve the basic characteristics of its own identity while constantly innovating across the rest of its product range; an example of this was the 2005 launch of the Calibre 360, a watch with a mechanical movement that vibrates more than 360,000 times an hour.

Along with this product innovation, a renewed advertising campaign is in place to support the brand on an ongoing basis, with many product placements at the cinema and advertising featuring such classic stars as Steve McQueen and Ayrton Senna, or even today's icons such as Brad Pitt, Tiger Woods, Kimi Raikkonen, Uma Thurman, Maria Sharapova, Yao Ming and Juan-Pablo Montoya.

Some products age much less well than others. This is because tastes change, technology moves on and designs evolve, but most of all, because the products themselves have not been watched closely enough. All sectors are affected. Therefore, although technology-based goods are particularly susceptible, they are not the only ones to be vulnerable to the repeated assaults of time. Consider, for example, the case of the Milky Way chocolate bar, a brand belonging to the Masterfoods group. In comparison to other Masterfoods products, such as Mars and Bounty, the Milky Way brand is, according to many retailers, a brand that has aged. Insufficient advertising, a low level of product and/or packaging innovation, and a narrower target market than the group's other products have been at the root of this progressive ageing. All this is despite the fact that in the mid-1990s a rejuvenation strategy was attempted. The brand is not dead; it simply seems to have slid gradually into oblivion.

There are other reasons for the decline of a product than simply negligence on the part of its brand managers. A product may decline and age, sometimes very rapidly, if it has not chosen to, or been able to, innovate appropriately. Innovation can be very expensive, and contrary to what one might think, adopting a 'follower' position is not necessarily any guarantee of safety. By constantly following without ever improving, the brand is rapidly imprisoned in the 'me-too' position and must therefore suffer the accompanying image effects; and ageing is one of these. Brands such as 3M have understood this fact, and have opted for permanent innovation across their entire product ranges. Naturally, their products are eventually undermined by the competition; but by the time this happens, 3M is already investing in new innovations.

Some brands have been quick to renounce their pursuit of quality; sometimes this is in an attempt to fight off competition from the sector, and often simply to improve the company's profits. There is a great temptation in this respect; while improving quality is an endless daily task, the opposite process is simple, and can produce results very quickly. Through the implementation of deliberate changes to areas such as raw materials or the manufacturing process, reductions in quality provide enormous scope for producing goods at a lower cost. Of course, it is not our intention to put such brands in the dock (and there are more of them than one might think); they have either already paid dearly for their mistake, or are doing so now. In some cases they have already completely disappeared; in others, they are now reduced to producing products for other brands (mostly the big retailers). To rely on a furtive reduction in quality is to commit the absurd crime of believing that consumers are so naïve and/or so dependent on buying a particular brand that they will meekly accept the change. With the exception of the rare cases where a monopoly exists, all competitive environments – even if the competition is not of the perfectly pure kind – are characterized by consumer choice. To leave a brand to age further and further is to nudge it gradually towards retirement; and the fact that consumers are now deserting the product in ever-greater numbers sometimes threatens to turn this retirement into a funeral.

The example of Adidas

In the mid-1990s, the general management of Adidas, headed by Robert Louis-Dreyfus, realized that the 'three bands' brand had aged significantly in consumers' minds. However, the fact that the new chairman, appointed in May 1993, immediately chose upon his arrival to set up his office not in some far-flung corner removed from the head office, but instead at the very heart of the marketing department, gave out a very clear and immediate signal as to the direction his strategy was to take. The fact was that Adidas, which had become used to competing mainly against Puma in the European market, had not been able to offer any suitable marketing riposte to the well-oiled war machines of Nike and Reebok. In particular, Adidas, famed for the quality of its products, had been unable to climb aboard the fashion bandwagon that was now dictating consumer choices. Luckily for the brand, the ageing process was a gradual one, for the new US market entrants (despite the fact that Reebok was actually founded in the UK) had done more than to just capture market share points; their new approach also helped to bring about considerable growth in the sports shoe market.

The new marketing strategy was implemented following the restructuring that began in the late 1980s. Adidas relocated its main centres of production to South-East Asia to take on its direct competitors on a level playing field. A new operational system of dividing the group by sport was introduced, creating a series of centres of profit. Considering the product innovation involved, Adidas adjusted its pricing policy, having realized that it was competing against entry-level products, whereas its competitors, and Nike in particular, were achieving comfortable margins in the high-end segments. Eventually, production itself was also reorganized in order to create smaller production runs, thus encouraging permanent renewal and also a reduction in stock levels and thus, ultimately, better profitability. The advertising account was given to the UK agency Leagas Delaney with the main stated intention of rejuvenating the brand. Adidas' new advertising approach thus became to create more of an emotive link with its public, rather than relying on the cognitive aspects (number of medals obtained, sporting image, technology, etc) that had been used until then. The new strategy was pan-European in scope, and was aimed at attracting new, younger segments.

PART 2

Rejuvenation factors

'Everything befits youth; it drowns ugly details in the uninterrupted stream of its lifeblood'
Franz Kafka
In the Penal Colony; 1914, 1919

In this section, we shall concentrate again on the brand as a brand, while remaining aware that the company name can sometimes also play a part. This distinction is an important one when demonstrating that if the brand manager, at a given point in time, chooses to intertwine their respective destinies, he or she must naturally accept the consequences; for this association is often profitable but potentially dangerous. After all, this shared identity naturally implies that they are united for better *and* for worse. A company brand could never expect to rejuvenate itself successfully if the company itself did not send out clear, powerful signals as to its own rejuvenation. But again, this is not some simplistic consideration of the chronological age of the company's CEO, the average age of its staff, the age of its corporate advertising, the age of its partners or even the age of its production resources in the widest sense. All of these are genuine potential causes of ageing. Once again, however, factors such as the company's positioning, message, values, management of its own social capital and innovation will each play their respective parts in determining the company's perceived age.

On the other hand, it should be understood that although the company's identity may be linked with that of the brand, any efforts to rejuvenate the brand will be futile if the company itself is abandoned to the mercy of time. If any proof of this fact were needed, it is easy to imagine an extreme case. Ethics – and indeed, morals – are now essential values for a modern company. To shun them is to send a strong signal to the various target markets of the company and/or the brand – a negative, disrespectful and naturally anachronistic signal, and an apparent throwback to a long-dead past. Is it conceivable that a company with a reputation for scorning ethics could then enjoy the benefit of a brand of the same name that was widely respected for its values and was presented by its advertising as being highly distinctive, probably at significant advertising cost? If they expect to be heard, listened to and, ideally, understood and appreciated, companies and brands with shared names have no choice but to develop a symbiotic strategy for mutual nourishment and promotion.

Success factor no. 1: a coherent strategy

The focus of this book is the battle against time, in order to reduce its negative effects. However, we should not lose sight of our goal. When it comes to doing everything possible to rejuvenate a brand, we are not advocating copying H G Wells and literally transporting the brand back to a past time in which it was chronologically, and logically, younger. If anything, our goal is even more ambitious – to alter the perception of the brand by its target market. We do not want to fight against its incontestable chronological age, but its perceived age. Furthermore, we want to achieve this not by masking its perceived age via a series of cunning tricks of which the advertising industry would be proud, but rather by deploying a solid strategy that will send out the appropriate signals for a young, dynamic, modern brand. Clearly, coherency is absolutely crucial in this case! When a company undertakes an audit of its image in order to establish its objective image (its actual identity), its subjective image (the manner in which it is perceived), and its desired image (the manner in which it would like to be perceived), there must be no attempt at concealment. Recently, Levine *et al* (2000) grabbed the attention of brand managers and company advertising executives alike with their very interesting investigation of the role of the internet in corporate advertising and the changes that advertising must undergo as a result.

The purpose of this approach is to take note of what the brand is and how it is perceived. It is sometimes possible that the two images will differ, either in a positive or a negative sense. Advertising can then re-establish the coherency in favour of the objective image. However, if we hope to use advertising to maintain this difference by artificial means and publicize on the outside something that does not exist on the inside, we are putting our faith in a naïve, costly utopia that is both outdated and highly risky. Backed up by modern advertising technologies, information is now increasing in volume and value in a way unlike anything experienced in the past. The internet removes all time and space constraints to provide exceptional accessibility to this information to anyone who wants it. For this reason, it is highly unwise to believe that individuals are still slaves to their own perceptions. Only genuine coherency between the actual situation and the perceived image can provide the company with any hope of achieving its goal. Its target market, advertising and products are no more than a reflection of the company's identity: an increasingly pure reflection, embellished with values, seen in a mirror that grows more and more faithful over time. Those who propose merely to alter the mirror's ability to reflect a specified image (instead of altering the actual object of its reflection) should be aware that they are creating an arbitrarily devised, fanciful burden for themselves that they will be forced to bear for the rest of the brand's life. Worse still, if the brand's perceived image does not fully and perfectly match its own stated values, it is likely to result in the opposite outcome: doubt and distrust on the part of the consumer. Where does a brand's fountain of youth lie? Which factors need to be worked on in order to rejuvenate a brand perceived as ageing?

The rejuvenation of a brand is an operation that sometimes requires the most sophisticated plastic surgery available. We seek to rejuvenate brands because a perception exists that they have aged. However, if they have aged, why not simply abandon them in favour of new brands? The answer is simply this: an audit of the old brand will reveal that the identity of the brand involved still constitutes an asset worth restoring, in order to make maximum use of its potential. Rejuvenating a brand entails making it more modern and contemporary. Sometimes, however, the identified ageing factors are so powerful that it may be necessary to reinvent the brand – but without losing its identity in the process. Modification is needed, but some fundamental characteristics must be retained. Rejuvenation is necessary, but not at the expense of the brand's history. These are the modest challenges facing the marketer. Logically, the art of a successful rejuvenation is to reinvigorate the brand's image without losing the capital of empathy it has enjoyed from its loyal consumers.

The example of Coca-Cola

On 23rd April 1985, Coca-Cola presented the fruits of several years of research and tests aimed at rejuvenating the brand – a new drink, appropriately named New Coke. Initially, all the signs seemed positive. So much so, in fact, that the new product was not a range extension, but a full-blown rejuvenation of the basic product.

However, despite the positive results of tests, the brand's hard core of staunchly loyal consumers dealt the plan a fatal blow. Mounting one campaign of opposition after another, they refused to accept the alteration to the identity of their favourite brand. The contamination effect was so rapid that on 11th July of the same year, top executives from Coca-Cola issued a live apology and announced the return of the 'classic' version of Coca-Cola.

Some will be quick to point out that this was only a half failure; despite having abandoned New Coke, the brand had benefited from an extraordinary media 'rejuvenation bath' with truly redemptive effects.

It should be understood that rejuvenating a brand means relaunching it, not launching it all over again as if it were a new brand. At the time of the operation, the brand already has its own existence, target market, positioning, etc. It is crucial to avoid making choices that are totally inconsistent with the brand's past history.

The example of Rockport

In the mid-1990s, rejuvenation was also the challenge facing the footwear brand Rockport. With its image of rustic, comfortable shoes capable of withstanding any treatment, Rockport had gradually aged. In order to win over baby boomers and the following generation of young adults, Rockport undertook the complete redevelopment of its footwear range.

However, although the stated objective was to sell models of shoe no longer totally associated with walking and mountain rambles, care had to be taken to avoid cutting the brand off from the image and identity that had originally won it fame. Rejuvenation is the art of changing while keeping the key elements the same.

It took the company a year to design a new line of products that retained the legendary Rockport comfort, but at the same time were considerably lighter to make the shoes suitable for everyday wear, and possibly even allow the brand to harbour aspirations of becoming the leader in its category. The objective was a laudable one. In practical terms, the operation posed a number of difficulties, since the upshot was an attempt to reconcile the technology of so-called 'technical' shoes with the design and style of contemporary shoes for everyday wear. It was therefore necessary to find anchor points in the leisurewear shoe trend which those familiar with the brand would be certain to seek out. Today, the task has been successfully accomplished. With new products appearing on a regular basis, Rockport is now a youthful and influential brand, albeit with a small competitive advantage: a carefully-preserved identity, which today forms the foundation of a strong image.

Back to the future: how do you turn the clock back at the right time?

Brands facing premature and/or undesired ageing often find themselves tempted to use tried and tested operational strategies intended to bring them firmly into the present, or even – in a perfect world – to propel them into a more comfortable future than they can currently expect. A little dose of the internet here, a big-name star there, a trendy, event-based advertising campaign and all is well again. We must be wary of operational tactics that do not form an integral part of a strategy tailor made to suit the company's own individual situation. The use of a singer worshipped by a particular teenage audience in a competitor's advertising may have placed that competitor in the limelight and rejuvenated its image enormously, but there is no guarantee that a similar approach will have the same effects on another brand. If the use of a pop star is a valid part of the company's new strategic approach, it may rejuvenate the brand and allow the brand to benefit from this rejuvenation. If, however, it is merely a tactic used to counteract the brand's ageing as quickly as possible, and is not backed by any particular strategy, its benefit – if indeed there is any – is likely to be very short-lived.

The rejuvenation of the brand must be seen in a specific environment – that of the brand. Four main areas for impeding the observed ageing process can be identified: enlarging the brand's identity, energizing its advertising, renewing its target market and expanding its product portfolio. None of these areas is better or worse than any other; and, besides, it is rare for any one to be implemented independently of the others. Only the chosen brand strategy can dictate the proportion and the subsequent nature of the rejuvenation operation to be implemented.

The example of Kmart

In the very early 2000s, the US store chain Kmart found that a section of its clientèle had become disaffected. The reasons? Outmoded stores, a product range essentially the same as that of its competitors, a rather old-fashioned image, to name but a few.

Over time, Kmart's positioning had become less aggressive than its rival discounter Wal-Mart. Combined with increasing consumer awareness – particularly with regard to the price variable – such weakness most certainly constituted a natural source of disaffection. Four key levers for redemption were put into place. Many hundreds of prices were renegotiated with suppliers in order to achieve a 'reference price'; that is, the Wal-Mart price. The second lever was a total logistics overhaul. There is no point in making changes to product ranges and their pricing if the store shelves are empty of stock. The third lever was the mobilization of company staff. The fourth lever was to put customer relationship management back at the centre of the strategy.

By early 2002, signs of the store's revitalization were becoming apparent. In 2003, Kmart exited Chapter 11 bankruptcy protection and in 2004, Edward Lampert, Kmart's chairman, announced a merger with Sears. This example shows how there may not be just one but many rejuvenation factors: a series of policies, tools and tactics that, when assembled in a carefully-planned way, will form a genuine brand rejuvenation strategy and allow that brand to find favour once again in the eyes of its consumers – knowing that the timing of the blend is just as crucial as the precise rejuvenation factors chosen.

6 Environment and nature of rejuvenation

In any examination of the factors likely to contribute to the brand's rejuvenation, the first port of call will very often be the brand's advertising and/or products. In some cases, the nature of the target market will also be analysed with the intention of effecting rejuvenation in that area too. Each of these components is a potential factor that may be actioned individually or in combination with others. However, it is also important to understand that if the brand has aged – or in any case, is perceived to have aged – it is not necessarily because the quality of its products has decreased or because its image has declined. In the first instance, it is because its environment has changed and it has failed to notice the fact and evolve accordingly. Lederer and Hill (2001) suggested an original approach inspired by chemistry. The aim was to examine the notion of a brand – and in particular a brand portfolio – with greater coherency. Their approach uses a model developed by Helios Consulting Group, which allows the brand and its environment to be represented in molecular form. This then gives a fairly clear indication of the brand's direct and/or indirect links with the various components of its environment, whether or not these consist of the company's other brands or competing brands. It then becomes possible to interpret some connections not necessarily visible until then. When a brand ages, its capital is eroded, and the rejuvenation initiative must contribute to the reconstruction of this capital; of course, this work has to take account of the brand's environment. We should also remember that when a rejuvenation plan for the brand is devised and implemented, it is not simply a question of 'repairing' the brand with regard to an identified fault, but of improving the brand by causing it to change within its environment and giving it the dynamism and youthfulness it lacks.

Apple's iMac was not designed as a replacement for an outdated or faulty computer. First and foremost, it was a symbol of the brand's renewal, offering more transparency and friendliness while still retaining its non-conformist positioning compared with other computer brands. The iPod was another beneficiary of this positioning, despite the fact that the product itself did not necessarily offer the best value in its market. The purpose of the Hush Puppies footwear brand rejuvenation during the 1990s was not a reaction to the collapse of the footwear market, but instead a rejuvenation of the image of a brand that, following its own successes in the 1950s and 1960s, had gradually aged without noticing the fact. It was time to move forward. As Keller (1999) has observed, the brand's decline and ageing process can both call for revolutionary supporting changes in the brand's development.

The example of MetLife

Insurance companies are often perceived by their clients as being old, cold, dusty ivory towers with no understanding of their clients' expectations. It is true that slow, gradual changes – stimulated by the arrival of new internet-based competitors – have had something of a galvanizing effect in terms of improving their image. However, once a signal of a younger, more dynamic image has been sent out and understood, the promise still needs to be kept in reality, and a genuine customer relationship management system must be implemented.

In 1985, long before the internet took off, the US insurance company MetLife had precisely identified the insurance sector's negative image. This is what prompted the company to accept a suggestion from its advertising agency, Young & Rubicam, to use the cartoon strip characters drawn by Charles Schulz: the Peanuts gang. These characters (Snoopy, Charlie Brown, Linus, Lucie von Pelt, Woodstock, etc) were young and friendly, sending out a discreet subliminal message that was beneficial to the company's image. As for adherence to the company's promise of satisfaction, this was expressed indirectly by Charles Schulz himself.

Dick Jones, who was at that time Vice-President of the Young & Rubicam agency in New York, comments:

> I always liked the fact that the idea of using those characters came from one of our creative staff, George Watts, while he was sitting in his office looking at a pillow he kept on a chair next to his desk; the pillow had a Peanuts cartoon on it. He sketched out a drawing of Linus holding his comfort blanket with a blissful look on his face, saying: 'Happiness is a thumb and a blanket'. In his mind, the caption became: 'Security is a thumb and a blanket'; and suddenly, we had the makings of a great advertising campaign. As for Charles Schulz, he'd been a satisfied MetLife client for 30 years.

The decision to rejuvenate is taken when an audit of the brand reveals two things. The first is the manifest ageing of the brand. The second is sufficient residual potential to justify the implementation of a rejuvenation remedy. However, this potential is sometimes difficult to identify, if only because it can vary considerably from one brand or sector to another. Even so, we propose to use here at least the five criteria put forward by Wansink (2000). Working at the Food and Brand Lab of the University of Illinois, Wansink conducted a detailed analysis of 42 brands that were successfully revitalized, and compared them with 42 other brands for which the rejuvenation plans were not a success. The results he obtained enabled him to advance five criteria (see Table 6.1) that, if combined, could be expected to allow an assessment of whether the brand apparently had sufficiently favourable assets for a successful rejuvenation. Wansink believes that if at least three criteria are not met, the chances of success will be limited. In the study, 32 of the 42 revitalized brands met all five criteria.

The aim of a rejuvenation remedy is to allow the brand to recover at least the proportion of maturity it has lost (see Figure 6.1). To do this, the brand must be backed by a rational environment. In other words, the start of the decline should not produce the immediate, unconsidered knee-jerk reaction of cancelling all marketing support simply because the brand is earning less today than it was yesterday. This happens much too often for the claim of having acted in ignorance to be valid.

To be certain of success, a rejuvenation plan requires a fully controlled environment. The brand has many facets. The aim of the rejuvenation in question is to obtain a new reflection from the point of view of the brand's consumers. If even one of these facets is overlooked, the entire rejuvenation plan is likely to fail as a result of a lack of coherency. Such control is a legitimate reaction. The brand is much too valuable to be left in the hands of the ignorant! As Norman Berry pointed out in 1988, if the brand has

Table 6.1 Criteria for the potential success of a rejuvenation plan

1. The brand's products are in the moderate to premium price range.
2. The brand's advertising and promotional exposure is lower, or considerably lower, than average.
3. Even if poorly stocked in terms of value, the brand is widely distributed in terms of volume and thus has a shelf presence.
4. The brand enjoys a long heritage which has created its capital of renown and empathy.
5. The brand has a distinct point of competitive differentiation (product, advertising, packaging, style, etc).

Source: Wansink, B (2000) Brand revitalization scorecard, *Brand Marketing*, August, p 78

aged, it is often because its values have been allowed to slumber. If we are to achieve success, an essential first step is to ensure that the environment in which its capital is managed is a healthy one. This must be done not only so that the progress of operations can be controlled at every step, but also to ensure that the errors that have led to this punitive situation have been eliminated and corrected *before* the revitalization of the brand in question begins.

For the brand manager, the fully objective acquisition of the ability to decide which brands are to be sacrificed and which are to be saved presents a genuine challenge. Naturally, it entails an element of intuition and experience. However, those skills alone are not sufficient in this case, considering the investments that have been poured into creating, developing and sustaining the brand whose fate is in the balance. The problem is often that the vast majority of companies that can claim first-hand experience of ageing and dying brands have no idea which factors caused them to age, and even less idea why they died – apart from pinpointing a single fatal decision taken on one particular day. Not enough time. Not enough desire. Not enough interest. Managerial wisdom is about planning for the future using the experience of the present. In this case, the past belongs to history, and history belongs to the past! And yet so many errors could have been avoided

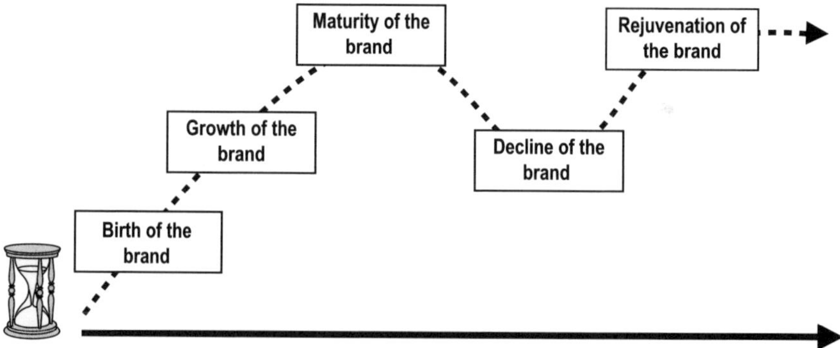

Figure 6.1 Life cycle of the rejuvenated brand

if only the time had been taken to identify and understand the factors that caused the now-defunct brand to age; and so many investments could thus have been saved if a timely *ad hoc* recovery plan had been implemented.

Although they have introduced considerable improvements by modifying their fittings and redecorating their interiors to blow the cobwebs off an image often seen by their clients as outdated, department stores are still sometimes feeling their age. In other words, the package they offer is, despite having changed considerably in a century of existence, generally perceived as an 'old' form of retailing. Following the example of Saks in the United States, when the German department store Kaufhof decided to rejuvenate its image, it had no hesitation in introducing 'little department stores' to meet its customers' expectations.

The advantages of constantly sustaining and revitalizing its brands were explained to the company in an article by Berry (1988). His solution was a seven-step programme produced by the advertising consultancy firm Ogilvy & Mather (see Table 6.2). It is interesting to note that the very first step of this programme insists that the goal must be a high level of quality. We must be realistic. A few decades ago, if brand managers had become aware of possible ageing in their brands, they would probably not have dwelled for too long on the subject. However, the environment has now changed considerably.

The first challenges to the established order were the store brands. With or without their own brands, stores noisily boasted a level of quality comparable to that of the national brands, allied with a price advantage intended to tip the consumer's decision in their favour. Some brands were wholly unable to compete in this area; but over time it was clearly shown that even in cases where the national brand refused to manufacture store brand products, the stores themselves would draw up specifications every bit as exacting as their competitors from the world of manufacturing and production. Furthermore, these store brands were naturally able to take advantage of the sort of in-store display and merchandising options the national brands could only dream about. And then, prompted by economic crisis, consumer demand and the arrival of hordes of hard discounters, these same store brands were in turn forced to compete against low-price brands, which the stores were then themselves obliged to offer to avoid seeing a section of their clientèle desert them in favour of the new competition.

This may only be a brief description of the facts, but the result was a new perception of the brand from the consumer's point of view. As a result of this new perception, brands and their prices were now obliged to justify themselves to the consumer. Of course, consumers have not stopped buying such brands. But armed with the new understanding of the power they wield in terms of choice, they now want to be given justification for their

Table 6.2 Programme for rejuvenating a brand, according to Ogilvy & Mather

1. New direction in favour of products and/or services with a high level of quality.
2. The quality of the product is backed up by its heritage, reputation, packaging and advertising.
3. Improve customer relationship management to benefit the brand.
4. Ensure that the brand value is clearly and completely visible.
5. Promote a unique point of differentiation.
6. Co-ordinate the various aspects of the rejuvenation programme.
7. Celebrate the end of the programme with a particular event, a relaunch campaign.

Source: Berry, N C (1988) Revitalizing brands, *Journal of Consumer Marketing*, **5** (3), pp 15–21

choice of brands. This is why, in most cases, the brand can only fight effectively if it is able to guarantee a high level of quality.

All the other points still apply today, whether they be customer relations in permanent support of the brand, a clear and distinctive image for the brand or even the need to deploy a coherent strategy (in other words, one in which all factors gel together to form a coherent movement). Quality, coherence and differentiation are indispensable springboards for obtaining an effective brand rejuvenation programme. It must be said that the criterion of differentiation is sometimes questioned by experts who maintain it is not fundamentally necessary as a distinguishing factor. For example, Ehrenberg, Barnard and Scriven (1997) prefer the concept of salience; or, to put it another way, the positive perception of a brand. Going beyond the simple question of rhetoric, it could be objected that two directly competing brands may not necessarily seek to be different from one another in reality. And indeed, the authors go still further, arguing that the spectre of advertising's influence is even greater in cases where the brands in question are similar. It is not our intention to reopen this debate; as the very fact that there is a discussion indicates that convincing cases can be made on either side of the argument. We will therefore accept the validity of both notions: differentiation, because brands are essentially similar (if only in terms of the nature of their offer), and salience, because we consider the concept an important one in terms of the brand's image, enabling it, at a specific time, to be chosen in preference to its competitors.

The example of Tesco

The case of the large UK retailer Tesco is worth considering for its textbook adaptation to its environment and ability to maintain a young image at a time when so many of its competitors were teetering on the brink of collapse and/or actually going out of business.

The Tesco brand, however, is a fairly old one. It was first created in 1924 by a highly dynamic entrepreneur, Jack Cohen, who, despite his knighthood, was described by his main successor and the principal architect of the company's success, Ian MacLaurin, as a Godfather-like character who operated a Mafia management style. Tesco took its name from the initials of the tea importer – **T E S**tockwell – which it took over, prefixing them with the first syllable of the founder's own name – **Co**hen.

Just as the Jivaro tribe are renowned for their skill in shrinking heads, Tesco is famous for its drastic price shrinking. However, although the UK retailer's image is permanently associated with price wars, it is a well-known fact that when this strategic option is the only one used, it is rarely either long-lasting or, ultimately, the source of the company's profitability. In fact, Tesco's young, highly dynamic image, which has enabled it to ascend to the top rung of the ladder in its highly competitive business sector, derives from a real talent for backing up its low prices with constant innovations in response to changes in the market environment. Tesco also boasts great attentiveness to the quality of its products, a wide choice for its customers, and all sorts of in-store services and facilities aimed at satisfying as many customers as possible and winning their loyalty.

Like most major retailers, Tesco took the opportunity of analysing its competitive environment as the tidal wave of the world wide web began to form far out in the ocean of the internet. Was it worth taking a gamble and plunging into the young, modern world of the internet, or risk allowing its image to age through its failure to stay abreast of contemporary technological innovations? In any case, it is interesting to recall two facts about the UK retailer. The first of these is that Tesco was far from being a pioneer in this area. The second is that in the mid-1990s, the company was heavily criticized by financial analysts for its 'wait-and-see' policy. However, when it came to the classic game of 'first or best', Tesco ultimately chose the second card, the 'best' option. Between 1996 and 1998, tests were conducted to see whether sufficient potential existed to make online shopping a realistic possibility. Next, in accordance with its intrinsic philosophy of profitability, the UK group trod carefully, and as late as 1999 – three years after the first online store opened – a mere hundred or so stores were offering an online service. Today, the existing network is able to reach over 90 per cent of the UK population living less than half an hour from a delivery point, and the group even posted its first financial profit in 2001. Taking the economic situation into consideration, this was a suitably impressive achievement for this type of activity, and was studied in minute detail both in the United States and across the whole of Europe.

Bucking the trend, Tesco realized that its internet venture would be a very expensive one if it opted for a hi-tech version in terms of electronics, logistics and the sort of sky-high advertising budgets commonplace in the first few years of the web. Unlike many competitors, with a bricks and mortar presence to match its 'clicks' business, Tesco opted for a rational, carefully-controlled approach – even with around 4 million orders per year at present, it has no enormous dedicated warehouses, but a number of staff assigned to a store shelf picking system. Furthermore, no attempt was made to put the company's entire product range online from the very start. Instead, the approach was to proceed step by step, gradually adding a new category once the previous one had been mastered.

Tesco's wise and highly strategic analysis even enabled it to brush aside the warnings of the doom-mongers and other high priests of internet marketing, the great majority of whom believed that consumers would never agree to pay for delivery. Tesco's financial and marketing analyses suggested otherwise; and today, the delivery price is not only accepted by all of its online customers, but also contributes to the firm's healthy profits. Once consumers have been informed of this fixed cost, their automatic reaction is generally to increase the value of their average shopping basket to 'offset' it.

On the other hand, the www.tesco.com website could be criticized for not being a model of cutting-edge graphic design and advanced technology (see the extract from the home page, Figure 6.2). It is sober and traditional, but also functional and effective. In other words, it does enough to allow Tesco to enjoy a modern image, offering its consumers a digital alternative to traditional retail and remaining fully consistent with the store chain's core identity of slashing unnecessary costs to offer the best prices every time. The intimate link between the virtual and the real (also known as internet/store) is one of the keys to Tesco's success, inspired by the triumph of Peapod in the North-Eastern United States with the support of the sales points owned by its parent company, Ahold.

> Today, Tesco is not only the best, but also the first... the first to have developed a 'new' internet sales strategy. The approach may have been more prudent (by re-routing to localized sales points geographically close to the customer), more rational (from a logistics point of view), and perhaps less ostentatious, but unarguably much more efficient and profitable. The objection is certain to be raised that in a business such as mass retail, where a few cents can make the difference between a profitable business and a loss-making one, the retailer ultimately had no choice. And yet store retail is hardly in danger of dying out any time soon! Tesco was able to develop one of the world's most efficient customer loyalty programmes in this respect. Examined in detail by Humby, Hunt and Phillips (2004), it has established the foundations for a genuine contract of trust with the consumer, and is now the envy of all of its competitors.

The exact nature of a rejuvenation can vary considerably from one brand to another. A bespoke strategy must be produced for each brand, and an appropriate blend of techniques found for the specific case in question. In this way, the correct approach for a mass retail brand may be substantially

Figure 6.2 Extract from the home page of the www.tesco.com website (2005)

different from that used for a clothing brand. Some readers will remember the bumbling escapades of the comedian Peter Sellers in the role of Inspector Clouseau of the French *Sûreté* throughout the 'Pink Panther' series of films; and the charisma and elegance of the actor Humphrey Bogart captivating the beautiful Ingrid Bergman in the truly classic film 'Casablanca' – which will always remain among the enduring and legendary images of the cinema. But what is the link between the characters these two actors depict and this book? What do the actors have in common? A simple raincoat as part of their on-screen persona. But not just any raincoat – a Burberry's raincoat.

The example of Burberry

It was back in 1856, when Victoria was Queen, that the young Thomas Burberry opened his small draper's shop in Basingstoke, Hampshire. It sold clothes, of course, but not just any clothes; these were items described as being intended for wearing over other clothes. Great success was to follow.

However, by the end of the 1990s, the brand had aged, and its inimitable tartan no longer appealed to the consumer. There were several reasons for this. The individual products had not been sufficiently modernized, and the range as a whole had aged in comparison to the dynamism of its competitors' ranges. But more than this, and in common with all other high-end brands, it was caught between the desire to expand its own business and the trap of straying into mass-market distribution, which would introduce the risk of altering its own positioning. While certain licensing agreements in Asia were certainly beneficial to the brand in the short run, the result was a wide-scale distribution of the brand bordering on the excessive, even leading to the emergence of a 'grey' market – a situation that never fails to compromise a brand's control over its own image and positioning. What was needed, therefore, was some sort of response, and the introduction of a brand rejuvenation policy. This was done in 1999, under the creative control of Roberto Menichetti and Rose Marie Bravo at the head of the company. The Asian contracts were all firmly renegotiated, and the brand's Spanish franchisee was bought out. At the same time, a decision was taken to remove the possessive 's' from the end of the brand's name. At a stroke, the brand assumed a more prestigious feel, while still retaining its name; there was no doubt that the new version sat more comfortably with a luxury brand.

The next step was to task Roberto Menichetti, in his capacity as artistic director, with the modernization of the entire brand. He devised Prorsum for Burberry, a much more dynamic clothing collection. However, for an apparel brand such as Burberry, the rejuvenation process was not a simple one, given that the very thing for which it had become recognized and renowned – that is to say, a specific motif and style – was deemed to have aged. The brand's mission, therefore, was to make changes while keeping it the same, and to ensure continuity while at the same time introducing renewal. Three floors of the brand's flagship store in Bond Street, London are now dedicated to the Burberry name, style and legend, from the famous trenchcoat to the classic scarf via the ubiquitous cashmere pullover and the standard plaid, but also extending the brand to cover underwear, short-sleeved shirts, jeans, shoes, perfumes and bandanas. Burberry has rediscovered its youth. The original target market has been reassured; the brand has retained its historical identity, legendary quality and distinctive style – while at the same time, the UK brand's products now appeal to new, much younger market segments. After all, how could tartan age while designers such as Jean-Paul Gaultier, Sonia Rykiel, Jean-Charles de Castelbajac and Vivienne Westwood can all be counted (albeit temporarily in some cases) among its loyal disciples? Even the ageless Barbie can now be accessorized with a Burberry skirt, trenchcoat, scarf and bag!

The final outcome of this rejuvenation initiative has been an increase of over 200 per cent in annual profits. The brand saw its image altered through an unintentional association with certain hooligans, but was able to shake this off by continuing to innovate. More than anything else, the factor that gives Burberry the ongoing youthfulness it now enjoys is the ability, throughout its history, to combine a distinctive high-end style with recognized everyday usability. It is true that the brand also has to incorporate features that express its own fashion aesthetic, but its new marketing strategy is able to take account of this. In 1910, Thomas Burberry gave his agreement for a brand advertising campaign encouraging women everywhere to forsake their furs for Burberry clothing and thus show off their figures… and their youth!

Time: an unpredictable rejuvenation factor

The nature of a brand's rejuvenation is therefore intimately linked with the brand itself; and, of course, with the company that owns it. Although some rejuvenation remedies can have almost immediate effects, this is not always the case. Sometimes time needs time to do its work.

For other brands, however, the effects of such work will only become apparent a number of years later. This may be because the symptoms of ageing were not the same, or because the brand existed in a different environment.

The example of British Airways

It took British Airways 10 years – the whole of the 1980s – to reinvigorate its image. Passenger growth rates were stagnant, the airline's staff were completely demotivated, and customer service had been entirely overlooked. The result was an aimlessly drifting brand and steadily mounting financial losses. Sir Colin Marshall and Lord King of Wartnaby – the company's CEO and chairman, respectively – then implemented a new and particularly aggressive marketing strategy based on the quality of the product (new products for business class, more comfortable seats, improved service levels, reduced check-in time, etc) and on new agreements with partner companies, allowing the UK company to offer its customers a full service for most destinations on the planet. Clearly, although some changes can be decided upon in an instant, it takes time before the actual implementation falls into line with expectations.

The reason for this is always thc samc. In order to be profitable, the brand's image must be a true reflection of reality. A new advertising campaign will help, but will not be sufficient on its own. For some brands, the minute details of the marketing mix need to be examined with a fine-toothed comb before it becomes possible to implement the advertising campaign intended to present these modifications. Logically, this poses the question of whether the brand's very identity needs to be modified.

7 Modifying the brand's identity

Randazzo (1993) explains that a brand has a spiritual heart, and that its core values can be shown to permeate all of the brand's other attributes. Randazzo uses the notion of a 'soul' to express his argument even more strongly. When a brand shows symptoms of ageing, there may be a strong temptation to change its identity for a younger, more dynamic version. Once again, this shows the fundamental importance of an audit which, as far as possible, should prevent errors of this kind from being made. It is likely that the rejuvenation remedy about to be applied to the brand will change certain characteristics of its identity. However, it would be a serious error of judgment to imagine that such a remedy will succeed entirely in eradicating the brand's old identity and replacing it with a new one. If such an outcome is desired, it would be better to kill off the brand in one way or another, and substitute a new one in its place. The Unilever group used such a tactic to focus its efforts on its star washing powders such as Omo and Skip, 'allowing' its leading washing liquid product, Wisk, to die a planned death.

Many brute-force attempts at repositioning have failed because the original positioning was such an integral part of the brand's identity that any alteration or deviation could only result in harm to the brand. For example, if the exotic dishes brand Suzi Wan were to decide tomorrow that it wished to renew its product range by marketing toad in the hole, Lancashire hotpot or steak and kidney pie, there is little chance that this modification of the brand's identity would be naturally and easily accepted by its target market. After all, what natural legitimacy could Suzi Wan claim for these products, which are so closely linked to UK eating traditions? Modifications to the brand's identity, no matter how urgent the need, should be undertaken only once careful consideration has been made of their consistency with the brand's existing perceived image. Although consumers are prepared for changes, they are often wary of violent shocks which suddenly remove the points of reference to which they had become accustomed. Under no circumstances must the customer's stability be threatened. In 2005, when IBM announced that it was giving up the production of PCs to concentrate on higher-value IT products and services, it sold its personal computing division – along with the temporary rights to the use of its name – to the Chinese manufacturer Lenovo, in order to ease this transition.

The example of Body Shop

Created in 1976, the Body Shop brand remains to this day clearly associated with the values of environmental friendliness and ethics, because its products are not tested on animals, some of its products can be refilled in-store to avoid wasting packaging, the component ingredients of its creams and other cosmetic products are natural, and so on. Body Shop's identity, so close to founder Anita Roddick's heart, is clear.

The problem is that modern consumers are not as altruistic as one might have thought or hoped they would become, or would like to seem. The 'personal pleasure' aspect of buying has neither disappeared nor been relegated to a supporting role. Obviously, consumers are well aware that the anachronistic exploitation of child labour in some African, Asian or South American sweatshops is hardly something to be proud of. But for consumers so far removed from the poverty which is regularly depicted by the media on TV and computer screens, does this really constitute a reason for not buying? We can all support solidarity, environmental friendliness and love for our fellow man when it costs us nothing to do so!

Body Shop's concern was that its competitors would also offer natural products, but in more modern packaging, with the backing of major laboratories, celebrity endorsements, large-scale media coverage, etc. After all, trade is nothing more than the promise of satisfaction, and the main goal of average consumers is to obtain pleasure for themselves. If their conscience can be massaged without any additional expenditure or particular effort, then why not? Otherwise, the approach would require careful analysis.

> The rejuvenation dilemma currently faced by Body Shop is clear. The brand cannot abandon its activist identity, because it constitutes its main point of differentiation. However, while at the same time remaining coherent, it must reintroduce a dose of marketing in order to stay fully competitive. The aim, therefore, is to move the brand's image along without betraying the individual identity upon which it is constructed.

If the brand's image has to be changed and/or other aspects of its identity must be modified, there is a need to justify, explain and follow up these changes. However evident it may appear to the marketer, the logic which led to the introduction of this modification will not necessarily be apparent to the consumer, who perhaps does not have the understanding of the ageing process which prompted the marketer to act. Although we must be wary of the conservative approach, which is always a natural source of ageing, caution is still highly advisable when it comes to decisions regarding the modification of the brand's identity and the way in which such a policy is implemented.

For example, advertising for cigarette brands is becoming increasingly standardized in many countries. If, say, Marlboro were to decide tomorrow to redesign its logo by abandoning the red/white/black colour scheme it currently uses, one would confidently expect that the brand's identity would be profoundly affected, since these colours are so naturally associated with it not only by the target market of smokers but also by other segments of the population.

Conversely, in the 1990s, when the leading UK retailer Tesco decided to stock a selection of top of the range products to attract new customers, it was careful at the same time to maintain its price argument across most of its product range. This image of low price and recognized own-label brands had allowed Tesco to become No.1; it would have been suicidal to change if to do so meant denying this essential component of its identity. An excellent analysis of the Tesco case and of the loyalty-inspiring power of the brand was conducted by Humby, Hunt and Phillips (2004).

Brand identity: a starting point for strategic analysis

In the early 1970s, a young advertising agency, Roux Séguéla Cayzac and Goudard (RSCG), named after its founders, devised a new strategic approach towards the brand known as 'brand personality'. Alain Cayzac and

Jean-Michel Goudard's aim was to consider the brand as a physical person and to treat and respect it as such, giving it its own life. The idea was interesting, but not necessarily original. A number of high-profile advertising gurus such as David Ogilvy, Leo Burnett and Marcel Bleustein-Blanchet had already, in one form or another, advanced the notion that brands needed to be considered as living beings. At RSCG, at the initiative of the always-creative Jacques Séguéla, brand personality took on the name of 'star strategie'. If brands are to be considered as people, then why not strive to make them into stars? The concept of star strategy recognized three dimensions to the brand: a physique, a character and a style. 'Physique' represents the brand's actual contribution to the product; that is, what it actually does. 'Character' opens the doors of imagination for the brand, resulting in appreciation or rejection. 'Style' represents the brand's method of expression, affirming the enduring character and codes of expression which allow the brand to be identified naturally and in the shortest possible space of time.

Nicholas Ind, a brand strategy and advertising consultant, prefers to talk in terms of personality – a personality which, as part of the brand's structure, forms the intermediary layer between the component parts of the structure's internal sphere and the brand's positioning. At Interbrand, the brand is first and foremost considered as a network of associations in the consumer's mind. 'Value' is the name given to the association – regardless of whether its basis is rational or emotive – which prompts the consumer to prefer the brand involved. The research company then produces what it terms the brand's platform, which comprises the structure of the functional attributes and values of the brand. Ultimately, this platform must provide better identification of the brand and a more strategic approach to predisposing the consumer towards it, associating the consumer's own values with those of the brand itself.

No academic or managerial consensus yet exists over the notion of brand image; and, in addition, the concept of identity has now complicated the perception of the brand a little further. Naturally, this new concept, which made its first real appearance in the 1990s, now has many supporters; although they are not all necessarily supporting the same thing. The only point on which everyone seems to agree is the fact that this identity is multifaceted or multidimensional. To define this brand identity, Kapferer distinguishes six dimensions, collaborating with Variot to express this concept in terms of a prism: the physique, the personality, the culture, the self-image, the reflection and the relationship (Kapferer, 1998; Variot, 2002). This view is an enriching new perspective on the vision of the brand, although it should be pointed out that the process of target market decoding is neither straightforward nor the same from one individual to the next, particularly since we are dealing with the brand's symbolic core. The US authors Aaker and Joachimsthaler (2000) identify 12 dimensions, divided into four categories. Six of these relate to the brand as a product: the scope of the product (products bearing the brand name, including extensions), the attributes of the product, the quality/value, uses, users and country of origin. Two relate to the brand as an organization: the attributes of the organization (such as innovation, the attention paid to the consumer, the expressed level of confidence) and the local character versus the global character. Two relate to the brand as a person: personality (for example, original, energetic, etc) and customer relationships. Lastly, two relate to the brand as a symbol: physical imagery and metaphors on the one hand, and brand heritage on the other.

In 1995, Upshaw devoted an entire book to determining and building this brand identity, based on the original and highly interesting idea that this identity is comparable to the formation of DNA, in which a collection of elements is assembled in a unique, decisive and final way – the way in which the brand will be perceived. The analogy is an appropriate one: at the heart of this identity, Upshaw (1995) places the essence of the brand in absolute interaction with six elements which, when brought together, form the total identity of the brand. The creation of this total identity is then presented by the author as the only way of protecting and increasing the brand's capital. She believes that this is the pathway to ensuring the loyalty of its consumers. Positioning is used as a 'compass' which shows it the path to follow if the brand is to grow and best meet the expectations of those who consume the brand's products, and do so in a way which corresponds with the image they have of the brand. 'When people think of brands, they imagine them among a sea of associations which constitute a mental whole, surrounding and at the same time including the brand. Its positioning is this "location" at the centre, among these associations,' Upshaw explains.

Put in simpler terms, we are saying that the brand's identity *makes* the brand, and represents it in the richest possible sense of the word. Many researchers have worked on this concept, and it would be difficult to favour one approach objectively over any other. Indeed, this identity is often diminished by being assimilated into the brand's personality. We believe that this too is a serious mistake. The brand's personality combines all of its character traits (dynamic, creative, independent, aware, caring, etc), distinguishing it from all other brands. This is the brand's own perceived value. Some brands have none of these character traits, and yet they still exist and have their own *de facto* identity. In the common sense of the word, we can subsequently say that a brand has a personality, without necessarily perceiving all of these character traits, simply because it clearly differentiates itself from its competitors.

The example of Cinzano

In 1995 in the UK, Cinzano was the subject of a rejuvenation initiative. A lemon-flavoured version was tested in different bars in York, while an orange version was tested in a number of establishments in Bristol. The objective was clearly to alter the brand's personality slightly by giving it two new flavours – but, of course, without betraying the brand's identity and its vermouth base.

Identity represents the entire qualified essence of the brand and all of the component parts of its physical manifestation, but also its image. It is a collection of components because, just as one generally struggles if asked to describe a person, a painting or a place in a single word, we need several components to obtain a precise description of this identity. We will therefore use 12 constituent parts which, in the light of expert interviews conducted for this book, we consider to be of crucial importance. Living on its name, its heritage, its codes of expression, its positioning, its status, its personality, its everyday behaviour, the beliefs it generates, its values, the image it projects, the attitude of its consumers toward it and its own attitude towards its consumers in particular, this patchwork identity represents everything that the brand is. To make profound alterations or brutal replacements would simply mean killing it. In his excellent book (2004) Haig analyses 100 successful brands. At first glance, the only factor common to all these brands is their success, for their respective identities are very different. However, the author concludes that ultimately, the true common factor is the clarity of their message. Their identity is specific enough to allow them to exist in a highly competitive world.

A rejuvenation remedy should permit the modification of one or more constituent elements in the brand's identity, provided the new created entity remains coherent and, above all, faithful to the brand's overall image of identity. Rejuvenation does not mean shattering this image. In such a case, it would be basically preferable to start from scratch and launch a new brand. Rejuvenation is a question of changing this overall image in order to keep it current in the consumer's mind. However, without the faithfulness to the brand's own roots, the points of reference used by the consumer as a guide simply disintegrate. And without points of reference there can be no clear identification of the brand, resulting in a fuzzy perception, a tendency for consumers to forget the brand, and the consequent advantage to competitors. We must never forget that although human memory is amazingly capacious, it still has limits. If the brand has been lucky enough to find itself a place there, it would be suicidal to seek to uproot it and replant it somewhere else. It would be far wiser to keep this place and continue to change its value.

The example of Babycham

In 1993, in the UK, the Babycham drink realized that it had aged. The rejuvenation plan was so profound and brutal that the brand was entirely uprooted and its identity torn to shreds – hardly surprisingly, considering the lack of respect which had been shown for the soul of the brand. A subsequent recovery plan was launched, restoring the brand's original identity and drawing on the more legitimate premise of nostalgia.

Although separate from one another, all of the component elements in the brand's identity are linked and interact with one another. This demonstrates why the brand manager's attention must not be focused exclusively on any one element, but spread equally between all of them. The manager's role must therefore not be reduced to acting as the 'guardian of value' for each of these components; he or she is also the head of the orchestra, conducting the music created by their association. The French brand specialist Lewi explains how difficult it is to create the perfect combination and how subtle the blend of each of the variables needs to be (2003). To obtain – and retain – legendary status, the brand must be able to question, re-examine, adapt and innovate if it is to change constantly while preserving the basis of its own identity.

The name

Without a name, no clear and unambiguous identification is possible. This is why that name represents the primary component part of a brand. Ask any individual about a brand that represents a particular category, sector or sphere, and in most cases his or her answer will begin with the first name that comes to mind. Furthermore, that name will also act as a point of reference for any additional descriptions the individual may give. The name is the basic component of the brand's identity; the foundation on which all the other components will rest. It is the trigger for evocation.

In the late 20th century, we witnessed the growth of sensorial and experiential marketing. Olfactory marketing is now becoming a subject of interest; the mystique which surrounded it was always likely to inspire loftier ambitions. Its main attraction was the range of emotions it was capable of releasing, in the manner of some Proustian marketing guru inspired by madeleine cakes and tea… but perhaps, to a lesser extent, because it targets the neocortex rather than the limbic system, it may be that the name already fulfils this evocative function to some extent. Without wishing to criticize any of the following brands, the stated positionings of which are very different from each another, does Peugeot evoke the same emotions as Citroën? Does Air France carry the same symbolism as Cathay Pacific? Certainly not. As the main perceptible component of identity, the name is the almost instant ambassador for the elements forming the brand's identity. It is the ostensible result of their amalgamation. This demonstrates the range of very different associations this combination can generate from one individual to another. It thus becomes apparent that the laborious work of homogenization, coherency and clarity on the part of the brand manager can assume its full meaning in the evocative power of this name.

Extract from a speech by Niall Fitzgerald, then Chairman of the Unilever PLC group, to the annual meeting of the Marketing Society in London, 18 June 2001

Brands exist because people want them to exist. Even if the word 'marketing' had never been invented and advertising was banned across the whole planet, there would still be brands, because people need them. The use of a brand is an instinctive, natural human creation – a way of simplifying a complicated world. With a brand, you have a symbol, a sign: you know what you're getting, and what to expect. When William Lever first cut up his soap bars into fixed-price pieces, wrapped them up and gave them the name Sunlight, he added responsibility – the first step towards protecting the consumer. Put a name on a product – brand the product – and yes, there is a long-term guarantee. If you like what you've bought, you know that you'll be able to buy it again and again. Also – and just as importantly – from the consumer's point of view, there's now someone to blame if things go wrong. If you don't like what you've bought, you know what to avoid – and what to tell your friends to avoid.

Heritage

Even an innocent newborn child, albeit unknowingly and helplessly, already has a heritage. Whether or not that heritage is known, it consists of a narration of former events. The past cannot be ignored. Even at a distant remove, it remains an integral part of a brand's identity. To deny it is to expose it to possible parasitic contradictions and disputes. To forget it is to lose its identity, little by little. To neglect it is to run the risk of missing potential opportunities for increasing its value. We are always responsible for our own pasts, whether or not we control them. In the case of old brands (that is, brands which are old in chronological terms), this can sometimes be difficult to manage, and may become increasingly so.

Barely a century ago, heritage had to make do with a handful of memory aids which were fragmented, sometimes fragile and often ephemeral. Today, it can call upon a wide variety of sophisticated and easily available tools designed to record all of the different possible versions of the brand's life for posterity. The heritage of a brand must be reconstituted, understood and interpreted, accepted and explained, to be given its maximum value. If we may respectfully paraphrase the thoughts of the philosopher Raymond Aron, the company may at the same time be both the subject and the object of historical awareness. It may not overlook its heritage, nor assign control of it to any party other than itself, for fear of being confronted with an interpretation with an intent other than that of portraying its identity in a favourable light. Its heritage is the physical proof of its life, the concrete evidence of its existence and – as far as possible – the practical demonstration of its contribution to the company to which it belongs.

There is nothing surprising in the fact that more and more brands are associating this heritage with specific places. After all, throughout history, origins have been assigned dates and geographical locations. Marketing has long since accustomed us to having to distinguish a Colombian from a Brazilian coffee, Côte d'Ivoire chocolate from Venezuelan chocolate, Indian tea from Burmese tea. Nowadays, a cosmetic products brand will claim to use oils from Madagascar, a perfume will have essences from Australian wood, a ready-prepared meal will be made from Argentinian beef, and a clothing product can boast Indonesian thread. However, this is a game that not only countries can play. Regions, and even towns, can also form anchor points for memory and/or imagination.

Codes of expression

If a brand called Mr Martin was identified sometimes as Martin, sometimes as Marretin, sometimes as Martine and sometimes as Marteen, it is highly likely that it would rapidly encounter many and varied identity problems, but in addition to its actual name, a brand usually possesses a logo which may or may not incorporate an emblem, also known as graphical characteristics. Any good brand strategy will therefore take care to establish a graphical charter specifying fonts, size, width, boldness, colour(s), proportions and layout of the set of semantic and/or graphical components which depict the brand. Compliance with this graphical charter must be enforced regardless of the individual circumstances under which the brand appears in each case.

The graphic symbolism for the brand naturally plays a part in both forming and classifying its identity; regardless of whether the device in question is an evocative iconic representation such as the Shell logo or the chocolate brand's old-fashioned clock with hands pointing to 'After Eight'; a metaphorical representation such as the crocodile in the Lacoste logo recalling the nickname given to the tennis player René Lacoste (the brand's founder), or the symbolic squirrel of the French Caisse d'Épargne Écureuil building society (*écureuil* means 'squirrel'). Or it may be a handwritten font suggesting elegance, such as the signature of Cartier, or a thick, dense font evoking power and stability, such as the one used by AT&T. Then there is the red of Coca-Cola, the electric blue of EDF and the natural green of Land Rover. Lastly, consider the red-checked cloth design used by Bonne Maman, the golden double arches of McDonald's and Jaguar's leaping big cat. Each of these elements plays its part in piecing together the identity of the brand and, in addition, the image that this brand will create in its consumers' minds and most of these codes of expression are protected by law. They are sometimes so well-established in consumers' minds that if they were to disappear, there is a danger that the brand's identity would be profoundly altered. Is it possible to imagine an Apple product without its 'bitten' fruit logo, a Peugeot car without a lion, or a Ralph Lauren sweater without its polo player? And never let it be said that such identities are the product of time alone; the Monster recruitment website is already attached to its characteristic mascot (see Figure 7.1).

Figure 7.1 Monster website character on each of the national versions of the site

Positioning

This is usually defined as the space occupied by the product in the minds of its target market. On this subject, Ries and Trout (2000) were prompted to observe that the company's positioning work was undertaken not on the product, but in the mind of the prospect. This is a long-term strategic task; its modification after the fact is often problematic to the brand, if not downright prejudicial. A brand's positioning constitutes not only a powerful factor contributing to its identification, but also an equally powerful instrument of differentiation. Its aim is to facilitate the brand's location in absolute terms; but more importantly, to enable it to be located in relation to its competitors. It thus constitutes a point of reference for the brand. No doubt some cynics may see this as an easy opportunity to point out that this reveals a weakness in the marketing, since it is marketing that is supposed to look after the upstream business of consumer needs and expectations. In such a case, where is the legitimacy in an attempt to differentiate, if the product would appear to correspond precisely with the expectations and desires of its chosen target market? One should always be wary of these flippant cynics, whose perception rarely extends beyond the limits of their own minds.

Pringle and Thompson (1999) concluded that in the 1990s, following on from judgment systems based on rational criteria in the 1950s and emotional criteria in the 1970s, the brand was now founded on spiritual or ethical judgment. The authors stated the importance of the brand territory in determining its positioning. This territory is located at the intersection of the brand's character (its status, and the beliefs and emotions surrounding it), the truth about the product (its objective competitive advantage) and the consumer rationale (the motivations and causes underlying their choices). The authors maintained that their aim was to use marketing research to discover which aspects of the brand's character could be combined with aspects concerning the truth about the product and the consumer rationale, resulting in a coherent positioning.

Status

Although some types of status may naturally appear more advantageous than others, no one status is more beneficial than another when it comes to lending value to an identity. The status of 'market leader' would naturally seem to be the most favourable of all. However, note the use of the word 'seem'. Experience shows that in all markets, there can be only one No.1 – and yet, in all markets, or at least in the vast majority of markets, there are other companies and brands which are doing just as well as, or even better than, the leader. Let us consider this in relative terms. A market-leading brand generally benefits from this status as a result of the fact that it is implicitly associated with a degree of success, giving its products a certain relevance compared to those of its competitors. Although we must be careful in this respect, as variations are possible from one market to the next, it is also often the case that a leader wields power – or in any case, more power than its competitors; this can be perceived as offering reassurance and making a positive contribution to the brand's image. Conversely, it can also be associated with the idea of detachment, or even outright domination, which do not make a positive contribution to the brand's image.

The key characteristic to bear in mind here is that of clarity. Regardless of the specific situation, this status must be clear, proclaimed, explained and justified, so that it may work to the benefit of the brand's identity. The classic case of the car rental firm Avis is a good example. The brand has always proclaimed its status as a challenger and the market's No.2, claiming in its own advertising that this motivates it to do more for its customers. Clarity removes most or all doubt, creating an environment in which confidence in the brand can grow.

Personality

Since the 1980s in particular, the question has often been asked: from whence does the company derive its personality? The 1980s are often used as a point of reference because it was at this time, aided by a rapidly expanding economic and financial press, that company bosses stepped out of their offices to declaim their own opinions before the microphones and cameras of the media. As with any new trend, excess often followed close behind, and the extent to which these CEOs were lionized by the media often far outstripped the publicity given to the other factors in the equation; that is, the company and/or the brand. This meant that the personality of the man or woman in charge became directly associated with that of the company itself; and since boss and company had thus effectively become fused together, the personality of the one merged with the personality of the other.

With the benefit of hindsight, it is easy to see the dangerous fragility of such an association; for if the personality of a company can be fragile, the same failing applies even more to human personality. Every alteration, contradiction and false move on the part of the human leader rebounds on the company, despite the fact that the protection of the company and/or the brand's personality is of crucial importance. A brand's personality is represented by its original character, its own value (creativity, intelligence, dynamism, independence, freedom of thought, etc). This explains the natural and logical assimilation which can occur between the brand and its leader. It is impossible to separate the two entirely, unless the company forbids any media publicity around its CEO – which, in a modern, media-saturated society, would be difficult to do in any case.

This brand personality is sometimes subtracted from the brand's complete identity with the goal of making it into an advertising tool – a strategy attempted by Gordon's gin in the early 1990s, although without any real success because the brand ultimately became too detached from the product itself. From 1994 onwards, a brand rejuvenation initiative was undertaken with a new advertising campaign produced by Leo Burnett, focusing on the product's distinguishing characteristic: its taste.

Everyday behaviour

This is probably one of the most recent strands of the brand's identity to be introduced. Certainly, a few decades ago the brand was, first and foremost, an advertising tool the purpose of which was to identify a product and, ideally, to provide information about its nature and perhaps also its quality. Today, companies generally enjoy greater and deeper recognition from their consumers, particularly if they operate in mass retail markets – another effect of the information society. With the changes in modern consumption and advertising this has brought, the brand has gradually moved further and further into the public eye. It has taken increasing care over the messages it sends out to its various audiences, and has gradually come to the realization that the cycles for this information were becoming shorter and shorter. The example of economic and financial advertising is probably one of the clearest cases in this respect. In the past, such information – if it existed at all – was mainly released on an annual basis, and was also targeted at an informed audience, thus generally confining itself to providing an absolute minimum quantity of raw data. In those days, it was claimed that instead of publicity budgets, advertising agencies worked with 'silence budgets'! In the more recent past, driven by market forces and demand from consumers who were constantly diversifying and becoming well-versed in the language of business, the brand instigated a genuine revolution in the way it communicated, reducing the period of time between operations and adding a little explanation to the statements it released.

Today, such communication is issued on a day-to-day basis, and aimed at professionals, amateurs and administrators alike. All brands – or, in any case, most brands – have come to the clear understanding that their brand image depends on doing this. The worst type of information is a failure to supply information. The brand's identity is not set in stone on the day of its birth; it is written daily, and each everyday act in its life plays a part in determining and changing the shape of this identity.

In December 1999, the tanker *Erika* sank off the coast of Brittany, causing a huge oil-spill. The tanker owner was Total and its CEO, Thierry Desmarest, had been named Manager of the Year just a few weeks previously. The press criticized him for taking too long to react and for failing to come and see for himself the damage caused by the oil-spill. As a result, Total's company image was tarnished in a matter of days. Comparison may be made with events on the evening of 2 August 2005, when an Air France Airbus A340 crashed in Toronto during landing. In the hours following, senior Air France managers gave a detailed briefing to the media and data was quickly put on the website. The following morning, 3 August, Air

France CEO, Jean-Cyril Spinetta, gave a press conference immediately prior to his departure for Toronto.

Beliefs

A simple etymological study of the word should be sufficient to inform the brand manager and encourage him or her to take the greatest possible care in this respect. Proof does not have to be produced, and nor must rational and verifiable evidence necessarily be supplied, before belief starts to take shape. This easily leads each person to his or her own opinion regarding the object of belief and (in the case which concerns us here) the brand. All brands, whether or not aimed at the general public, are surrounded by beliefs. These beliefs may be beneficial or detrimental to the brand. A belief consists of the emotional, descriptive and qualitative components an individual will associate with the brand. The factors creating these components can be very varied, ranging from actual experience of the brand to a rumour that has been given credence, and including subjective and/or objective as well as conscious and/or subconscious impressions. It is thus easy to see why the brand manager must precisely identify these beliefs in order to manage and nurture those he or she considers favourable to the brand's desired identity, but also to use facts and advertising to combat those which reveal themselves to be detrimental to that identity.

In December 1994, Intel was hit by a crisis when it was discovered that its latest Pentium microprocessor was making calculation errors. The error only affected a handful of sophisticated calculations where floating-point precision after a number of decimal places could be incorrect; and furthermore, the average rate of its occurrence had been calculated at 1 error every 27,000 years for an ordinary user – and yet, for several weeks, Intel faced a barrage of criticism and abuse. The beliefs that comprised its identity had been profoundly altered. A microprocessor's function was to be powerful, precise and exact in all its calculations. Regardless of how infinitesimally small the alteration of these beliefs in reality, an alteration had still occurred!

Values

Ever since companies started claiming social awareness credentials for themselves, a wave of ethics has gradually seemed to immerse the world of economics. Clearly, however, not all companies have been affected! However, the more lucid among them have already realized that the responsible consumer – who must, after all, live in the same society as the brand – now expects to deal with companies that show responsibility in terms of their obligations and duties as economic entities within society.

Evidently, companies will always be subject to economic factors, and it is understandable that they are driven by profit. However, among the many paths which can lead to making money, some are more praiseworthy and respectable than others. Safety, the environment, human rights, freedom, ethics, knowledge, trust – these are just a few of the values which, if they are adhered to and clearly publicized by the brand, can have a beneficial effect upon it. Once companies had come to understand that economic salvation was to be found in loyalty to the brand by the greatest possible number of its customers, they also began to consider the idea that to achieve this, they would need to create win-win relationships. Their goals can no longer be restricted to merely satisfying their consumers at the time when the good is consumed. Their aim must be to go much further, because such satisfaction, while necessary, is no longer sufficient to win the consumer's loyalty. Consumers now need to know that they can trust the company; that as well as providing them with the products and services they require, it will also share their own civic values. Some will be quick to denounce this vision as utopic, given the manifest existence of 'rebel' consumers for whom civic responsibility is – and is likely to remain – an abstract notion with no real meaning. No matter. It is illusory and dangerous to attempt to please everyone. However, everyone must be treated with respect. And this respect usually takes the form of adherence to the noble principles and values which, because they benefit consumers in general, will also ultimately benefit the company in particular. One might point at this juncture to a commendable and original initiative taken by one major retailer: in 2001, Auchan introduced a new clause into its specifications aimed at its own-brand producers, whereby these producers were obliged to stamp the name of the Auchan own-brand product in Braille on the packaging of all the store's own products.

Projected image

This is the image that the brand desires and that it presents to its consumers – the image that forms the basis of the advertising strategy. If all goes according to plan, the perceived image of the brand will be a faithful reflection of the projected image. However, as we have already observed, this is only possible if, from the beginning, the projected image is itself a reflection of the brand's objective image. This is a simple issue of coherence. The brand's advertising must strive to create, project and maintain this image. It should be pointed out that this is no short-haul task. While it might be conceded that a brand's renown can last indefinitely in the minds of its consumers – albeit subject to a considerable effort of recollection, given the depth at which the information seems to be buried away in the long-term memory – the same is not true of its image. The image is 'only' a reflection of its own identity. It contributes to the process of establishing this identity in the mind of the individual, and – if maintained – allows value to be derived from its existence. The image is not eternal, and it is certainly not immovable. Separated from straightforward renown, it can be either positive or negative; a very well-known brand can still have a very bad image, while a low-profile brand may enjoy an excellent image. This projected image must therefore be closely monitored with consistency, real-life accuracy and permanent effort if it hopes to retain a positive place in the mind of the target individual.

Attitude of the brand's consumers towards it

In recent years, price wars between brands – fought either unwittingly, or out of the need to confront their competitors on a battlefield the brands themselves had unknowingly chosen – have simply ripped apart any notion of loyalty upon which the brand might have hoped to build a durable relationship with its customers and/or consumers. Today, a very large number of brands are perceived by consumers as factors that serve to identify the product in question, but certainly do not symbolize any particular value of this brand. The brand's image is not – or to be precise, is no longer – a piece of information released by the brand and received by the consumer. The relationship between the brand and the consumer is now, by necessity, an interactive one. In other words, the way in which the target market will perceive this image and the attitude it will consequently develop towards the brand will constitute factors which, in return, will influence the image of the brand. To understand this point fully, it must always be borne in mind that a brand only exists in any real sense inside the minds of its consumers. If, despite the best efforts of the brand, its consumers remain hostile, its image will suffer.

Attitude of the brand towards its consumers

A brand which fails to study, include and respect its customers and/or consumers is highly likely to accelerate the process of its own impending ageing. Marketing should no longer be considered as some minor sub-branch of management sciences. It is essential to any company that aims to identify, understand and create a dialogue with its customers and/or consumers. Given the imbalance between supply and demand, which structurally favours excess demand in the vast majority of cases, the company has no other choice. Benezra (1996) noted that the average rate of failure for new products was 94 per cent. This shows clearly that the chances of success are uncertain, even for products which would seem to be based on fresh foundations. The brand must use rigorous, appropriate market research to address the perceived expectations, needs and risks in its consumers' minds, while at the same time managing to create, nurture and maintain not just one, but all of the emotions that will give the brand its values and positive connotations. The brand's aspiration is to enter the world of the consumer. It should be understood that apart from a few rare and marginal cases, it will achieve this goal not by brute force, but by persuasion. 'Permission marketing' is not an invention, or even an innovation. It is no more than the now explicit revelation of a shift in the balance of power in which the consumer comes to be considered as a significant individual and informed participant in a relationship built on respect, as opposed to the old model of a homogenous unit whose only choice was imposed by another party. The brand is free to decide whether to ignore this fact, or act upon it. However, it must bear in mind that although it may still retain a choice, it no longer exercises full control over the consequences of that choice.

The example of Laura Ashley

During the mid-1990s, the Laura Ashley home decoration brand experienced a number of economic difficulties. A detailed analysis of the reasons for this situation revealed that the brand was ageing – in relative terms, but persistently. The changes adopted by the brand were considerably more conservative than the previous set of changes, which had been made for the same reasons. The intention in the former case had been to achieve a dramatic rejuvenation of the brand by distancing it from its traditional floral image. Just as dramatically, the brand found itself cut off from its core identity, thus removing all points of reference for the faithful consumer and confusing the image which other consumers may have had of it.

From 1995 onwards, the new rejuvenation strategy incorporated the requirement that it had to be possible for the loyal consumer target market of the 1980s to re-associate the brand with what had made Laura Ashley home decoration famous, while at the same time winning over the 1990s target market of more modern consumers by offering new products without compromising the brand's quality standards. A brand rejuvenation programme must take account of each of the component parts of the brand's identity; if it does not, there may be many potential outcomes, but perfect coherence will not be one of them.

Generic brand names: an imperative need for rebirth

Is there anyone who has never talked about 'doing a spot of hoovering'? Who has not, when trying to get to an upstairs floor in a department store, wondered where to find the escalator? Haven't we all at one time or another asked for a roll of sellotape when wrapping presents; or opened the fridge door? And yet the vacuum cleaner in question may not actually be a Hoover; just as the moving staircase might not have been manufactured by Escalator, the adhesive tape you used may have come from a firm other than Sellotape, and the refrigerator in question will most likely not have been produced by Frigidaire.

Is it not legitimate for any brand to wish to become a generic name and, in the best of cases, to achieve immortality through a dictionary entry? Can there be any more absolute form of recognition than being automatically – and usually subconsciously – named by a consumer when referring to a whole category of products to which the brand belongs? There is no doubt that this is a sign of success. But what kind of sign? A brand needs to be known and recognized in order to have a presence in the consumer's mind at the moment when a product from the category in which it has earned its name is bought or used. But does this mean that it is wise to do everything possible to obtain the absolute recognition which comes from the 'brand as generic name' phenomenon? Certainly not! Masson (2000) rightly pointed out that this was 'an advantage which could rapidly become a handicap'. A handicap, indeed, which has even prompted some brands to change their name in order to avoid being relegated to generic status as a result of the ubiquity of their name.

The example of Xerox

Most Americans use the verb 'to xerox' when referring to the act of photocopying a document. It was Chester Carlson who, in 1938, produced the first Xerographic image, but it was not until 1959 that the term truly entered into common parlance. In that year, the Xerox company launched the Model 914, the first automatic photocopier to use ordinary paper, which was the direct ancestor of all such machines in existence today. This photocopier was to become the best-selling item of industrial equipment in history. Thanks to this invention, Xerox became the world leader in reprographics.

Today, the brand's success can be measured by the fact that when someone talks about 'a xerox', it is understood that he or she means a photocopy – even though there is no guarantee that a Xerox machine was actually used in the process.

This success was such that the brand dropped its guard and failed to spot a number of markets in the 1970s and 1980s, not realizing the potential of the inventions its own engineers had devised – one of which was no less than the personal computer itself. While Xerox continued to focus on sophisticated, very high-end products because of the margins they commanded, its competitors were at the same time making inroads into the enormous entry-level and mid-range market, compensating for lower margins with much greater volumes. Their products and brands thus gained ground while Xerox's dwindled.

In 1994, Xerox decided to rename the company. Thus was born The Document Company, the stated objective of which was to distance itself from the photocopying segment alone in order to become a global partner in the management of its client companies' documents. However, a change of identity implies that the company's personality is also changing, its strategy has been adjusted and its objectives redesigned. Today, Xerox is no longer even the leader in its original market. The market has continued to change.

A brand **must** be managed; if it is not, there is a risk that the market will step in and do so in the place of companies that abdicate their own responsibility. Naturally, this is not in any way to suggest that Xerox has ever been guilty of a lack of goals for its brand. However, the leap from strategic analysis and practical application is rarely made – or if it is, it is made badly. Now, after much restructuring, Xerox is much more in step with the expectations of its market, and has once again become a significant brand.

An audit of the company's image should allow the brand manager to identify what constitutes the foundation of the brand's identity. In other words, the intangible aspect that must, like Ariadne's ball of thread in the Minotaur's labyrinth, always be present, removing all doubt from the minds of the brand's consumers. This includes anything that constitutes the brand's core identity and which, if it is adhered to, will enable the brand to preserve its aura.

The example of Dior

Few brands have been able to preserve their fundamental characteristics more successfully than Dior. Yet the haute couture company, founded on 16 December 1946, owes its existence to the fact that Christian Dior had accepted the financial support of Marcel Boussac, a French clothing manufacturer; a fact that might, somewhat unjustly, encourage the supposition that such an industrial link may have been detrimental to Dior's luxury image. The reality, in fact, was quite the opposite. Very soon afterwards (in 1948), the Christian Dior perfume company was founded and is now one of France's most successful luxury brands at rejuvenating its image over time without losing its own identity. When it comes to haute couture, talented young designers such as John Galliano and Hedi Slimane are no strangers to working with the brand. And as for the perfume itself, a new advertising campaign has done the rest.

As we will explain, the brand can and must change, precisely so that it can avoid ageing in a negative way. However, it must not deny its own identity, or else it may be misunderstood; at which point disappointment and oblivion will logically follow.

Brand characters

Advertising has led the way here, offering brands that took this option a chance to obtain an embodied identity. For the advertising executive, it is a simple matter to devise a real or imaginary character that corresponds exactly with the brand's aspirations and is given the task of embodying that brand, putting a face to its name and giving it life by proxy. Furthermore, most studies show that when the choice is coherent with the brand's message, the results obtained with a brand character are better than average.

In this way, the brand can acquire an everyday face and its identity may take a physical form. The history of advertising contains many examples of brands that have been 'humanized' to add life and bring them closer to their consumers. To name but a few, one might think of the legendary Milky Bar Kid for Nestlé Milky Bar, I Helford for Viking Direct, Baron Wrangel for Hathaway shirts, Germaine for Lustucru, the Jolly Green Giant for Green Giant Sweetcorn, the Marlboro cowboy, M Plus from Bahlsen, Uncle Ben for Uncle Ben's, Commander Whitehead for Schweppes, Titus Moody for

Pepperidge Farm, Joe Isuzu for Isuzu cars and Betty Crocker for the brand of the same name... the list goes on and on. However, beware: in some cases, such as Isuzu and Viking Direct, the face of the brand is unique; or at any rate, nearly unique. The brand is embodied by a real person. This can pose a problem over time, as the person ages. And yet, in other cases such as Marlboro and Uncle Ben's, what matters is the character's own attributes as opposed to his actual identity, and actors can therefore be replaced at will, provided the basic attributes remain the same. The advertising manager David Ogilvy explains that doing so can even help to strengthen the authenticity of the product.

Some brands, in their constant pursuit of an identity with a higher profile and more differentiation, have even adopted a first name. Not all brands are able to take such an approach. However, many old brands have names deriving from one or more of their founders. Even so, although the origin of this 'loan' may have been apparent at the time of creation of the brand name and for a number of years afterwards, the same is not necessarily the case today. This is why, when faced with the chance, some brands are quick to seek out the 'missing first name' in order to humanize the brand character and thus make it less industrial, more up to date and, naturally, closer to its consumers. In addition, many will be quick to take the opportunity to acquire a face for the character symbolizing this forgotten first name. In some cases, authenticity is the most important factor – even if this can only be achieved through the use of archive images.

The example of Lipton

This is how Sir Thomas became the main spokesman for the tea that bears his name – Lipton. From a sociological point of view, the approach is a very interesting one in that the image of a conspicuously dead character is being used to promote the merits of a product. However, the collective unconscious does not trouble itself overly with such a 'detail', preferring to focus on heritage, origins and roots – in a word, identity. Yet the Lipton case is a special one, given that Thomas Lipton, who was born in Glasgow in 1850 and died in 1931, had a sufficiently rich and media-friendly life to supply his brand with plenty of visual archives, despite the fact that only limited recording means were available at the time. An energetic businessman, he was even knighted by Queen Victoria in 1898. A keen sailor, he participated five times in the America's Cup; and although he never managed to win the cup itself, his name remains associated with it.

In other cases, there is insufficient visual evidence to enable appropriate use to be made of this approach. In this way, Bridel is able to stipulate that its Camembert cheese be named after Émile. Likewise, Lindt paid tribute to Rodolphe, offering a genuine guarantee of the quality of its chocolate through his portrayal by an actor. Similarly, Panzani gives the nod of recognition to Giovanni Panzani, whose first name and likeness now appear on the firm's pasta packets. In the same way, Gervais discovered Charles, whose odiously divine character also acts as a guarantee as to the quality of the brand's products, but whose face has so far never been seen. A first name is a simple, easy way of humanizing the brand. The case of Gervais was, in addition, a rather unique one compared to others: the Gervais brand was 'shared' between Nestlé (for ice creams) and Danone (for milk products). The introduction of the first name 'Charles' allowed these two identities to be differentiated a little more. The additional value of these forenames from the past is that they have no specific age other than the heritage of tradition and quality. It can therefore be presumed that there will be no particular difficulty in managing them over time.

8 The dynamizing of advertising

Every marketer knows that as soon as the slightest suggestion of an economic recession appears, the advertising budget is one of the first – or indeed the very first – to be cut back to a basic minimum, if it is not simply dispensed with altogether. However, every marketer is also familiar with the maxim stating that a brand that continues to invest during a crisis increases its own chances of surviving the crisis better than its fellow brands. Yet while these are brave words, the theory is often difficult to put into practice. Even so, advertising is probably one of the essential factors in the rejuvenation of a brand – if only because there is a risk that any interruption will add to the vicious circle of the negative effects of the ageing process. In the mass retail products sector, it is a basic truth that if the media advertising plan is halted, the result – within a very short space of time – is the partial or total de-stocking of the product by a number of large retailers. Not stocked means not seen. Not seen means not bought. Not bought means forgotten. Forgotten means an old image. And an old image means a gradual death. This sequence is not necessarily inevitable; but if care is not taken, it can certainly lead very quickly to a sad end.

If the brand audit identifies ageing through the brand's advertising, there is always the option of changing creative teams or even advertising agencies. Some advertising and/or marketing managers tend to do this as a matter of course as soon as they start their new job, without first conducting an objective study, either as a practical way of showing that changes are afoot, or simply to switch to the same agency they worked with in their old job. One might have thought that more rational criteria would be needed for such a decision! A lasting relationship between an agency and an advertiser is central to maintaining, protecting and nurturing the brand's image. The brand needs innovation, but also stability. Not change for change's sake, but change for the sake of growth that is supported by strategic analysis.

Furthermore, some identity changes cannot truly be described as such; the modification is so subtle that it can virtually go unnoticed. However, the approach is a deliberate one, usually with the aim of not altering this identity – and yet the result still brings about a rejuvenation of the brand. This can take the form of a very slight change to the name or logo, which may even in some cases receive little or no media coverage, in order to increase its acceptance by the entire target market still further. However, such modifications generally come under the heading of an anti-ageing strategy. Once it has been observed that the brand is ageing, rejuvenation work must be perceptible; and, if possible, perceived. Of all the rejuvenation factors open to a brand, advertising is one of the most widely used because it is probably the most flexible, and the quickest to implement. The brand's target market cannot be renewed overnight, nor is it possible to rejuvenate an entire range of products over a similar period of time. However, it is possible to set up an initiative to dynamize a brand's advertising in a very short space of time. It is probably wise in this case to be wary of the marketing trap of concentrating exclusively on this factor as the sole means of salvation from the ills besetting the brand.

Favouring advertising above all other tools

The brand is a marvellous advertising tool all on its own. And ever since poster advertising turned into publicity and thence into modern advertising as we now know it, it would seem that anything is possible once the strategic marketing instrument of advertising is pressed into action. Furthermore, the teachings of gifted advertising executives such as Alex Osborn, Raymond Rubicam, Roy Durstine, David Ogilvy, Bill Bernbach, Bruce Barton, Philippe Michel, Marcel Bleustein-Blanchet and Jacques Séguéla now reinforce the modern marketer's hopes for miracles on demand. Are studies showing that the brand is perceived by its target market as having aged dramatically? Just run a few well-chosen advertising campaigns, and all is well again! It is understandable that a green, young advertising apprentice might still harbour such a belief; experience will soon bring him or her round to a more rational, tangible version of reality. However, let a brand manager even dare to think such heresy and he or she is to be immediately consigned to the dungeon of sales negotiations with leading retail stores for having committed the unforgivable sin.

Advertising is potentially a powerful and wonderful method of communication. It acts as an amplifier, attracting the attention of consumers and – in the best of cases (to complete the old faithful AIDA sequence) – to win their interest, stimulate their desire and ultimately prompt them into action.

Ewing and Fowlds (1995) demonstrated the potential power of advertising in rejuvenating a brand through its contribution to increasing the brand's identity capital. This is even more important for products with basic characteristics that are hard to alter. Take, for example, the case of an alcoholic drink, the taste of which is difficult to change. Clearly, range extensions can be created, but the taste of the core product itself cannot easily be altered: a rejuvenation of this kind would risk losing a portion of its core target market.

The example of Allied Domecq

In the late 1990s, marketing research conducted among the consumer target group and also with barmen and serving staff revealed something of an uncertainty with regard to the exact nature of tequila, and with particular reference to the factors of distinction between one brand and the next – unlike, say, whisky, which has several centuries of history behind it and therefore an almost natural justification. By contrast, tequila had only recently received mass-market interest from consumers, and among young adults in particular. Consequently, many brands had been launched on the market without the appropriate steps to educate the consumer.

Domecq thus launched an educative advertising campaign aimed both at consumers – helping them to recognize a 'good' tequila from an entry-level product – and at professionals (staff in bars, restaurants, night clubs, etc), enabling them to offer real added value by providing information to their customers; for, despite the fact that both the ultra-premium and bottom-of-the range brands bore the name 'tequila', there was a world of difference between the two. Such an approach gave Domecq a chance to claim a legitimacy throughout the entire category and, ultimately, the hope of winning the loyalty of discerning customers for its products, while at the same time informing professionals about the complexity of manufacturing high-end products and the difference in terms of the raw materials used. In this way, Domecq was able to make them into ambassadors for the group's brands, adding dynamism to its product range.

Advertising acts as an amplifier, and therefore care must be taken over precisely what is being amplified. The natural aim of an advertising executive is to amplify only the brand's positive points; but sometimes, entirely unintentionally, the advertising can deviate from its initial objective and become a sounding board for unfavourable opinion aimed at the brand. Once again, this is all a question of degree, and of controlled renewal.

If it is to differentiate itself, the brand must establish distinct codes for its advertising in order to differentiate its own message from those of its competitors. These codes are specific, and have become utterly indispensable if the brand is to exist among the cacophony of advertising that assaults the poor consumer in the form of several hundred messages every day. However, a code represents an anchor point in time – which means that if it does not change, it is in danger of being an unwilling contributor to the brand's ageing. Furthermore, the stronger the codes, the heavier the temporal anchor. Kookaï is well aware of this fact. The brand's advertising codes are very powerful, and – in addition – purely corporate. However, the brand has so far always been able to reinvent itself through innovation, backed up by highly original and differentiating campaigns.

The brand is not some mere variable to be tinkered with to facilitate advertising. It is – and must remain – a most precious resource, to be preserved and developed with the assistance of advertising. Clearly, in most cases, a rejuvenation strategy will require its assistance to promote and broadcast the efforts being made elsewhere. But with the exception of the fairly rare cases in which this ageing is attributable entirely to out-of-date advertising, rejuvenation primarily takes the form of the management of strategic marketing factors that are symptoms of its own ageing. Naturally, this approach is much more difficult. It is easier to change advertising agencies and draw up a new brief than it is to rethink the entire range from top to bottom, to modernize the whole distribution network, to shift the brand's current positioning; or even to reshape the target market for that brand. However, this is the cost of deploying an effective rejuvenation strategy. A brand cannot choose which ageing factors it will be affected by. It must, however, try as hard as possible to decide objectively how it will apply the appropriate *ad hoc* rejuvenation tools. This choice must not be guided by the line of least resistance, nor by the lowest-cost solution, but simply by the actions the brand needs, as revealed in the audit. Here, the problem itself must be allowed to dictate the nature of the response; and it is to be hoped that the marketer in charge of the brand will have sufficient talent to find the right way of expressing this.

Using celebrities to rejuvenate a brand

Among the plethora of advertising theories, strategies and techniques, one consists of using a famous personality; that is, a person already famous before appearing in a promotion for the brand. Such a tactic can be very profitable in revitalizing advertising for a brand that has aged, for a number of reasons. In most cases, the use of a celebrity comes as a surprise. Most scientific studies conducted in this area confirm that the star can be expected to provide a significant additional impact. For an ageing brand, this constitutes an opportunity to change its tone and thus attract attention. The brand's ambition is therefore to benefit to some extent from the star's celebrity and image. The star can also constitute a weapon against channel-hopping.

On paper, it would appear that nothing could be easier than simply parachuting a celebrity into an advertisement for the brand. In reality, there may be many delicate issues surrounding the use of that star. Firstly, it has to be decided what role to give the star. Should he or she provide evidence of one of the brand's qualitites? Will he or she become its official spokesperson? Is his or her appearance the result of a sponsorship contract? Is it justified because the star is a recognized expert in this product category? Is the star extolling the product's merits because he or she runs the company that manufactures and/or sells it? Is he or she being called upon to act as a mere figurehead in the brand's advertising? Naturally, each role corresponds to different choice criteria and – more importantly – to different types of use. However, celebrities still remain the weapons of choice when it comes to rejuvenating the brand. They create an impact, and the brand in question is likely to benefit from the extra attention. They represent image, and image is precisely where the brand requires rejuvenation. Furthermore, celebrities are constantly reinventing themselves; and so it is always possible to find one who will meet the requirements of the advertising strategy in terms of rejuvenation. In terms of age, target market, area of business, the professional longevity of the star in question and the extent of his or her celebrity, a star can be chosen to fit perfectly with the brand's needs in the fight against its own perceived ageing.

A study of all types of celebrities taken together (actors, sports stars, singers, musicians, managers, etc), looking at the use of stars in advertising over a century, indicates that 60.85 per cent of celebrity figureheads used were men, compared to 39.15 per cent women. This study is based on purely statistical observations, and is not meant to imply that such a disproportionate representation is linked to greater powers of prescription in men, nor that the impact obtained by using a male spokesperson is any greater than it might be with a female spokesperson. In addition, this study covers an entire century, with the 'smoothing' effect this implies; it is apparent that the status of women has changed considerably over this period. Sport is probably one of the areas in which the most visible changes have occurred. A mere 20 years ago, famous sportswomen were a rare sight in advertising. Their 'value' was not as great as that of their masculine equivalents, because they had received less media exposure, both on and off the pitch. Even now, the balance is still far from being redressed. For example, compare the media coverage of the women's Tour de France to that of its male counterpart. Unlike men's football, broadcasting rights for women's football are rarely fought over, and it was not until 2001 that a US channel (CBS) first broadcast the ladies' final of the tennis US Open at peak viewing time.

Many brands looking to bounce back and/or stay fashionable in terms of celebrity endorsements have made astute associations. For example, the US tennis stars Serena and Venus Williams have already lent their images to Wilson, Nortel, Sega, Reebok and Avon. As well as achieving rejuvenation, the use of famous sports personalities can be a real anti-ageing tool for brands that exercise this option. For most sports, there is a quick turnover; much quicker than used to be the case. By regularly replacing their celebrities, brands that base some or all of their advertising strategy on their testimonials remain associated with the media coverage surrounding the latest winning sports personalities. This allows them to hope that the transfer of celebrity, status and image will rub off on the brand. Nowadays, the brands mentioned above face the problem of finding the resources to keep renewing their advertising contracts with new rising stars in the relevant sports. This is why, with just a few exceptions, this type of advertising is reserved only for the leading brands with the financial ability to play this game.

When the celebrity is used to rejuvenate the brand's advertising, care must be taken to avoid falling into the trap of the knee-jerk reaction. Many advertisers claim that stars are only used when the brand has nothing else to say. The use of a celebrity must be considered as an additional asset, and not as an end in itself. If it is the latter, there is a strong chance that the advertising investment will serve to maintain the star's own celebrity without generating any benefits for the brand or contributing to its rejuvenation. Lastly, brand characters who are a sort of star created by and for the brand, are not exempt from rejuvenation remedies themselves. For example, Captain Birdseye, Don Patillo and Mr Clean have all been given facelifts of varying magnitude to retain a youthfulness compatible with that of the brand. We will note in passing that the use of a cartoon or virtual character, as opposed to a physical one, naturally has an anti-ageing benefit, since its appearance need change only when it suits the requirements of the advertiser, rather than in submission to the will of time.

As a final point, an original use can sometimes be found in product placement or brand placement in films. Via these means, and depending on the film, celebrities and, of course, conditions of use, an ageing brand or product can rapidly improve its image among a wide audience and/or be completely relaunched. At the very least, many studies show that recall for the brand is assisted considerably by a sufficient presence in the film; and keeping the brand in a strong position in the target market's memory is an essential prerequisite for preventing the brand from ageing.

Using education to combat ageing attributable to competitors' dynamism

Some brands age not because their products are out of date, their target market has aged or their advertising does not seem particularly modern. They age simply because of their relative lack of image; or in other words, because their competitors are much more dynamic than they are. In this way, the causes of ageing stem not from a single discernible point, but gradually, through the conscious or subconscious comparisons the consumer makes with the brand's competitors.

Advertising can be an effective rejuvenation tool for combatting such ageing. Of course, the best idea is always to revitalize this advertising in its entirety. But in this particular case, it is also recommended that the positioning of the brand and its products be reaffirmed in comparison to the positioning of its competitors. Such an approach is justified mainly by the fact that this type of comparative ageing generally affects market-leading brands. Because they are leaders, and thus comfortably ensconced in a dominant position, they are not particularly concerned with the possibility of ageing problems. Meanwhile, followers (and in particular the challenger) are often striving to outdo one another in terms of innovation and the production of more dynamic, and comparatively more modern, advertising. A good example of this is the fizzy drinks market, in which Pepsi-Cola's advertising is often considered to be much more modern and creative than that of the leader, Coca-Cola. It may thus be useful to resort to category-based advertising; that is, advertising that places much less emphasis on trumpeting the merits of the brand itself than it does in promoting the product category as a whole. The aim of this is not to advertise your own competitors' products, but simply to 'take the high ground', in a sense, to distance yourself slightly from a purely commercial approach. In this way, advertising for the brand can stand slightly aloof from that of its competitors. When applied carefully, such an approach reinforces the legitimacy of the brand, gives it a distinctive positioning and helps to revitalize it, lending justification to its position as leader. Clearly, there is sometimes a need to educate – or re-educate – the consumer from scratch in terms of the product category or some of its features. However, this task is by no means an impossible one.

The example of Eagle

The case of the US sweetened condensed milk Eagle is an instructive one. Having been introduced before the Civil War, it had aged, and its owner Borden decided to sell it off in the late 1990s. It was relaunched with the backing of a large, dynamic advertising campaign in 1999. Reading the results of the marketing studies conducted at the time, it was apparent that there was a need to educate the consumer as to the different possible uses of the product. An eight-page booklet was thus inserted into *Better Homes and Gardens* magazine, presenting simple recipes using Eagle milk. Studies had shown that although the brand still had an extraordinary image, modern consumers were a little intimidated by the prospect of making pastries and desserts. The various recipes produced were simple. They were aimed at mothers at home, who could make them on their own or with their children. The internet was used to make more recipes available, and to bring the brand a little closer to other more contemporary brands partnerships were signed with Hershey for its chocolate brand of the same name and with Unilever for its margarine I Can't Believe It's Not Butter.

Educate the consumer: the exhortation would appear a simple one at first glance. However, putting it into practice can sometimes be a delicate matter from an advertising point of view, if one is to avoid falling into the trap of boring academic sermons – which could harm the brand still further. This is why the approach must be founded on a rigorous study of the motivations of the target consumer group. The confused perception of the brand's positioning arises from insufficient or unclear information intended to enable the consumer to re-establish the relevant competitive positioning, hierarchy of quality and/or trend-based classification. It therefore becomes necessary to start with a very clear analysis of the exact causes of this confusion, in order to establish what the *ad hoc* responses will be, as well as the techniques and media that seem appropriate for use in passing on this information. Such an advertising initiative sometimes means that the brand must communicate separately yet in a linked way with not only the consumer but also the retailer; if such confusion has appeared, it is often partly because the brand's retailer – the company's customer – has itself not been in a to supply the consumer with adequate information.

Co-branding: an original solution requiring careful attention

Occasionally, some brands form associations for the duration of an advertising campaign only. There are also longer-term partnerships, whose content and components can vary over time. Fast-food restaurant chains, for example, often set up such partnerships to complement children's 'toy meals', the constant purpose of which is to keep winning over a younger audience. This allows the fast-food chains, during these partnerships, to remain up to date, jumping from one fashion effect to the next without any need to commit themselves to binding long-term agreements or suffer the effects of decline phases.

Other brands are prepared to throw in their lot with another brand on a short-term basis via co-branding exercises (exercises where two or more brands become associated with one another). This association can take the form of the development of a joint business initiative to be presented under the auspices of both brands, for the launch of a co-branded product or range of products, or with a view to an advertising campaign featuring both brands. A variety of studies has confirmed the validity of the co-branding approach, the concept of which was very clearly explained by Cégarra and Michel (2001). The work of Desai and Keller (2002) has confirmed this validity, although it also notes that the host brand does not create any long-term capital as such, which could prove damaging in the medium to long term.

If it is to succeed, this association must be based on a logical synergy between the two brands, which is sadly not always the case when it comes to co-branding. When Nivea joined forces with Philips to enable the latter's Cool Skin electric razors to use and promote the use of the former's shaving cream, there was perfect, logical and coherent synergy. When Subaru and L.L. Bean teamed up, the same synergy was found in the common 'outdoor' theme: the cars of the former and the clothing of the latter were complementary.

Obviously, co-branding only works if it results in a win-win relationship. The same is true when rejuvenation is being attempted. Co-branding then takes the form of an association in which the old brand seeks the dynamism and youth of a young brand. In exchange, the young brand must be able to benefit from the renown and established status of the old brand. When Renault's Twingo paired up with Perrier in 2001 for a limited series of vehicles, the car manufacturer obtained the benefits of an associate with a modern image almost entirely restored following the so-called 1990 benzene crisis. On the other hand, Perrier, which had still not entirely rediscovered its former growth rate in the years following 1990, also benefited by acquiring a youthful, rewarding form of advertising.

Not all associations even between major brands, are inevitably destined to succeed. In 2001, two giants, Procter & Gamble and Coca-Cola, announced their intention to collaborate. In this way, Coca-Cola's worldwide distribution network was to serve as a springboard for P&G's food brands such as Pringles snacks and the Sunny Delight drink. Yet after a few blissful weeks together, the two parties came to the conclusion that the marriage was not as simple in practice as it had appeared in theory, and it was annulled by mutual consent. Several years previously, something similar had happened with Yolka (frozen yoghurt), which had brought Danone and Motta together, but had not succeeded in winning over the consumer.

Rejuvenation by modernizing the brand's visual identity

Brand rejuvenation can also take the form of a change in its name and/or its logo. We should also recognize the impressive power a name can possess; with a slight alteration, a name can give the brand an entirely new image and play a very significant part in its rejuvenation.

Many companies, as a result of mergers and restructuring, a renewed focus on specific business areas, or simply because they wanted to restore a certain youthfulness to their business, decided to change their names; examples of this abounded in the final years of the last century. This can be explained by the fact that, ultimately, no mergers or alliances are ever carried out 'just for the sake of it', but rather because the competitive environment, technological progress or even the economic health of one or both of the companies requires it. This then raises the key strategic question of what the new entity's name will be. These are not simple choices. Of course, we once again need to consider what are the strategic goals of this new entity in order to determine whether either of the two brands or associates potentially make a positive contribution. However, we must also consider the characteristics of each of the two brands' identities. They are, by nature, different; and so it is frequently the case that the merger has not only structural and cultural but also economic repercussions. There is usually a transitional phase of varying length during which the two names are juxtaposed, once a decision has been reached as to the order to be followed for the juxtaposition. Generally speaking, however, what we see in such cases is a compromise solution that is rarely satisfactory from a strategic point of view; hence the frequently adopted strategy of creating an entirely new name and identity. This often costly solution means that the new entity can be founded on a new – and therefore neutral – strategic identity base. In addition, it has the enormous advantage of showing no favour to either of the old brands. In this way, the respective identities and consequent standings of the individuals representing the two entities may implicitly be respected.

The decision to adopt a new name can also simply be imposed by a company's decision to switch its focus to an area of business other than the one that previously formed its core business and, in some cases, may have been explicitly stated in its name. In 1987, American National Can could hardly have retained its name when the US company ceased manufacturing metal containers. Moving instead towards a service-based business, it adopted the name of Primerica. To distinguish itself from Arthur Andersen, Andersen Consulting became Accenture in 2001. When the French company Seita merged with the Spanish company Tabacalera, they opted for the new name Altadis. In 2001, when the steel industry union between the Luxemburg firm Arbed, the Spanish company Aceralia and the French firm Usinor ended, the three companies adopted a new name: Arcelor. One might also think of Ciba-Geigy and Sandoz and their new name of Novartis; Philip Morris Companies opting for Altria; Framatome, Cogema and CEA-Industrie transforming into Areva, and the disappearance of Dow Jones Reuters Business Interactive in favour of Factiva. The Greco-Latin connotations in these names are not accidental: a 'trendy' (or at least highly contemporary) name can age very quickly, and very badly. Conversely, having its origins in the distant past, the 'new' name can have an 'established' feel to it, and thus be reassuring without actually sounding old. Most importantly, however, it is of course better equipped to face the future and protect itself against the effects of ageing.

The fact that many examples of name changes can be cited shows that a name appears to play such a key role in announcing a new start; a new life; a new identity. Delano (1998) draws the manager's attention to the care that must be taken over the media migration from one name to another, in order to maximize the new name's chances in terms of recognition and image. In addition to the brand name alone, the logo is a major component that can be susceptible to ageing. Some shapes, colours and fonts age better than others. In such cases, they perform a simple and redeeming act of rejuvenation.

The example of New Man

The New Man brand is a great classic of its kind, and a perfect illustration of this point. A regular word-processor user may enjoy installing new fonts on his or her computer. The procedure is a simple, quick one, and the choice on offer means that styles can be varied almost infinitely. However, budding graphic designers excepted, that user will generally realize very quickly that despite the hundreds or even thousands of available fonts, only half a dozen or so are in regular use – and always the same half a dozen. The eye is a creature of habit. Exotic and/or sophisticated fonts may be a valuable advertising technique for drawing attention, but there is a risk that they will age much more quickly than the brand carrying them. In 1967, when the New Man brand was created to identify a small clothes shop in Rue de l'Ancienne-Comédie in Paris, the all-out Western-style logo (see Figure 8.1) was no surprise to anyone, given the company's chosen positioning. Unfortunately, when New Man sought to expand beyond the borders of France and into other product ranges, it became more and more apparent that the identity bestowed on the brand by its logo – and more specifically by its font – was likely to prove a liability in the long term. It was therefore decided in 1969 to rejuvenate the logo, and the task was given to Raymond Loewy, a talented designer who has always adhered to the philosophy that 'ugliness doesn't sell'.

Figure 8.1 New Man brand logos

Distribution: a lever that naturally complements advertising

Clearly, distribution is often linked to advertising, and vice versa. They must, therefore, both be planned and developed jointly.

The example of Beiersdorf

Unlike L'Oréal, the Beiersdorf group – another sector leader – has opted for a highly strategic delimitation of the areas in which the various brands of its cosmetic products are sold. Furthermore, although the L'Oréal group emblazons its name across most of its own products with the aim of creating an umbrella brand, the Beiersdorf brand is sometimes unknown to consumers of the company's products, so we must dig down further to identify the level at which the group's umbrella brands are successful. Among them, although the well-known Nivea brand distributes most of its products via the supermarkets and hypermarkets channel, Eucerin (on the international market) and Nobacter and Onagrine in France operate in the specialized pharmaceutical products distribution channel. Complementing these first two channels perfectly, the selector is used to market the group's extreme high-end brand, La Prairie. The positioning and price levels for these products are a perfect fit for this approach, which gives Beiersdorf better control over the implementation of its marketing strategy. Furthermore, advertising can then be sectioned off entirely into appropriate media, avoiding any substantial degree of cannibalization. In fact, Nivea now acts as its own umbrella brand, unifying a variety of different products with different positioning and advertising.

For other products, such control sometimes suggests a greater involvement in the distribution of the brand's products. Indeed, even the trendiest of advertising campaigns will be worthless if the product is distributed badly and/or through points of sale that are out of date or even overlooked entirely by the target market. Sometimes, this prompts brands to handle their own distribution in order to give their products the space and attention they are perceived to deserve. This need for an *ad hoc* sales environment is seen particularly strongly among brands positioned in the luxury sector. For this reason, Louis Vuitton, with nearly 30 global stores worldwide, is proud of this initiative, which enables it to present its entire range in selected locations, and (more importantly) in an environment entirely consistent with the positioning and image to which it aspires. However, the products of the luxury sector are not the only ones affected. Once again, when the product in question is a technological one, it is by nature far more exposed to the potential effects of ageing. With 'generations' that have a life span of only a few months, the technology sector is in a very vulnerable position.

The example of Apple

In 2001, Apple Computer won a new gold award for the design of its latest computer, the Titanium Powerbook G4. The Industrial Design Excellence Awards (IDEAs) are presented annually by the Industrial Designers Society of America; and adding up all the gold, silver and bronze awards won by all companies over the last five years, we find Apple on the top step of the podium alongside the Korean firm Samsung.

Since its birth in 1976, and more specifically since the launch of the Macintosh in 1984, Apple has always adopted a positioning which is out of step with the rest of the IT industry, constantly introducing technological and aesthetic innovations. In 2003, the iPod reinvented the portable music market. Even Apple's publicity material has always conveyed a surprising creativity and very distinctive tone. In terms of the distribution of its products, Apple has always tried to convince its stockists that, while they may not have been exclusive Apple channels, it is still important that they set aside a specific area for the brand; a 'corner' in which they show off these computers and their extreme distinctiveness in comparison with the PC family of computers. This is particularly important in light of the fact that the average prices of the brand's computers are higher than those of their indirect PC competitors, which goes some way towards explaining their market share of below 5 per cent. Apple encourages its potential clients to 'Think Different', primarily because that is what it does itself. These are, therefore, different products for which it uses a different advertising strategy – and which it hopes to sell in a different way.

One particular piece of received wisdom about ageing is often encountered: the belief that this phenomenon – which can be very damaging to a brand – targets only weak prey, thus implying that market leaders are immune to the ravages of time. Let us make this absolutely clear: ageing is a relentless process that can affect any brand. Is there any more accomplished marketing operation than the Procter & Gamble group? And yet even its own brands are potential victims.

The lever of distribution is essential if the brand is to carry its image forward as effectively as possible, all the way to the point of contact with the end consumer. If this mechanism is not permitted to operate fully and freely, the brand's other efforts are likely to be futile and its investments nothing more than losses.

The example of Essilor

The fact that Essilor is now firmly established as a market leader is due not only to its constant innovation, the billions of different optical glass combinations it manufactures, or – thanks to its highly efficient information system – the widely-acknowledged first-rate quality of its products, resulting in it supplying some 200,000 opticians worldwide with tailor-made lenses within 48 hours. It is also because Essilor exercises the strictest control over not only its production units but also its distribution outlets. In many cases, distribution is the brand's physical 'shop window' onto the world, and thus also reflects its own age and, by this token, any signs of its rejuvenation. In the context of an ageing Western population (particularly in the United States and Europe), there is a natural growth in Essilor's potential target market. Needless to say, however, its competitors remain watchful – and thus it is imperative for the French brand to pay close attention to both its products and its image.

The lever of distribution is often neglected because the company believes – wrongly – that the product-advertising combination alone will be sufficient to relaunch the brand. When Levi's realised in the late 1990s that its brand had aged in the minds of potential consumers, its main response was to launch a widespread programme to renovate its points of sale while at the same time making changes to its product range.

It is obvious that advertising in its many forms has a very positive role to play for the brand. However, it should never be forgotten that advertising and brand strategy are not the same thing; rather, advertising is just one variable in the mix that may be called upon to serve the brand. There are charismatic brands, such as the Donge soap brand in France or US brand Starbucks coffee, that have created for themselves a very positive image and still maintain that image without having to spend the same sort of sums as their competitors on advertising. Advertising, in all its guises, is a useful tool for conveying the values underlying the promise delivered by the brand. It does not permit substitution. Even the most creative and impressive advertising campaign will have a very short-term effect (if indeed any effect at all) unless it conveys a genuine promise. Advertising can be a very powerful ally, but it must not be confused with overall brand strategy! Furthermore, only an audit of the brand will provide any degree of certainty as to what is useful for the brand and what is better left behind.

Too much advertising = guaranteed boomerang effects

Advertising is an extraordinarily powerful, and often overlooked, marketing lever. For this reason, it sometimes wrests itself free from the control of its users. The effects of this can be very damaging to the brand and its products.

The example of Calvin Klein

In 1995 in the United States, the advertising crisis experienced by the Calvin Klein brand was a hotly-contested issue. Clearly, its advertising made use of a very up-to-date fashion effect, but the outcome was not entirely in line with expectations. Accused of using 'paedophile chic' by showing partially naked adolescents in suggestive positions, many consumer associations responded by calling for boycotts of the brand. However, the brand was already a past master of provocation, having already used the adolescent actress Brooks Shields in 1979–80 in its jeans advertisements, in which the actress announced, 'There is nothing between me and my jeans'. Not to forget Kate Moss, who, at the very start of her modelling career, appeared totally naked on a divan to promote the Obsession fragrance. Lastly, consider the 1999 case of another campaign. This one used very young children for the brand's underclothes range, and brought down the wrath of a great number of associations upon Calvin Klein. However, considering that the brand has always maintained such a provocative position, it seems likely that it will be safe enough with its core target market, provided it stays within certain limits.

Although some brands are partly protected from their own worst excesses by the tolerance of their core target market, the same cannot be said for all brands in general, especially the ones that suddenly decide to adopt a provocative approach, in total contrast to their usual advertising. This can lead to very negative boomerang effects.

The examples of Marks & Spencer and Unilever's Dove

In the UK in 2000, the Marks & Spencer store chain, faced with the serious ageing of its overall brand and the St. Michael brand in particular, opted for a new advertising stance with a provocative publicity campaign – a TV commercial featuring a model running naked through nature, with the theme backed up by a poster campaign. It immediately provoked howls of protest, particularly among the religious community, and, despite a ruling from the Advertising Standards Authority allowing the campaign to continue, the outcome was not a particularly favourable one for Marks & Spencer's image. Even a few years later, the UK retailer was still struggling to come up with a clear marketing strategy either for its food or clothing business. In the meantime, in spite of heavy restructuring work, the brand equity is being inexorably eroded, making the task of a much-needed rejuvenation a much longer and costlier process.

It is interesting to note that the 2000 Marks & Spencer's advertising campaign based on a 'real woman' did not succeed. A mature model was used, whose proportions were said to reflect the size 14 of the 'typical' British woman. The female audience at which the campaign was directed, however, failed to identify with the ad, perhaps perceiving the model as being rather too close to reality for comfort.

In stark contrast, just a few years later Unilever's Dove launched an ad campaign using women (not professional models) of all sizes, ages and colours. Using real, naturally beautiful people (see Figure 8.2), Dove contributed to its permanent rejuvenation. On a dedicated website, Unilever offers the possibility of voting electronically for the consumer's preferred look. Dove also achieved an authentic vision with this campaign. As psychologist Dr. Joyce Brothers observed in *Ad Age*, 1 August 2005:

To me, this is positive, partly because how we feel about our looks, our overall appearance, is more apt to reveal our true self and esteem, whereas the term 'beauty' usually involves some comparisons with others, as if we were in a continuing competition, or as if others were judging or determining the correct answer, as if the definition of beauty itself was exact and limited, which it isn't.

Figure 8.2 Dove 2005 ad campaign

Finally, these advertising excesses must always be seen in their historical and sociocultural context; it is quite possible for a daring campaign to go unnoticed at time 't' in the life of a brand and attract furious censure at time t + n. Similarly, something easily tolerated in one culture may come in for heavy criticism in a different culture.

The example of Marlboro

Marlboro is a cigarette first produced in 1924 by the Philip Morris group. The cigarette originally had a brown tip, the purpose of which was to hide lipstick marks, as these were considered unbecoming when left by the made-up lips of a woman on the white paper of a traditional cigarette. In other words, at the time when it was launched, Marlboro was a cigarette aimed at a female market. Although not exactly a failure, the product never really succeeded in attracting its target market.

Thirty years later, Philip Morris decided to reposition the product completely. To achieve this, it created a new packaging, the design of which was left to designer Louis Cheskins. Philip Morris also added a filter as standard, and repositioned the cigarette for the male market. It was an ambitious gamble. The new box packaging was more utilitarian than aesthetic, and was designed so that men (considered to be less fastidious than their female counterparts) could avoid crushing their cigarettes in their pockets. The job of advertising the product was entrusted to a publicity genius, Leo Burnett. Despite the popular legend, the idea of the famous cowboy did not arrive immediately. In fact it was 10 years before that particular identity was established; and it was not until 1954 that Marlboro adopted the new iconic symbol that won the brand its sector-leading position. The cowboy image – a symbol of independence, freedom and an almost savage masculinity – is now recognized across the entire planet.

The power of this image, and Marlboro's ability to adapt subtly to local tastes, were so great that the brand was able to keep prices steady (and even increase them) at a time when its competitors were struggling just to cover their own costs. However, the magic was not enough to sustain the brand's own excesses; and on the notorious date of Friday 2 April 1993, Philip Morris was forced to announce a drastic 40 cent reduction in its price, representing nearly 20 per cent. The Philip Morris share price immediately fell by 23 per cent, dragging down a number of other key Wall Street performers with it. In the following weeks, Michael Miles, the CEO of Philip Morris, announced a restructuring plan that would lead to the closure of 40 production units and the layoff of 8 per cent of its workforce – nearly 14,000 people at that time – at an estimated cost of US $2.3 billion. Friday 2 April will live in the memory of financial analysts as 'Marlboro Friday'. A successful rejuvenation does not grant a brand a licence to indulge in excess.

9 Renewing the target market

Does a brand have to be the same age as its customers? Not necessarily, but it is true that the average age of the consumer base influences the perception of the brand's age, in addition to its own actual age. In this way, there is often a great temptation to renew and – if possible – to rejuvenate brands. The decision is a strategic one, and is thus a more delicate matter to implement, deserving some thought. Renewing the target market is in no way the same thing as deciding to increase prices. It is a marketing strategy affecting several variables of the mix that, in the best case, will bring about the renewal of the target market.

Based mainly on the financial belief that it was more expensive to win new customers than to secure the loyalty of existing ones, companies have – at last – recently begun implementing genuine customer retention strategies. In the vast majority of cases, securing customer loyalty is indeed necessary for the reason given above; but a company will not survive for ever if it neglects the also essential function of prospecting, which brings in new customers. Renewing a target market does not necessarily imply changing it completely, but instead regenerating it – and ideally, expanding it. Some authors have protested that the variable of age created far too much segmentation to allow cooperation, renewal and expansion. However, the expansion that accompanies renewal does not necessarily imply the addition of different age bands: nowadays, segmentation can benefit from variables other than simply age. Furthermore, it is sometimes possible to achieve a spread of ages within the same target market. In marketing, one should always be wary of any logic that is too cut and dried, remembering at all times that the main purpose of marketing is to allow the company to adapt to its environment as successfully as possible. Kapferer (2004) speaks of 'dual marketing' (recruitment/loyalty), which is so obvious, logical and necessary that discussion of its usefulness is superfluous. The Petit Bateau fashion brand is no longer confined just to children: it has understood, and taken advantage of, the interest it had generated among young girls (and even young women).

Rejuvenation by adding more young people to the marketing mix: a logical move

The instinctive response when formulating an advertising strategy for brand rejuvenation is 'to use a few young people'. There are many scientific studies supporting the theory that most brands used young people in their advertising to target older consumers. To name but a few: Gantz, Gartenberg and Rainbow (1980), Smith and Moschis (1985), Greco (1989), Zhou and Chen (1992), Peterson and Ross (1972), Langmeyer (1983), Roberts and Zhou (1997). Other studies, such as Deutsch, Zalenski and Clark (1986), Mazis *et al* (1992), and Sawchuck (1995), confirm that advertisers fear alienating themselves from the younger segment of the target market if they use older people.

It seems logical to suppose that if a brand can succeed in attracting a few more young people, it will renew its target market and thus its image. The idea is an attractive one, but it is not necessarily guaranteed to succeed. The strategy may also be indirect, such as the one adopted by Renault. The French car maker is using its Renault Toys brand for a range of replica model Renault cars and trucks, some with pedals and large enough for children to sit in. This move is partly based on the idea that children might influence the choice of the family car using their toys as a reference point; but also, who knows what effect on the unconscious this first contact with the brand will have when these children come to buy their own car?

At Toyota, another strategy was used to seduce young potential customers.

The example of Toyota

At the end of the last century, the car manufacturer Toyota came to the realization that both its brand and products were perceived by young consumers as being too old. This was in no way a criticism of the firm's prices or quality. However, the cars' shapes, styles and positioning made them unattractive to young drivers, thus automatically associating them with an older client base. In Japan in 1987, 45 per cent of all cars purchased by 20-year-olds were Toyotas. In 1998, this figure was a mere 30 per cent. This was such a significant decline that it resulted in the erosion of some of the brand's market share, with young drivers preferring models with a 'younger' image, such as those produced by Honda.

Given the serious nature of the problem, Toyota even considered the advisability of creating a new brand, prompted by the inspired strategies adopted by the Japanese car industry in the 1980s, creating brands such as Lexus (Toyota) and Infiniti (Nissan). The brand's differentiation strategy was a successful one, given that the firm's image as a 'general-purpose' manufacturer had excluded it from the profitable high-end market sectors. However, the solution was a costly one; and Toyota's problem with regard to the rejuvenation of its brand image could not be expressed in the same way, as the target market was not the same. Not only that, but many analysts still believe that the young people's car market should not be of any great concern to manufacturers, as the market is essentially a second-hand one. For this reason, it was decided to develop new models benefiting from a much more aggressive advertising strategy and design, in line with the tastes of young drivers. This resulted in the creation of the Platz, FunCargo, Will, bB (black Box), Vitz, Allex and Matrix. However, it should be noted that the distribution variable was tested across the whole mix. In Japan, in order to promote the idea of a specific distribution chain, a number of sellers were renamed 'Netz' in order to draw a little more attention to the rejuvenation brought about by the new products. The brand's strategy is thus entirely in line with its objectives. The models are very modern in style, and the selling price remains relatively affordable to the target market, because their platforms are not specific but instead borrowed from other models in the Toyota range. Even the advertising has been revised in order to correspond more closely to the 'codes' of the youth population.

However, a word of caution when attempting to rejuvenate a brand using young people: we need to understand in this case that the youth population, currently used and/or described without further qualification, is in fact a hyper-segmented population; and not just in terms of age criteria. We must therefore ask ourselves some specific questions regarding precisely which young people the brand wishes to attract to rejuvenate its target market.

This preliminary step is all the more essential in light of the fact that this group of heterogeneous tribes has evolved out of its subgroups, each with their own codes, signs of recognition and languages. This is not a question of parachuting a 'young person' into the brand's advertising by dropping them into an environment not designed for them and making them speak 'youth language'. Not only would the commercial nature of this strategy be immediately apparent; but also, the resulting rejection of the brand would eventually accelerate the ageing process against which the brand is attempting to fight. Yet despite this, sociologists teach us that trans-tribal characteristics exist, such as a language that is often pared to the bone and focused on key meaning only, and also the importance of music and – more importantly – rhythm. However, although these suggestions may act as guides, all approaches of this kind must be rigorously tested as part of the marketing strategy.

Rejuvenation by ageing the marketing mix a little: a paradox?

Although the stated objective is to rejuvenate the brand the rejuvenation factor that interests us here is primarily the renewal of the target market. This naturally means that we should take the term 'brand rejuvenation' to mean the redynamization of the brand. The implication is that the company will seek not necessarily to attract younger consumers, but – more importantly – to renew its existing customer base, which is either shrinking, deserting or may never have been interested in the first place. Petit Bateau, the well-known French fashion brand for children, migrated with total success to the older 'young adult' sector, drawing in these new consumers with its new advertising. The new target market was attracted by the quality of its clothes, and consciously or unconsciously drawn to the brand's ultra-young image. Ultimately, if the rejuvenation is a total success, the brand can even hope to increase its overall number of consumers. In this way – as paradoxical as it may sound – it is entirely possible to seek to rejuvenate a brand by setting out to win over new consumers who are older than the brand's existing customers.

Today, a good number of studies – including Schiffman and Sherman (1991), Mathur, Sherman and Schiffman (1998) and Carrigan (1999) – incorporate the notion of cognitive age, and recommend that it be taken into account when producing advertising material. This does not mean using people who are systematically younger or older than the actual age of the target market; but rather, people whose actual age is close to the cognitive age of the target market. Taking an average for the over-50 target market, this cognitive age is generally between 10 and 15 years below the actual age of the same target market.

A vital step: involve the brand's internal target market

A company's employees, and especially its public-facing staff, *are* the company – regardless of their seniority or level of responsibility within the company, and regardless of the job they actually do. For a period of a few minutes, the checkout operator at your local supermarket bears the weight of the brand's entire image on his or her shoulders. For a brief time, the call-centre operator providing after-sales service for your domestic appliance personifies the entire brand. For a few miles, the driver of the delivery lorry bedecked in the brand colours, driving alongside you, represents every single aspect of that brand. Throughout his or her entire sales pitch, your insurance company's representative or broker symbolizes the entire company as a whole. Throughout the entire car-buying transaction, the seller becomes the custodian of all of the brand's values. A modern consumer, who now has a better understanding of marketing techniques and the brand's obligations in the competitive environment within which it exists, is well aware of the power he or she wields. Any disappointment with regard to the perceived image of the company – and the selection of that company – could potentially drive that consumer to switch to a competitor. For this reason, it is vitally important to make the effort to inform staff and involve them fully in company strategy. Failure to do so may result in considerable effort being reduced to nothing in a few seconds, however flagrant the contradiction may appear between a company's official position and its projected image on the one hand, and reality – the space in which the consumer is actually engaged after initially having been won over and attracted – on the other. Davis (2000) talks about establishing an internal culture based on the brand. Such a culture, he states, must be conducive to a change of mindset within the company, resulting in a change in actual practices, that must become focused upon protecting the brand and giving it lasting value. Of course, an internal change of this kind cannot be forced; it must be encouraged up to a point where staff embrace it, make it their own and protect it. The motivation thus generated must therefore, by definition, produce genuine involvement.

Does this mean that to appear young we will need to hide or even dispose of staff above a certain age deemed to be inappropriate for maintaining a young (or at least suitable) image? Of course not; this would be to misunderstand the nature of the problem. However, we should not deny that there may be cases where the actual perceived age of public-facing staff may potentially represent a handicap. For example, can you imagine a fashion brand such as Zara, H&M, Gap or Pimkie with an entire staff, without exception, made up of people in their fifties? Not easily! Considering the fairly young core market targeted by these brands, it would be a contradiction in terms if the sales force did not belong to this same core group – if for no other reason than because it would make the 'advice and recommendation' function more difficult and, in many cases, less credible. Conversely, can you imagine a firm of financial advisers dealing mostly with the corporate market in which the entire sales force visiting prospects was in the 20–25 age bracket? Again, not easily! What would happen to the notions of credibility, confidence and experience that are legitimately expected to be found in such a case? These may be extreme examples. However, they account for more cases than one might think.

It is now common knowledge that baby boomers have largely overturned the stereotypes of age. By pushing back temporal boundaries and destroying cognitive distinctions, they have called the entire traditional frame of reference into question. This means that in the case currently under consideration, actual age is a genuine concern only in the extreme cases stated above; especially considering that e-commerce has helped to create a virtual distance between seller and buyer, which serves to mask a potentially negative gap in actual age – an advantage that is difficult or impossible to obtain in the real world. By contrast, perceived age may become a genuine handicap if the variable is not fully incorporated into the company's strategy and staff are not seen as a true strategic resource. Ind (1997) draws company managers' attention to the need to improve horizontal communication within the company. Too often, however, a strictly vertical approach is favoured; and the narrower this approach, the less scope staff are given to participate and express themselves. Hence Ind's insistence on the vital need for interaction between staff and managers, supporting the brand in a collective, organized, coherent and synergistic way and conferring upon it the advantage of a young, dynamic perceived age. This is a restatement of the notion of interrelations put forward by Porter (1998) as a source of competitive advantage.

In practice, therefore, this assumes the need to explain, educate, train and update the knowledge of contact staff to reflect these new requirements, in order to make the best possible contribution to the brand's youthful image. In this way, they will act as a logical, coherent extension of the brand's work elsewhere. Managers who remain reticent, fearing that they will incur unnecessary education and training costs, need to understand that ultimately, the issue at stake is a simple question of coherence. At every point of contact, staff act as the vehicle through which the company's image is reflected. If the prism it represents is badly constructed or positioned, the reflected image will be blurred or, worse, distorted – but through no fault of the prism itself! The prism is a multifaceted one (including knowledge, culture, fashion policy, behaviour, language, etc), in which the nature and intensity of the training depend on the nature of the contact. Care should therefore be taken to ensure that each such action contributes to the faithful construction of the image desired by the brand. A company's staff is a formidable asset; firstly, because it consists of human capital. To recognize and value it as such is to build a genuine partnership, and perhaps even an understanding in which both the individual *and* the company are able to succeed. If, all things considered, a modern company is not able to create emotive links between its staff, its values and its culture, it will never be able to create such a link with its target market. It is not an easy goal to achieve, but it is an ambitious one. Naturally, since the workload itself is shared, such a strategy will work only if the return on the investment is, in one form or another, also shared.

Can the brand become a factor of absolute differentiation?

McAlexander, Schouten and Koenig (2002) produced a very interesting redefinition of the notion of brand community using ethnographic data. In terms of marketing involvement, their work was significant in that it was based on the now-evident observation that competitive advantage based on differentiation is an endless pursuit that rapidly becomes exhausting. Hence the notion of brand community, bringing together satisfied customers who are loyal to the brand to the point of becoming its evangelical advocates. Ultimately, if such brand community is maintained, it can become resistant to changes to the brand, even in the event of exposure to a better offer.

Nature has dictated that all consumers grow old over time. Consequently, the client loyalty strategies advocated by some observers, if successfully implemented, result in the natural ageing of the target consumer group. As this group grows older, will it always be attracted to/interested in the same products and brands? There is no simple answer to this, especially as the group's needs are constantly changing. Firstly, there must be clear differentiation of the product brand. Although the product itself can change, it is easier for the brand to expand its range and offer new products. However, can a brand easily offer products to consumers right across the entire '10 to 90' age range? The task is difficult, but not impossible. A wide range can be expected to make the task easier. The narrower the product range, the more delicate the coexistence.

The simplest solution is to resort to differentiation through the brand – a strategy particularly advisable in cases where the segments to which the brand aspires are distant ones. However, be warned: aside from capturing additional client share, the strategy is really only of any use if it enables certain economies of scale over the full range of volumes in question. And this is really where the problem starts; for in many cases, to produce these economies of scale, brands tend to reduce the product differentiation and thus, whether consciously or not, lay the way open to commercial cannibalization. The result is that these products and services no longer differentiate. This is to some extent the problem encountered by the US fashion group Gap, with its Gap, Old Navy and Banana Republic labels, when these were no longer perceived by the consumer as being differentiated. In addition, it may be observed that in the fashion market, players who may be tempted by such diversification are now more circumspect, and are quick to focus on niche markets to avoid any such cannibalization. This results in the targeting of much narrower age groups, or even a positioning aimed at well-identified communities.

The example of Inditex

The case of the little-known Spanish firm Inditex is, without question, one of the most interesting success stories in the fashion sector. Over time, Zara, the group's flagship brand, was joined by other labels, such as Pull & Bear, offering young items with an increasing sportswear and leisurewear focus, taking a leaf out of Gap's book; Massimo Dutti, whose more traditional range was aimed at older men and women than those targeted by Zara; Bershka and Stradivarius, aimed at young Generation Y (born 1979–1994) women and the younger end of Generation X (born 1964–1979); Oysho, the lingerie brand; Kiddy's Class for children; and even Zara Home for home interiors. Each different yet complementary, these labels allowed Inditex to diversify its client base and maintain a clear set of images and positioning. However, it should be noted that whatever the underlying motivation, the key is that brand differentiation should be clearly conveyed by product differentiation. Does anyone still believe that customers are gullible? Although it is true that some may be, consumer associations are constantly on the lookout for pseudo sub-brands to 'name and shame', with the aim of making the aforementioned consumers aware of the marketing ploys directed at them.

Of course, differentiation by age is no panacea for rejuvenating the brand. The mere fact that Gap has launched Gap Kid does not magically restore its youthfulness. On the other hand, having noted the growth of the teenage market, many players have recently gone down the road of differentiation by brand, targeting 'generations' or, to be more precise, age segments that are younger than their original target market. In conjunction with strategic advertising, this may (with luck) result in the transfer of clientèle from one brand to another as the consumer gets older. Of course, we cannot take this transition for granted: it implies very well-demarcated positioning, as well as a rigorous, coherent advertising strategy for each different area. The fashion sector is a promising target for such a strategy, and many examples have sprung up over recent years, particularly in the United States. The Limited Too chain has, for example, opened the Seven stores; Abercrombie & Fitch has developed the Hollister store concept; Claire's Stores, which had been aimed at teenagers, is attempting to target a younger market with the Velvet Pixies store chain; Hot Topic, which remains the emblem of the MTV generation, is now targeting young women in the 15-29 age bracket with its Torrid stores, and so on. Large stores are also getting in on the act as they seek to rejuvenate their target market, and thus their own image, with smaller surface areas once again devoted to fashion in one segment or another. Consider, for example, Thisit, launched in the US by the famous store Macy's. And Europe is not to be outdone, either. The large stores that sometimes try their hand at diversification are also naturally attracted by fashion, which targets the younger segments of the public. They do this by directly opening new specialist stores such as Sfera Centro, the new brand in this field from the Spanish retailer El Corte Inglés, or Le Bon Marché, who opened the Balthazar store in France. At a time when brands that generally use small store areas or corners, such as Celio, Adidas, Etam and Nike, are starting to open superstores, the strategy is a highly interesting (and paradoxical) one.

The rejuvenation of a brand makes use of tools that are simple and fairly well known to the marketer. Ultimately, however, these tools – which are available to any operator – will not bring about the rejuvenation of the brand on their own. It is generally only when they are blended together in the correct proportions that they become potentially capable of reversing the ravages of time on the brand. In other words, even with the right tools, there is no guarantee that the facelift will be a success.

10 The growth of the product portfolio

The brand does not age: only its products do! This statement may be a simplification of the truth; however, it is rarely entirely wide of the mark. By turning the logic on its head, we are left with an apparently obvious statement. What brand could survive the ageing of its entire product line? Most brands suffering from the ageing process consist of products that have aged in the eyes of their consumers. There are two key strategies for avoiding this problem. The first is to introduce a policy of constant innovation, linked directly to consumer expectations; the second – which should complement the first where appropriate – involves expanding the range to include products with a much younger, more dynamic image. The theory is simple; putting it into practice is much less so. This is especially true where the company image has been built on one or more flagship products that *are*, and still *make*, the brand. The strategy may be difficult to implement, but it is not impossible.

The example of McDonald's

In 1961, seven years after having founded their hamburger business in San Bernardino in California, when Maurice and Richard McDonald sold the operating rights to their fast-food system to Ray Kroc, he opened his first restaurant in Des Plaines, Illinois. Over the following years, McDonald's built its image as a hamburger specialist.

The fast-food chain (Speedy Service System) continued to grow; and 50 years later, 31,000 restaurants represent the brand all around the world, serving 50 million customers daily.

However, McDonald's does not merely develop more and more variations on the traditional hamburger; menus at local branches often feature products that are perfectly integrated into the local culture, after having been rigorously tested; particularly in countries where local culinary traditions are far removed from the typical US fast-food model. Of course, McDonald's is – and will always be – McDonald's. However, although this positioning, with the accompanying image it conveys of the US consumer society, was good enough in the early 1970s, McDonald's decided to introduce a parallel range of Japanese-inspired specialities when it expanded into Japan. Who would have thought 30 years ago that McDonald's would introduce rice dishes? And yet, Bento is just such a product, designed to win over the Japanese market. Since the early 2000s, McDonald's has been offering a range of salads (adapted to local tastes) worldwide. The concept was originally launched in France in 1987.

The success of McDonald's, despite the 'junk food' allegations flung at it by certain anti-capitalist naysayers, is based simply on good old-fashioned marketing. It is the type of marketing that adapts constantly to its environment, and innovates as a matter of course. The 'twin arches' brand is well aware that even its most loyal customers occasionally appreciate variety in their meals, and thus the portfolio of brand names now owned by McDonald's now also includes Aroma Café, Boston Market, Chipotle Mexican, Donatos Pizza and Prêt A Manger. Faced with such a list, who would now dare to say that there is little choice available at Ronald McDonald's?

Innovation is often considered to be one of the most relevant factors in a brand rejuvenation strategy. All things considered, this would seem logical. Are a brand's products not its ambassadors, after all? If they grow, rejuvenate and continue to stay abreast of the times, then the brand will benefit, and will be able to reap the rewards of a facelift.

Range extensions and brand extensions: rejuvenation solutions?

Renewing the product portfolio does not necessarily mean abandoning the products that had been sold up to that point and replacing them with new ones. Renewal may – and generally does – take the form of additions to the range, which will (if necessary) provide a gentle way of retiring certain products considered to be too out of date, or too unprofitable, to remain on sale. In 2001, with the aim of attracting new, younger consumers in the 15–35 age bracket, the Maxwell House brand launched new cappuccino products under the Maxiccino name, flavoured with hazelnut, vanilla, caramel and chocolate. When performed with care, range extension enables the current core target market to be retained, while at the same time attempting to win over new customers or consumers. Amor Lux – also known as Lumière de Bretagne – became famous in France with its classic, comfortable fishermen's jerseys. In 1995, the brand diversified, creating Terre et Mer, a fashion line with a sports slant, while still retaining the marine theme on which it had built its reputation. And the brand also remained true to its basic identity when it decided to rejuvenate its range by collaborating with the Japanese stylist Zucca, a former assistant to Issey Miyake.

Through the use of range extensions, the brand can rejuvenate itself while still gaining the maximum benefit from its core assets (recognition and image). The range extension consists of developing additional products (new shapes, colours, sizes and packaging, etc) bearing the brand name. Specifically, it can be said that a range extension confers a threefold advantage: impact, cost, time. The new products benefit from the same brand and thus carry an additional impact that is significant in terms of image. Since the brand is already well known, the launch cost is lower than the investment that would have been required with a brand that had not yet forged a reputation for itself. Lastly, because of these advantages of recognition and image, the success of the new product can be achieved more quickly. Indeed, some of Kapferer's work even suggests that the survival of products after a four-year life span is more likely if they bear a recognized brand name as opposed to that of another brand – 50 per cent against 30 per cent (Kapferer, 2004).

Furthermore, if the results of the research carried out by Keller and Aaker (1992) are to be believed, we see that the success of extensions even contributes to improving the consumer's opinion of the brand in question. Experience shows that these extensions can be expected to allow the brand to renew its range of products and/or services, and thus to present a certain dynamism capable of offsetting potential ageing factors. Despite this, a little

caution is necessary; some brands move very quickly from range extensions to brand extensions without always paying attention to the requirements of sensible practice first. Brand extension consists of extending the brand name to cover products and/or activities different from those the company has previously offered. The definition of brand extension can, however, vary from author to author; and in some cases, come very close to that of range extension. Consider, for example, the warning issued by Trout (2001). 'Brand stretching' may be a good idea as long as it remains strategic and based on consumer expectation. It is essential that the brand extension should appear a logical, coherent one. In this way Taillefine, a chilled-food products brand launched in 1964, was able to incorporate a range of low-fat biscuits under its umbrella in 1997, as consumers of LU biscuits – another brand belonging to the Danone group – had reduced their biscuit consumption, conscious of the effect on their waistlines. Following on from this success, Danone went one better in November 2000 with a mineral water containing 0 per cent sodium, also called Taillefine.

As one might imagine, such strategies are accessible only to powerful brands with the capital strong enough to survive being divided between a number of products. However, care must be taken not to alter the nature of this capital, as this would cause the brand to lose its identity. Today, Hermès is acknowledged as a brand that has carried off its brand extension strategy perfectly, taking care not to alter its capital. The designer scent has found its own niche without in any way diluting the original Hermès capital. After all, such strategies are not guaranteed success. Pierre Cardin is often cited as an old label that has lost its soul, although it is merely a figurehead for a variety of other brands that were never able to find the right balance between profitable extension and necessary protection. When partner Sergio Galeotti died in 1985, a number of analysts were dubious about the managerial ability of the creative stylist Giorgio Armani. Today, he has won respect for his skills in both areas, generating around US $1 billion for the group. In addition, the Armani label – despite having lent its name to items as diverse as sunglasses, cosmetics, furniture and watches, as well as the original fashion brand – has been able to increase its capital strategically, always achieving a perfect balance of opportunity and risk in its extensions.

As for range extensions, they primarily represent a distillation of the consumer requirements that drive companies to carry out such extensions. Once again, however, overall coherence must be maintained. Too wide a range could, of course, potentially weaken the brand's identity, if the result was that its positioning no longer seemed clear. Hence Trout's insistent recommendation that the brand manager must show the greatest possible discipline. If not, the result in some cases could be the dilution of the brand that, far from remaining young, would see its image diminished in the minds of its consumers. This is why it is crucial to have a genuine marketing strategy and to carry out consumer acceptance tests. Lastly, the brand equity must of course remain carefully controlled. Regardless of whether the question is of a brand extension or simply a range extension, subcontracting production is always one possible solution. But the brand must bear in mind that a product bearing its name makes a contribution to its image, regardless of which organization actually manufactures it. A very strict set of specifications is therefore required. After all, any failing will be blamed upon the brand, with all the resulting negative consequences.

We could have dwelt on the fact that a proliferation of extensions can sometimes naturally create a phenomenon of commercial cannibalization. However, this problem – although serious – is trivial compared with the possible distortion of the brand and the likely alteration of its image capital. With all of its various representations, the band ceases to appear coherent; yet such coherence is one of the key factors indicating the stability of the brand over time. Such stability should not be confused with immobility, which can lead to ageing. This stability forms the basis of the identification system used by the consumer to store memories of the brand, fix it in its own space and bring together the various components constituting its identity. A wide variety of extensions may also be perceived as concrete evidence of a diversification strategy. From a more positive perspective, it also allows a company to spread its risk over a more diverse area. Having perceived that the footwear market was too narrow for large growth, the Burlington brand moved successfully into knitwear pullovers, and then, in the late 1990s, into polos and shirts. However, from a negative point of view, such a choice can also turn out to be costly if too much diversity starves the company of an obvious core speciality and requires more and more work in multiple markets, all the while playing a part in imperceptibly wearing away the brand's identity.

The example of Sony

During the 1990s, under the influence of its chairman Nobuyuki Idei, Sony underwent a complete transformation, shifting from being a company that specialized in audio-visual products to a company with a presence in all fields of information technology. However, information technologies are resource-hungry, and the strategic goals they pursue are as changeable as the trends that drive them. Sony's power was eroded as a result of too much diversity in sectors that, although considered to be complementary, had very low profit margins, so that the company gradually appeared to be ageing and unable to react simultaneously to the developments in the multiple markets in which it competed. Sony saw itself shifted away from its former position as a dynamic innovator and towards comparison with the lumbering, stereotyped conglomerates that make strategic changes slowly and not always wisely. Beginning in 2001, the Japanese giant resolved to respond to this trend, and decided to step up its restructuring plan, drastically reorganizing itself or simply purging secondary lines of business that should have been subcontracted long before. This was done in order that the brand might rediscover its former coherence and image; a move that was long overdue, since industry observers had already discerned unmistakeable signs of ageing, even though the vast majority of the general public had not yet truly observed such a phenomenon. In 2005, to breathe yet more new ideas into the company, and for the first time in its history, Sony appointed a US CEO, Howard Stringer, whose career had previously been spent at CBS.

The specific case of store brands

Today, very few mass retail brands have yet to seize the strategic opportunity presented by store brands. As Sordet, Paysant and Brosselin have analysed in great detail (2002), store brands have now become genuine brands in themselves, gaining a little in importance every day. And the authors encourage these 'new' brands to go even further in adopting a full-on marketing approach, conducting detailed studies into consumer preferences and attempting to win their loyalty. In the past, some distributors have even experienced success in this area, such as Marks & Spencer with St Michael. Others have put the emphasis on the label, such as Ikea, Castorama and Home Depot. Still others have opted for a private label associated with the brand name, which then becomes elevated to the status of an endorsement guaranteeing the product's quality. Today, this last category now contains the majority of mass retailers, whether food-based or not. Tesco uses Tesco Finest, Carrefour's main contributions are FirstLine and Tex; Sainsbury's offers Freefrom and Taste the Difference, Safeway favours The Best, Asda recommends Extra Special, and so on. Some retailers offer a whole series of these private labels, over which they know they will have 'more control'; such as Décathlon, for example, which launched Quetchua, Tribord, Fouganza and Domyos.

The store brand can come to represent a genuine strategic advantage for a distributor that, as the ordering customer, has extra leverage over its producers to direct their production and thus precisely match the needs of its target markets, assuming that it really is involved in a genuine marketing approach and not just a sales process. Of course, if the retailer decides to invest in a genuine marketing approach – which, to be fair, is not often the case – the store brand may become a supple tool under the control of the retailer's strategy. Note that this is not a blind criticism of mass distributors for not adopting a genuine marketing approach. The low margins generated in France go some way towards explaining why resources for designing and supporting such a strategy are not always available there. However, it is clear that today, almost all mass retailers suffer from a lack of identity. Certainly, they all claim or 'support' a vague image with little differentiation in reality from one retailer to the next. But what about the concept? Can any operator currently boast that it has a concept that genuinely differentiates it from the competition? Trapped as they are in the snare of short-term operating strategy, the major retailers are now prisoners of this lack of identity. Clancy (2001) published the results of a very interesting study into the factors responsible for killing off US brands (a fact that was beyond doubt). For most of the categories analysed, the clear observation was that consumers perceived no real differences between the leader and the No.2 in a given market. The reasons underlying this observation certainly had something to do with homogenization of supply; but more importantly, as Clancy noted, it was about the use of price reductions as a primary factor for differentiation, prompting the head of the Copernicus consultancy to observe: 'The practice of price reductions informs your loyal customers that they are wrong to pay any attention to the brand, which is just a waste of time [...] Price reductions erase the main point of difference compared to the competitor's products.' If the big-name French retailers also find themselves in this situation, it is to a great extent because they have all, at one time or another, fallen into the classic trap of price wars.

Do you always have to follow or create the fashion to achieve rejuvenation?

Barthes (1967) explains that 'fashion essentially appears – and this is the ultimate definition of its economy – as a system of signifiers; a business of classification; an order which is far more about semiology than semantics'. The clothing sector is one in which fashion often plays a critical role. However, an excess of fashion is not necessarily a desirable situation for the brand either. The debate is a well-rehearsed one, and has adherents in both camps. Is it possible to create fashion; or is the best one can do to follow an effect, a movement, a trend that is already – or will later be described as – fashion? Sommier (2000) says that 'if they feed on the symbolic codes belonging to the fashion area on which they have focused to increase their impact on the market, brands will become dependent on the growth of recognition of this area by consumers.'

The example of Coach

Less well-known than some of its competitors such as Prada and Gucci, the Coach brand has nonetheless been a source of informed inspiration in terms of rejuvenation strategy. Its CEO, Lew Frankfort (MBA Marketing, Columbia University), has a clear understanding of the machinery of the mastery of time and the pressing need for a company to expand its product portfolio (handbags, wallets, shoes, belts and other fashion accessories). At the heart of Coach's success has been a heavy emphasis on marketing research, and consumer research in particular. It is now some time since Coach was known only for producing wallets. Nowadays, detailed analysis of consumer expectations has allowed the company to expand its range of products and offer handbags of all kinds, shoes, fashion accessories, jewellery, clothing, etc, all renewed from one season to the next. The diversification has been such a success that it has been able not only to rejuvenate the brand's target market – nearly a third of buyers are now under the age of 26 – but also to attract new business; these days, around 37 per cent of purchasers of a Coach product are new buyers.

A modern approach to manufacturing (the outsourcing of 85 per cent of production, compared to 25 per cent in the mid-1990s), while retaining process control, remains the absolute watchword. In this way, the selection of subcontractors is an extremely rigorous process; on average, for every one new provider accepted, five are rejected. Lew Frankfort is well aware that a fashion-based positioning, good public reception and significant media support are a useful springboard, but they will not be the making of a brand in the long term. They will certainly play a part; but they mainly constitute an opportunity to achieve good short-term results. If quality does not follow, then fashion or no fashion, media publicity or no media publicity, the brand will ultimately find that its clientèle gradually turns away from its products in favour of more serious competitors and/or will be obliged to fight a constant battle to win new clients. Material and aesthetic quality is therefore a non-negotiable matter for this US company, which has also had a presence on the internet since 1999. For one thing, its industrial partners know that they are likely to receive a surprise visit for an on-site manufacturing check at any time. Furthermore, Coach is quick to call upon designers such as Reed Krakoff, formerly with Tommy Hilfiger, to renew the product ranges constantly and diversify styles in order to satisfy a multiplicity of diverse requirements as revealed by consumer studies. It is this type of strategic movement that has enabled Coach to add depth to its range, while at the same time limiting its risks; the number of handbag lines has thus increased from 80 to more than 130 in just a few years.

Fashion is without any doubt a prime niche market for keeping the brand young. However, this advantage also brings its own significant demands; it is highly unstable, highly unpredictable, and highly contested. A complementary marketing strategy is therefore a source of relative control and thus of greater stability. Coach's customers are regularly interviewed for their opinions on the image of the brand, its positioning, nature and quality, and the status of its products. This regular exercise gives the company the ability to spot trend changes more easily, and thus, usually, to predict what many competitors will only become aware of in a few months' time. Operating in a fashion niche, nothing is for certain. Although a professional soothsayers' licence is not supplied as part of the marketing research tools package used for the consumer surveys, these same tools can still often help to define the probable territory a little better, identifying those that are clearly outdated and/or at risk. Travis (2000) confirms that no infallible crystal ball exists, but he does maintain that the brand manager should stay a little ahead of the game; or better still, as Peter Drucker recommends, that he or she controls the change.

Rejuvenation with the help of brand revitalizers

Some companies specialize in rejuvenation plans. They scan the market and analyse the life cycles of brands, performing audit after audit, attempting to identify the brands that have aged, yet still appear to possess a certain potential. Sometimes they are merely passionate individuals who, because of that passion or simply because they have glimpsed what others believed no longer to exist, choose to get involved with setting up a rejuvenation plan for brands that had seemed to be in terminal decline. The tactic consists of buying an outdated brand at a knock-down price and implementing *ad hoc* rejuvenation techniques to bring it back to life, strategically reinvigorating its image.

One of the great masters of this approach in the United States is The Himmel Group, named after its founder Jeffrey Himmel. Brands such as the chocolate drink Ovaltine, the toothpaste Topol, the Porcelana brand and the Lavoris mouthwash have been reinvigorated and rejuvenated by The Himmel Group to the point of enjoying a fresh lease of life. Jeffrey Himmel has now been implementing this approach for more than two decades. It consists simply of drawing up a suitable marketing strategy backed with concerted advertising pressure. Naturally, such an approach can only achieve positive results with brands that Jeffrey Himmel describes as possessing 'dormant capital'; in other words, brands for which an audit reveals genuine residual potential. In most cases, these brands are the orphans of mergers. They have had their moment of glory; but the growth of the company, the merging of several business areas and the strategic reorientation of these business areas – or simply neglect – have allowed them to fall by the wayside; and naturally, they have started to age in the minds of consumers, who have gradually turned away from them. Clearly, the brands most commonly affected are those that first and foremost need a boost in recognition, since they are still clearly capable of earning substantial profits, but the gradual ageing of which has deprived them of shelf space, causing them to age a little further, which deprives them of a little more space, which causes them to age a little more, and so on, and so on.

As part of its strategy, The Himmel Group itself designs new advertisements, which are manifestly not the last word in creativity and originality. However, they are not intended to be. The main focus is on the brand name itself. The components that result in the brand satisfying the consumer's need are emphasized and expanded upon. The advertisment never fails to show a very clear 'pack-shot' (picture of the product). All of this is condensed into a very short time, to make regular repetition possible. When the New York group bought Topol toothpaste in 1973, it paid US $200,000. A mere 10 years later, Topol was earning US $23 million a year in sales. In 1992, after its buyout, the *Blitzkrieg* approach used to advertise the Ovaltine chocolate drink took the form of a presence on 30 different radio stations and six commercial TV channels. Sales doubled in the first 100 days. And although Ovaltine had only an 11 per cent market share in 1992, it now accounts for around 29 per cent, generating nearly US $40 million in turnover. The advantage of the *Blitzkrieg* approach has been indirectly confirmed by research work from Keller (2004), confirming that a multiplicity of messages under various different forms can dilute the brand equity and lead the confused consumer into confusion.

Of course, the point is not to pull off a one-off 'coup' and then leave the brand to age again once it has shown a profitable return on investment. This – the brand auditing stage – is probably where Jeffrey Himmel's real genius lies. Its main purpose is to determine, as precisely as possible, how much potential the brand has. Not only in the short term, once the *ad hoc* rejuvenation strategies have been implemented, but also in the medium to long term, within the context of the deliberate, careful management of the brand. Once the train has been put back on the track and appears to be working once again, why not take the opportunity of adding a few more carriages? A rejuvenated brand can then be the subject of range extensions, which will ideally complement the original promise. These range extensions will (of course) be the result of a genuine marketing strategy; that is, they will be capable of satisfying identified consumer needs without altering the core values of the brand. This is, for example, what happened with the Gold Pond brand. Originally, Gold Pond was simply a powder with pharmaceutical connotations. Today, other products have been launched under its umbrella; baby products, anti-itching powders, etc.

The Himmel Group has shown undeniable talent for rejuvenating certain brands in which it has spotted hidden potential. However, a discussion of its success should not simply serve to inform the current brand manager that it may be possible to create a rescue plan for the purpose of rejuvenating a brand. It should also – and most importantly – draw the manager's attention to the importance of managing the brand appropriately, as Jeffrey Himmel does, after having rejuvenated it. All of this begs one obvious question. Could such a rigorous management strategy not have been implemented for the brand previously, to prevent it from having aged in the first place? In other words, surely some anti-ageing strategy could have been implemented earlier? There are good reasons to think that the answer is 'yes', and this is the subject of the third and final part of this book.

PART 3

The strategy to prevent ageing

'Each age has its own beauty, and that beauty must always constitute freedom.'
Robert Brasillach
Les Sept Couleurs, 1939

We have shown that it is possible, in some cases, to rejuvenate a brand by acting on the right factors at the right time, and investing the necessary resources to allow this to happen. However, as we have already said, the first step in rejuvenating a brand is the sad task of examining how it has aged. In other words, we must conduct an assault on the effects of time's ravages that have been – rightly – diagnosed as detrimental to the brand in the longer term. However, cause and effect generally go hand in hand. Given that this is the case, rather than doing everything possible to turn back the clock, surely we should instead attempt to slow it down and prevent the brand from ageing? The idea appears even more attractive when one observes, as we have already noted, that the potential causes of ageing are many and varied. A strategic approach based on prevention should increase vigilance and give us the ability to react at the slightest sign of a problem. Naturally, such an approach presupposes a genuine desire to act.

The example of Polaroid

Edwin Land was inspired to make his extraordinary breakthrough when, in 1943, on his holiday, he was stumped by a naïve question from his three-year-old daughter Jennifer, who asked him why they had to wait to see the photograph he had just taken. History records that he solved the basic technical problems the same afternoon. However, it was not until 1948 that the Model 95, a camera weighing around 2 kg, first appeared. This revolutionary device was the first camera able to take photographs – although only in black and white – that would develop instantly. An extraordinary series of technical developments were made to subsequent models, improving the cameras' weight, compactness, image appearance time and, of course, photographic quality. In the late 1990s, however, as digital photography moved from its launch phase to its growth phase, the brand aged at a cruel rate. Because the brand had failed to anticipate the likely ageing this would induce, Polaroid found it very difficult to adapt; and a series of restructuring operations were needed to drag the brand into the digital era.

If just one argument were to be advanced in favour of such a strategy to anticipate the possibility of future ageing, it would be the undeniable economic advantage it offers. It is much less expensive to develop a preventative anti-ageing strategy than to perform a methodical identification of the existing causes of ageing in the brand and to undertake a strategic initiative aimed at one or more rejuvenation factors. In addition, brand rejuvenation work is often conducted with an urgency imposed by the desperate need for salvation. Sometimes, therefore, the brutality of the measures implemented in some areas can be detrimental to the initial spirit of hope in which the initiative was undertaken. The reason for this is a simple one. What we are dealing with in this case is not a recognition problem, but an image problem pure and simple. Although there is no reason why recognition and speed should not go hand in hand, image needs to be lent a 'helping hand' by time. Researchers at Newcastle University suggest that some aspects of human ageing can be overcome by DNA modification, working with PARP-1 (poly(ADP-ribos) polymerase-1). Their recent work has shown that overexpression of the PARP-1 genes in the cells protected the DNA strands from being altered. The advantage of a preventative anti-ageing strategy is that it can be superimposed upon the brand's overall strategy – and, in the best cases, merge with it entirely. It is not a separate path to be followed, but simply a set of complementary choices that guide, inform and improve the choices already established for the brand.

Because the brand is one of the company's most precious resources, it **must** be protected. None of the brand's competitors – not even the most formidable – is as powerful, perfidious and devious as time itself. The main reason for this is that time is invisible, intangible and infinite. The creation and development of a preventative strategy against ageing assumes an understanding of the exceptional emotional advantage a brand's image provides, and the fragility of that advantage over time. A brand that builds relationships with its consumers solely on the cognitive basis of its promise is a brand with promise that will always be prey to the direct or indirect challenges of its competitors. A brand that, in addition to this necessary cognitive base, is able to develop a powerful emotive link between itself and its consumers has acquired a weapon invisible to its competitors, yet real enough for that link to reinforce a brand identity that goes well beyond a mere commercial relationship. A conscious or subconscious understanding can then take shape and guide the anti-ageing strategy developed by the brand manager. Without this emotive link between the brand and the consumer, the brand's magic cannot operate – and the differentiation supposedly suggested by the brand will not be fully perceived. In a study conducted for the Young & Rubicam group, Agres (1990) clearly showed that in advertising terms, the combination of an emotive benefit and a material benefit produced superior results to the outcomes of either one of these benefits in isolation.

The question of image

In addition to recognition, rejuvenation must address the question of image. The modern internet – that is, the internet as we know it today, as opposed to its original military and scientific manifestation – appears to have half-opened a door into a fourth dimension of time. Hours, days and months appear to have little meaning on the net, and have no value for use as a frame of reference – events now occur with bewildering speed. Apart from traditional 'gadget' products, the life spans of which were already preprogrammed at their time of launch, never in economic history have we seen concepts, businesses, firms and brands age as quickly as they have since the advent of the internet.

It used to take years – or even decades – to establish a brand in the so-called old economy. With the internet and the new economy it ushered in, Amazon, Yahoo and AOL were able to gain recognition around the entire planet in less time than it took to devise the marketing strategy to make it happen. However, despite this handful of examples known to every web user and repeatedly quoted as evidence of the internet's clear advantage in this area, the information highway is strewn with innumerable failed brands that aged before they had even had time to grow. Not all disappeared for the same reasons, but it is still possible to identify one common factor that applies to most of them, and could be described as a 'recognition complex'. Reading the business plans created by the many now-defunct start-ups, it is clear that they could never have grown, or indeed have worked at all, without an exceptional advertising strategy and the full arsenal of marketing expenditure this implies. All these fledgling businesses were in fact obsessed by the idea of recognition, convinced – often with sincere naïvety – that it was not merely a precondition but instead an essential end in itself. From unknowns yesterday, they would become the market standard today, simply as a result of the fact that their names were on everyone's lips.

What is a brand? Granted, it is a name. But after all, these start-ups were obliged to have names, since their names also represented their network addresses. Why then so much effort to increase the recognition of that name, instead of the recognition of its underlying meaning? A brand's image does not emerge by chance. It is the (always uncertain) result of an alchemy of chosen behaviours and constant work on the part of the brand. In a free, competitive economy, a product can survive without a brand, but certainly not without an image. Sadly, discouraged by a complete lack of recognition, the 'click' companies lost sight of what the brand itself constituted. What it is. What it promises. What it offers. What it allows. What it communicates. For each of these characteristics, the name is merely the component that is immediately apparent. However, it is also the component that must inform its viewer of these same characteristics. People are loyal not to brands themselves, but rather, to the characteristics and attributes of those brands. The brand itself is no more than the identifier that allows this loyalty to operate. Without any attributes corresponding to the genuine conscious or subconscious expectations of internet-based consumers, the 'click' brands were able to generate the initial traffic that provided them with abundant recognition. However, once this stage had passed, not only did the actual or implied promise fail to materialize; but also, the *Blitzkrieg*-like consumption of their resources left them unable to maintain the costly investments in their public recognition. And yet, some 'clicks and mortar' brands did learn how to use the net strategically and benefit from its reinvigorating effect.

The example of Volvo

In 2000, in the United States, Volvo decided to launch its new model, the S60, on the internet only. This could have smacked of a 'novelty' ploy tacking an internet element onto a traditional launch campaign to effect a magical rejuvenation of the brand. It was nothing of the kind. The tactic turned out to be a genuinely strategic approach to the problems posed by launching this new model. Clearly, the internet had been used for the connotations of modernity it carried with it, naturally representing as it did a highly contemporary means of advertising. More importantly, however, the marketing studies conducted by Volvo had shown that 80 per cent of its target clientèle was already online. Lastly, this was not simply a question of buying a few banner advertisements here and there to announce the S60. Instead, it was an orchestration of the entire launch strategy around the internet, including links to AOL in terms of information, links to websites participating in the launch, games and competitions, etc. In other words, the internet was for once being viewed as a meta-medium offering a whole panoply of different methods of communication that could be united and combined into a genuinely synergic whole. This was not about gimmicks, but about strategy, in a real attempt to produce coherence and image.

11 Staying young: a need or a desire?

Are there any brands which refuse to stay young? Probably not; although a really hard search might reveal one or two intentionally or inadvertently suicidal exceptions to this rule. However, there is a clear difference between wishing to stay young and failing to notice that one has grown old. On the one hand, the brand's aspiration is to avoid suffering the effects of ageing. On the other hand, it does everything it can to avoid such a situation. The gap between the desire and the need may be likened to the distance between a rejuvenation remedy and an anti-ageing strategy. In the present case, it is possible, using the analysis grid shown in Figure 11.1, to identify three separate situations. These situations are represented by three contiguous areas in which the brand will be located after its characteristics have been analysed. Ultimately, the results of the analysis will translate into a variety of actions ranging from long-term approaches that have been carefully thought through strategically, to quick fixes that are usually imposed by the need to react quickly to existing real-world situations.

This grid provides an approximate way of establishing the extent to which the brand is exposed to ageing. The closer its profile comes to Area 3, the more care the brand manager must take to identify the slightest sign suggesting impending ageing, as this will indicate that the brand is one of those with the highest exposure to the feared ageing process. By contrast, a brand located mainly in Area 1 will be more naturally resistant to the effects of time, thus allowing its manager to devise and implement an anti-ageing strategy under optimal conditions. There is no rigorously scientific foundation to this grid. It has been created with the assistance of the many

Desire	Area 1 Regular methodical analysis for structured reaction	Area 2 Precautionary monitoring for pre-emptive initiatives	Area 3 Extreme, constant vigilance for maximum reactivity	Need
Basic product				Sophisticated product
Luxury products market				Mass retail market
Wide target market				Narrow target market
Low-innovation sector				High-innovation sector
'Follower' company				'Leader' company
B2B business				B2C business
Old brand (chronological age)				Young brand (chronological age)
Low-technology business				High-technology business
Few competitors				Many competitors
No.1 share of voice				Residual share of voice

Figure 11.1 Analysis grid showing degree of brand exposure to ageing

professionals called upon to help produce this book. It is a simple, quick way of obtaining information, and its purpose is to attract the attention of the brand manager to the potential fragility of his or her capital, encouraging him or her to take a proactive approach rather than a reactive one. Reactions are often dictated by the harsh reality of the environment, and thus impose a real need to act urgently.

Area 1 is located firmly within the framework of the company's desire to anticipate any possible ageing. A brand situated in this area is not greatly affected by the pressure of time, and so there is plenty of room for strategic deliberation. The anti-ageing action undertaken by the company on the brand can be fully scheduled at the appropriate time intervals, and is thus often much easier to control. Area 3, however, is located in the sphere of need, and compels the company to maintain extreme vigilance at all times if it is to be able (where necessary) to readjust the relevant factors in its preventative anti-ageing strategy as quickly as possible. Between the two is the intermediary Area 2, in which the company maintains a precautionary state of alert in order to have time to react if needed, but without being forced either to accept or to forego a prior methodical analysis procedure. Like all intermediary areas, it is not strictly defined. In a similar way to what happens in Area 3, the current situation does exert a certain amount of pressure, but its urgency is still low enough to allow a carefully considered strategic analysis.

To find out where a brand is located, we must do more than just ask about the company's desire to implement an anti-ageing strategy. In reality, the area in which a brand is situated is dictated mainly by a number of different variables that enable us to produce a graphical profile of the brand. The more this profile tends towards Area 3, the more the brand may be considered to be potentially sensitive to time (see the example of a fictitious brand of printers in Figure 11.2); and the more the anti-ageing strategy needs to enable a high degree of responsiveness to changes in the brand's environment. In cases where the profile appears to bounce from one side of the grid to the other, it is possible to calculate a rough average position for the brand by disregarding any weighting between the variables. Each position is therefore allocated the area value, and the sum of the values can then identify the rough average area and the consequent recommended action. The variables that should be considered in an analysis of this type are varied, and can differ from one sector to another. However, it is possible to select 10 main categories, representing 10 keys to better

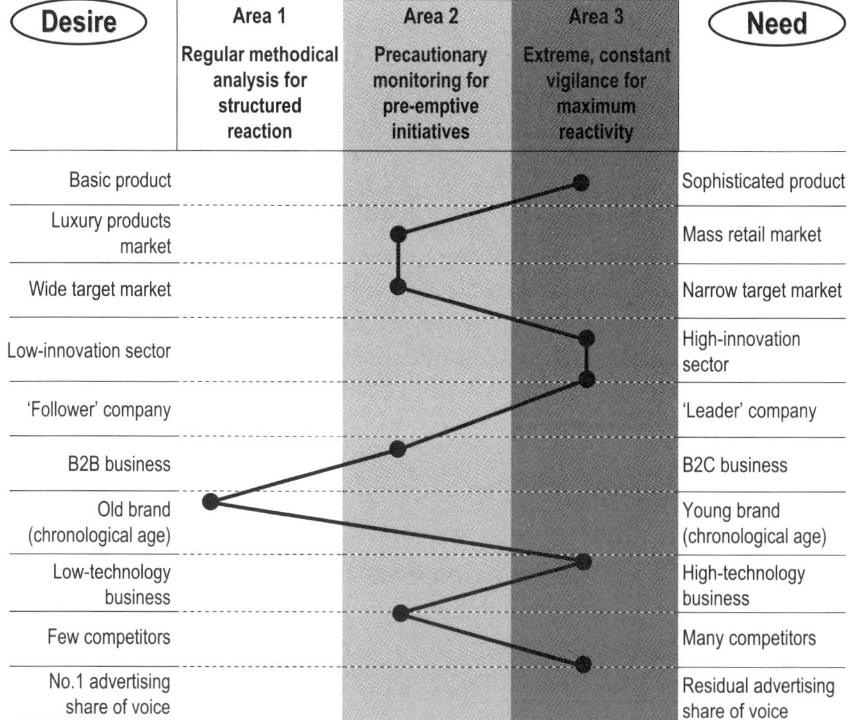

Figure 11.2 Fictitious example: brand 'Alpha' printers

understanding the approach the brand should adopt in deploying its anti-ageing strategy.

The first variable relates to the **product** itself. In other words, the more sophisticated the product, the further it will be removed from the base product, and the more it will be likely to suffer from ageing. For example, while the classic French baguette endures over time, the various other speciality breads may become the subject of a passing fashion and age much more quickly than their creators could have imagined possible.

The example of RCA

In 1999, research carried out by RCA (a brand used by Thomson in the United States) showed that it enjoyed very high levels of recognition. However, the brand also realized that it was not naturally associated with high technology and innovation. In a sector such as mass-retail audiovisual equipment, these characteristics are important for retaining a young, dynamic image. The most frustrating aspect was that this perceived image was not a true reflection of real life. Thomson thus started a programme to promote its new products better, and launched an advertising campaign to ensure that, in future, the objective and subjective images would be entirely in synchronization with one another.

The second variable relates to the **market** in which the company operates. As we have already said, the phenomenon of ageing affects mass-retail goods that are based mainly on demand-led marketing more than luxury products that, for the most part, are based more on supply-led marketing. Products from the latter category are not entirely spared by the potential ageing of the brand; but because of nature and the positioning of the products in question, time generally has less of an effect. A number of companies occasionally operate both at the high end of the market and in more mass-market segments.

The example of Coty

An example of such a company is the perfumer Coty (a subsidiary of the Benckiser group since 1992). Coty now manages such varied perfumes and cosmetics brands as Jovan, Aspen, !excl.mation, Stetson and Vanilla Fields, as well as brands or licences bought by

Benckiser from the Beecham group: Lancaster, Davidoff, Margaret Astor, Adidas, Jil Sander, Joop and Manifesto. It is easy to understand that the management of prestige brands such as Monteil and Lancaster will not require the same attention as a brand such as Rimmel, which Coty acquired in 1996. This is not in any way a pejorative or negative statement, but simply an appropriate strategic approach.

The **target market** is the third variable. The narrower this market is, the greater the chance it will be homogenous. Subsequently, if the brand falls prey to a perceived ageing process, the phenomenon is in danger of spreading more easily throughout the entire target market. By contrast, a brand in the same situation but with a wider target market will have more chance of seeing the various segments that probably constitute this market reacting differently over time.

The example of Leica

Great names from the photographic world, such as Robert Capa and Eddie Adams played their respective parts in making the Leica camera brand into a legend. But from the early 1970s, aggressive marketing and technological dynamism from Japanese brands such as Canon and Nikon seriously undermined the foundations of the brand, whose target market then shrank over the years, including among professionals. The brand could still boast that its luxury image was being promoted by the Sultan of Brunei or Queen Elizabeth; yet this was not enough to prevent the brand from ageing slowly but surely. New, less luxury-oriented products were developed from the late 1990s onwards, and a new advertising strategy was implemented to resurrect the target market.

The nature of the **sector** in which the company sits in terms of innovation forms the fourth variable. The more the sector is carried – or even driven – by innovation, the more the risks of ageing naturally increase. By contrast, in a sector with low innovation, the brand generally has the time it needs to follow or even lead an evolutionary change.

The example of whisky

The whisky sector is not a particularly innovative one; and furthermore, it is one that has always traded on great age, which is synonymous with the quality of the drink. In addition, this is a sector that – with the exception of a few well-known names – has a highly fragmented market and a gradually ageing clientèle. Thus, taking into account the fact that the sector is structurally low on innovation, urgency is not the order of the day. It is true that many brands have tried to rejuvenate their image – mainly through their own advertising, such as Johnnie Walker, Dewar's and Glenmorangie – to attract younger consumers. However, although action is clearly necessary, it is not yet imperative. This is particularly true given that consumers in the core target market are now frequently retired, and thus more loyal.

A corollary to the previous variable, but this time looking at the **company** itself, the fifth variable concerns the company's market position. If it intends to retain the initiative, a company in a market-leading position must be continually renewing its product range to avoid the effects of ageing. Note that we are talking about a leader here, and not a monopoly situation. The mobile phone sector was a real surprise in terms of the speed with which it attracted a target market of users that, in some cases, is now larger than the number of subscribers to land-line network services.

The example of Nokia

Nokia, a leader in this sector, has understood this point clearly; and while the competition introduces waves of technical innovations under a variety of different forms, the Finnish giant adopts a fashion-based angle for its own products – at the same time remaining constantly on the alert for ways of winning over younger segments, and also the most profitable sector areas. Nokia is aware that the slightest let-up would allow its challengers Samsung, Motorola and SonyEricsson all the space they need to capture a few points of its market share.

The sixth variable is related to the nature of the company's **business**; and more precisely, to the nature of its primary target market. While on this subject, it should be pointed out that companies with a B2B business (that is to say, companies whose clients are other professionals) enjoy a cycle spread out over a longer period than those with a B2C business (in other words, companies whose clients are individuals). Spreading the business cycle over time in this way generally provides more thinking time for planning and/or a more comfortable amount of reaction time in which to deal with a perceived ageing problem. Of course, companies that find themselves with the same brand in both of these types of business should always take the least favourable approach into consideration, and therefore examine the pressing needs that apply to their B2C business.

The example of AT&T

In the late 1990s, when the US giant realized that it needed to implement a brand rejuvenation plan, it approached the Young & Rubicam agency, whose BrandAsset Valuator tool has proven itself time and again. Results showed that AT&T no longer offered a degree of value that truly differentiated it from its competitors. Naturally, in a highly competitive market, this was liable to develop rapidly into a major handicap. AT&T thus devised a new offer, the purpose of which was to promote a more tangible added value for the brand, which was subsequently presented as being a true ally to its clients. A wide range of project fulfilment checks were put in place to check that commitments were being met; these were tailored in each case according to the type of client (professional or individual).

The seventh variable is represented by the brand's **chronological age**. The older the brand, the more the ageing process will impact on the identity and history of the brand. However, this does not represent some sort of absolute shield; but rather, unlike a young brand that has not yet proven itself and established its own individual identity, the chronological age of such a brand can constitute a significant advantage, enabling the brand to react more gently to the attacks of time. In addition, as we have already explained, the brands that fare best through a rejuvenation plan are those with a long history that can be expected to have left a firm imprint in the memory of consumers; this can be used to the brand's advantage.

The example of Leffe

Leffe beer can trace its origins back to around 1240, when the monks from the eponymous abbey first created the drink. Today, even among consumers of other-brand beers, Leffe enjoys majority recognition and even approval. If the brand were to suffer from the effects of ageing, it would probably be in a very gradual way, since its long history allows it to cushion such effects very comfortably. Conversely, if a new beer were to be launched tomorrow, it would first need to justify its existence, added value, differentiating characteristic and promise. If it were to choose to establish itself on the back of a fashion effect, in order to benefit from positive media contamination which served to boost its recognition levels, it would have to exercise extreme care that it could identify the tiniest symptoms of ageing at a sufficiently early stage.

The eighth variable relates to the level of **technology** within the business. The more the business relies on technology, the more it will be subject to constant changes in that technology. Over recent years, some sectors, such as IT, electronics and biotechnology, have proven – if any proof were needed – that they have an amazing ability to push back the limits of progress on a daily basis. In future, the more the company's business is linked to this technology, the more the brand will find itself under time pressure.

The example of Samsung

Retail electronics is a sector in which the ongoing need to impress the public dictates that constant technological innovation must be a way of life. For the past few years, the Korean giant Samsung has spared no effort to ensure that its image – which still has some progress to make in the West – benefits from the constant innovations the brand is bringing to market. This is because Samsung is not the usual stereotypical Asian company that routinely follows and copies where others lead. In both the electronics and the IT sectors, Samsung's lifeblood is invention and innovation. In addition, premium advertising for the company itself accompanies product advertising that emphasizes the brand's innovations.

The brand's **competitive environment** determines the ninth variable. The more the brand has to battle against competitors and the greater the pressure they exert on the variables in the marketing mix, the more the brand will tend to suffer from ageing. By contrast, in a market where competitors are few and operate on a relatively small scale, there will be fewer opportunities for comparison, and the pressure will consequently be reduced.

The example of General Motors

At the end of the 1990s, General Motors (GM) gave two models from the Oldsmobile brand (Aurora and Alero) a specific mission to fulfil: to position themselves as rivals to foreign brands with a younger, more dynamic image. Their goal was to win over a younger clientèle, which GM was lacking. Unfortunately, although product modifications were made, no real brand rejuvenation plan was put into action – despite the fact that studies clearly showed that Oldsmobile was not a brand with which young drivers wished to be associated.

Remember that the marketing function does not deal with absolutes; but rather, with relatives. In reality, it is misleading almost to the point of incorrectness to say that a brand ages; for it is extremely rare that a brand actually ages in an absolute sense. It only seems old when compared with its competitors, direct or indirect, and these appear to be younger than itself. This is why it is essential to monitor the competition as closely as possible at all times if an anti-ageing strategy is to be successful.

The tenth, and last, variable concerns brand **advertising**. Our aim here is not to assess the quality of the advertising, but simply the volume it accounts for as a proportion of the advertising investment made by brands in the segment as a whole. The greater the brand's own share – and especially if the brand is the leader in its segment – the greater the visibility of the brand, and therefore, logically, the more exposed it will be to ageing: the actual potential for ageing actually operates in reverse. In other words – almost paradoxically – the risk is greater than it would be for a brand with less visible advertising. However, this criterion does not take the actual nature of the advertising into consideration; it merely assumes that by advertising, the brand is showing the world that it exists.

The example of Heinz

In 2000, H J Heinz perceived the need to relaunch its Heinz Salad Cream product in the UK. A large-scale rejuvenation plan backed with a £10 million budget was agreed to reinvigorate the brand's advertising. It consisted mainly of a repositioning of the brand further up-market, an increase in the retail price, a large advertising campaign and various internet initiatives. Heinz recognized that the brand had been somewhat left behind in the previous years, while products from the mass food-retail sector, particularly in the UK, had been facing the massive onslaught of store brands. This made it all the more critical that the brand should be defended as a source of genuine differentiation and, to this end, ensure that it enjoyed the full benefits of advertising backing.

The grid shown in Figure 11.2 is simple to use. The area number can be used as a score that – when compared to an average score – allows the brand to be located in one of the three areas. The brand manager thus learns whether his or her strategy is based more on a desire or a need. By consulting the reference area he or she is also informed as to the associated action that needs to be taken.

Approximate average position
for the example of 'Alpha' printers = 3 + 2 + 2 + 3 + 3 + 2 + 1 + 3 + 2 + 3 = 24 (or Area 3)
Interpretation of care needed:
Average score of 10: brand located in Area 1
Average score of between 11 and 20: brand located in Area 2
Average score greater than or equal to 21: brand located in Area 3

Clearly, the results produced by this approach are not rigorously scientific, and cannot provide the brand manager with a set of ready-made solutions. However, even considering their lessons with hindsight can give the brand manager a more precise idea of the degree of caution that needs to be adopted. Once again, each brand and each company constitutes an individual case. Even so, a multi-criteria analysis of this kind does give an impression of which area the brand may be presumed to inhabit.

Brand identity or product identity: which should we pursue and protect?

There is often a tendency to confuse the age of a brand's products with the age of the brand itself. Seen in its simplest form, this observation stems from a piece of received wisdom that needs to be contradicted, for fear of attacking the problem in the wrong place and ultimately failing to rejuvenate the brand. Clearly, the perceived age of a brand's products has a considerable influence on the perceived age of the brand itself. However, a more in-depth analysis of cases of this type reveals that the original problem is a little more complex, and sometimes a little more difficult to identify. Brand identity creates an institutionalized mindset. However, any strategy has to be worth implementing. Obviously, opting for an institutional brand identity makes it possible to bring all a company's business and products together under one umbrella, reduce advertising costs and even create an institutional endorsement for the brand. However, as pointed out by Hatch and Schultz (2001), in this case the company must manage to bring together three basic elements: a vision, a culture and a brand image. This is where the brand identity becomes essential. And as Lindstrom (2005) argues, brands will increasingly need to establish and defend this identity.

When a company experiences an economic slowdown, its first reaction is often, understandably, to implement a cost reduction plan as rapidly as possible. However, the first of these 'costs' to be put under the microscope is often advertising; and among advertising expenditure, costs relating to institution-based advertising – that is to say, advertising for the company itself that is not directly related to its products and/or services. It is not my intention at this point simply to state yet again that advertising is not a cost but an investment; and that for this reason, it is one of the items of expenditure that should be preserved come what may – and even increased when times get hard. The fact is that institution-based advertising is now of key importance to most brands. It enables the brand to exist, to gain value and, by means of positive contamination, to serve its products and/or services. Most importantly, it allows the brand to exist as a pure brand, alongside its products and services. It allows it to establish itself relative to the actual product – and, indeed, to create a reasonable distance between the two so that it is able to distinguish itself. Furthermore, experience shows that this distance can be profitably used for marketing purposes. By remaining distinct from its products while at the same time retaining a natural association with them, the brand can advertise with perfect synergy, strengthening its own identity and the identity of its products at the same time. The example of Danone illustrates this point perfectly: its advertising for the group itself and for its children's institute, for example, constantly strengthens the existence and image of the brand while at the same time adding value to the image of the group's products. The result is the creation of a positive permeability.

The risk that the brand's identity will be imperceptibly and gradually lost without warning signs is not only a problem for producers. Mass distributors can also suffer in this way as a result of their reduced margins. Since all these distributors are locked together in fierce competition, there is now little distinction between the offerings of one distributor and those of another. Even their price positioning is similar. Their stores are located in centres of population, and are almost never the sole presence in the area. Their advertising is based on similar strategies that they use in turn, and perhaps even symbiotically. Why, for example, do the major textile retailers such as Gap, Abercrombie & Fitch, Zara, Kookaï and Benetton place such emphasis on this identity? Why have they not fallen into the trap of a complete loss of their own identity, like their elder siblings in the food retail market? The most obvious reason, of course, is that they are able to differentiate themselves much more easily in terms of the products they offer. But more importantly, it is because their ability to react enables most of them to bring to market a successful model 'inspired' by the competition in a matter of mere weeks, or sometimes even days. They now understand that in order to avoid ageing – and to age is to die in this business – what they need is a clear, distinct, positive and well-maintained identity. The brand outlives its products and can protect them, umbrella-like, from the danger of being confused with the competition's products.

Bernard Arnault, CEO of the LVMH group, interviewed by Suzy Wetlaufer, editor of the **Harvard Business Review**

A star brand is timeless, modern, grows rapidly and is very profitable. [Finding all four together] is rare. In my opinion, there are fewer than ten stars in the world of luxury brands. It is very difficult to achieve a balance between these four characteristics at the first time of trying – after all, rapid growth and strong profitability are often mutually exclusive – but that's what makes them stars.

The brand, regardless of whether it is owned by a producer or a retailer, is cruelly dependent on remaining young; but to do so it needs to be distinguishable from its products, while at the same time remaining faithful to them. In this way, it becomes possible to make regular changes to the brand concept, while at the same time introducing innovations to its products and/or services.

Brand rejuvenation via the internet

Since the collapse of the speculative bubble of 2000 and the domino-like collapse of a great many websites, a large number of brands are now asking themselves whether it is even truly necessary to maintain a presence of one kind or another on the mighty internet, let alone develop some form of sales activity there. Despite the fact that past experiences can always enrich our understanding of this extraordinary meta-medium, the future of the internet often remains difficult to imagine with any clarity or accuracy. However, no-one will deny that whatever form the internet takes in future, its arrival has made an indelible mark on modern consumer society – particularly with the advent of the world wide web – and that it is here to stay. In 2001, Professor Don Schultz, a US specialist in integrated marketing communication (see Schultz, Tannnenbaum and Lauterborn, 1993), lamented that despite the obvious lessons of the 'dot-com marketing fiasco' and the bankruptcy of e-brands that had seemed guaranteed a glowing future, such as pets.com, boo.com, etoys.com and furniture.com, there seemed to have been little improvement in the strategies being implemented by brand managers on the internet. Schultz observes: 'Unfortunately, it would seem that the marketers still haven't learned their lesson. Or, if they are learning, they aren't learning very fast. Or maybe the truth is that they're not learning the right things.'

The internet is a meta-medium. In other words, as the combination of media, the combined knowledge concerning those media is not sufficient to be used in a relevant way. The internet is a combination of media that calls for special consideration and a specific approach involving the rethinking of everything. Even more importantly, however, the fact that life takes place in real time should never be overlooked. Without a strategic approach, the brand is left defenceless, at the mercy of the uncertain events of the market and circumstances. This is a sad situation to see; for when dealt with correctly, the internet can be an extraordinary vehicle of advertising and growth for the brand, even today.

The example of Pepsi-Cola

Pepsi-Cola invested in the internet at a very early stage, harbouring very serious marketing ambitions. In February 1996, at a time when the web was still in its infancy, Pepsi-Cola opened its Pepsi World site. Of course, the aim of this was not to sell cans of Pepsi live on the internet. Its goal was to use the modern internet as a genuine method of advertising. The US drinks manufacturer's target market is mainly a young one, with the core market made up of young people under the age of 25. Indeed, for the most part, this target sector was the first to make use of the internet. For Pepsi-Cola, therefore, not to have a presence on a modern technological advertising medium such as the internet would have represented a significant potential ageing factor.

However, Pepsi-Cola's investment rapidly turned into a strategic plan. The Pepsistuff.com website is the means through which all advertising and promotion operations by the company are conveyed, while at the same time it acts as a point of entry to the other drinks brands owned by the group. To have a young image, it is essential to know what young people consider to be 'young' at any given time. The site allows visitors to collect contact details for Pepsi drinkers and communicate with them.

Once it has been inserted and integrated fully into a strategic plan, the internet can become a formidable lever of recognition and growth for the brand. The internet is not only a modern, dynamic and relatively inexpensive method of communication, but also a potential source of rapid, direct information about a brand's consumers. Two attributes now make it a virtually indispensable component of any anti-ageing strategy. Only five years ago, when a company was 'connected' – regardless of whether it just had an e-mail address or, better still, its own website – it immediately appeared to be at the cutting edge of technology. By definition, this made it a dynamic, modern, avant-garde, young company. Nowadays, being in possession of these same things no longer automatically confers the same positive status. By contrast, the lack of an internet presence immediately consigns the company to an archaic, dusty past, potentially damaging its image. It no longer comes down to a choice of whether or not to have a presence; but instead, 'simply' to decide what is the most effective means by which to be present.

12 Anti-ageing: rejuvenation cost vs ageing prevention cost

Is it preferable to invest in an anti-ageing strategy, or is it more sensible to take action regarding rejuvenation factors only when brand ageing starts to become noticeable? The question is an important one: costs can vary significantly between these approaches. There is also an assumption that the question will be asked as early as possible, in order to provide freedom of choice; otherwise, the only remaining option regards the precise details of a now-necessary rejuvenation 'remedy'. From a strictly financial point of view, we quickly run into the classic dilemma of brand advertising. If the brand invests on a daily basis in a preventative anti-ageing strategy, an advance cost is incurred, and the return on this investment will be very difficult to ascertain in the event of success, as it will have enabled the brand to avoid ageing. However, a 'non-result' investment of this kind can be declared a success (or not) based on what becomes of the brand. Inevitably, though, doubt will remain as to the exact reasons behind the preservation of this youth and the actual correlation between it and the investment made in this respect. Conversely, if the brand ages anyway, it will then be possible to calculate the return on investment with considerable accuracy, as it will be negative! Comparatively speaking, the rejuvenation strategy offers the

Table 12.1 Comparative cost characteristics according to type of action taken

	Cost characteristics		
Types of action carried out	**Decision**	**Price**	**Timescale**
Rejuvenation remedy	Forced	Often high	Taken on immediately
Preventative action	Calculated	Variable	Scheduled in short term
Anti-ageing strategy	Chosen	Depends on company	Spread out over time

advantage of allowing a more precise understanding of the result obtained, using factors implemented to rejuvenate the brand. Once again, however, doubts remain as to cause-and-effect relationships (see Table 12.1).

The main difference between the cost of remedial rejuvenation and the implementation of an anti-ageing strategy lies in the choice offered. In general, rejuvenation implies an emergency reaction, dictated by the brand's environment. It becomes necessary because an analysis of the problems faced by the brand has identified the cause, or causes, of the ageing process. Such causes often come as a surprise, because no-one had noticed that the brand was ageing. There is therefore an urgent need to mobilize resources of the appropriate scale, depending on the magnitude of the observed ageing, to effect the rejuvenation. An anti-ageing strategy, for its part, is the result of a measured strategic analysis, at a time when the brand does not seem to have been under threat from ageing. It therefore provides an objective way of establishing the nature and size of the investments to be made. Ultimately, the cost of this approach will not always be lower than the first. However, it does have a threefold advantage: it is chosen by the company; it can be more easily adapted to the company's financing ability; and, taking the proactive aspect of the strategy into consideration, it can much more easily be spread out over time.

We must also take the deeper implications of ageing into consideration. In some cases, ageing may be the result of symptoms that have been ignored for so long that the remedy is powerless to bring about a miraculous short-term solution. Even though no direct correlation necessarily exists between the timescale scheduled for the rejuvenation work and the cost, it is easy to see why an overall long-term rejuvenation plan is, in most cases, more expensive than preventative short-term action such as a simple packaging facelift.

Finally, we must also consider the goal the company will set itself in order to evaluate the relevance of its investment in hindsight. It is often considered that the goal is attained by measuring the growth of business activity and/or the profits recorded. A firm may also initially be satisfied with the acquisition of image, or simply added recognition. Lastly, extra market share points may be preferred as an immediate outcome in favour of short-term profitability. In this way, the cost may vary from one company to another as a function of the goals each individual company sets itself. This is especially true given that some companies opt neither for a pure rejuvenation remedy nor a pure anti-ageing strategy, but instead for a hybrid solution, because the position in which their brand finds itself permits them this choice. This case is a commonly-encountered one today, and is often confused with an anti-ageing strategy simply because it involves a proactive approach. In reality, the goal is not to devise and deploy an anti-ageing strategy, but simply to implement one or more preventative actions because it is felt that the ageing may soon be noticed by the target market.

When we encounter the notion of the cost of a brand anti-ageing strategy, there is a strong temptation to resort solely to brand advertising. This is an error. It is a basic misunderstanding to believe that brand strategy is based solely on the most skilful blend possible of advertising techniques. Of course, the advertising component is one of the more important variables in this respect; yet it is far from being the only one. To avoid growing old, a brand has to outwit time itself. Not only is this battle an unfair one, but it is difficult and relentless. On the other hand, human intelligence is said to be limitless – which is why all companies engaged in the fight against time are constantly on the lookout for a solution that will grant them a few more instants of this precious time. It certainly has to be admitted that since the start of the industrial age, considerable progress has been made to enable companies to be, as far as is possible, the masters of their own time.

The example of Dell

To explain the insolent youthfulness of the Dell brand in a market in which so many other brands have disappeared over the last 20 years, we need to cut to the very heart of the company. Dell's 50 largest suppliers, which account for around 95 per cent of its component purchases, are in constant contact with the company, with production figures sometimes being sent several times a day in order to keep throughput at maximum levels. Computer management of the process allows Dell to set schedules for every production line at each one of its production sites around the world every two hours or so. If it were ever possible to produce a visual representation of mass personalization, this is without doubt what it would look like; for of course, it is hardly ever the case that the computer ordered by a user filling in a form on the company's website actually exists at the moment that user clicks the 'Send' button at the bottom of the page. The exchange of data via the internet enables constant contact with suppliers, but the growth in sales of its products through that same internet means that customers can also be kept informed in near-real time. Holding an average of only five days' worth of stock, Dell is the envy of the vast majority of its competitors. Every day, as it replaces more and more of its physical stock with electronic information, Dell – like its competitors – dreams of improving its systems; and researches ways of getting that figure down to two days as quickly as possible. This exemplary mastery of time enables Dell to retain a young image – mainly because its products spend so little time in its hands that they have no time to age.

13 The policy of continuous, controlled innovation

The example of Cinzano

In 1970, the famous vermouth brand Cinzano produced an advertisement that has gone down as one of the all-time greats. The picture showed a tiny town building, on the bottom floor of which was a café adorned simply with the Cinzano logo across its front. This little building was flanked on both sides by two enormous, dull-looking skyscrapers; and standing at the threshold of the café was a waiter in traditional dress, with a nonchalant look and leaning against the doorframe, arms crossed. The caption on the poster read: 'The good old days haven't gone: you just have to know where to find them', and the bottom of the poster was adorned with a message attached to a bottle of Cinzano, stating: 'Cinzano bitter: We'll never change.'

Would anyone dispute the fact that the world is changing? A group such as Procter & Gamble is a market leader today mainly because it has succeeded masterfully in adapting to a world that is in a state of permanent movement. However, despite the fact that most of the fundamental principles of modern marketing have originated from this Cincinatti-based group, the main reason why its products are so popular with consumers today is that it has been able to reinvent its marketing strategies on a permanent basis.

Marc Alias, French External Relations Manager for Procter & Gamble, for the Mr Clean brand

It is possible for a brand to age with its users. This is why care must be taken to ensure that brand user 'generation renewal' takes place. The problem lies in accomplishing this renewal without losing the brand's loyal user base. To achieve this, you have to innovate while at the same time remaining faithful to the brand's legacy. Mr Clean was able to do this when it launched cleaning wipes to appeal to younger consumers while at the same time retaining the brand's unique historical character, based on an understanding between the brand's figurehead character and consumers.

For a number of years, we have been seeking to recruit users to the brand and win their loyalty by taking advantage of the capital generated by the friendliness of the Mr Clean character. In this way, we produced a new poster campaign which points out the brand's effectiveness, while at the same time strengthening the understanding between Mr Clean and his users. In conjunction with this 'brand equity' work, we have maintained our approach of 'relevant innovation': Mr Clean was the first brand to launch cleaning wipes in 1999. Nowadays, wipes have turned out to be a big hit with consumers, and account for more than a third of Mr Clean turnover. Along with the new advertising campaign, they have played a huge part in rejuvenating the brand and its consumer base.

Whether the issue at stake is its product or products, their packaging, distribution and/or advertising, no modern brand can afford the luxury of not changing. We are not proposing that the brand's identity be denied or destroyed; quite the opposite. Innovation, at all levels, is an integral part of the life of the brand. It is an essential precondition for preventing the brand from remaining frozen in a different era to that of its consumers. Hamel (2000) exhorted company directors to make relevant innovation a way of life and to manage their companies by adopting an often disruptive approach. It was, however, a strategy recommended by the chairman of Strategos as promoting factors such as internal talent and being linked to a great ability to adapt. Innovation, in a form that is perceptible, real and appreciated by consumers, is probably one of the most high-profile guarantees imaginable, because it shows that the brand is trying to differentiate itself from its competitors and remain contemporary. The US bicycle firm Schwinn, a leader in the US market since the 1960s, has aged very badly over the years through a simple lack of innovation. Competitor brands arrived on the market with lighter products including technology that seemed 100 years in advance of anything Schwinn could offer. Innovation is a strategic choice that stems from a twofold decision. It is on the one hand a financial decision, because there is a cost to innovation and therefore innovation requires investment. On the other hand, it is a marketing decision, because innovation for innovation's sake is an out-of-date notion. The aim must be to innovate in line with the conscious or subconscious expectations identified among consumers. The more closely the brand is associated with the product, the more meaningful the innovation aspect must be.

In 1992, in the United States, Nestea's act of abandoning the metal can – a traditional aspect of the soft drinks sector – in favour of a bottle played a major part in redynamizing the brand, which then gained an advantage over Lipton. Sophisticated marketing studies and accelerated processes (R&D, design, development, tests, marketing) have now produced a situation where most business sectors have experienced the rapid homogenization of their product ranges. Under such circumstances, innovation is a necessary solution to send consumers the strong signal that points to a dynamic brand. However, this innovation must constitute a direct or indirect response to the conscious or subconscious expectations of the consumer. Not only do consumers need firm points of reference; but in addition, they are no longer willing to pay the price for pseudo-innovation that adds nothing genuine to the use of the product and/or its aesthetics. Innovation, backed up by marketing tests, is the only factor that can make a lasting and positive contribution to the brand's image. It provides it with the time it needs to assert its leadership, during which – if that time is used well – the brand can clearly demonstrate its distinctive added value compared to its competitors, as claimed by Michon (2000). There is no doubt that these periods of time are now relatively short, particularly in sectors where technology plays a dominant role. However, the narrowness of this time window of value must be considered as a spur to hard work in this area. Yet if we admit that innovation can become something of an antiageing factor, an innovation of this kind cannot be decided and managed without being adapted and monitored.

The example of Ikea

The image of Ikea is, by definition, the same all over the world, and it would be tempting to try to make it into an icon of globalization. Clearly, some products sold by the world No.1 in furnishings are available in all of the various countries in which the Swedish giant operates. However, it would be wrong to believe that Ikea is a perfect example of globalization. In the first place, most of its products are manufactured locally – or at least regionally – in accordance to an extremely strict set of specifications, to reduce the cost of warehousing and transportation. However, perhaps even more importantly, the job of advertising for the brand is given to small local agencies. The theory is that by working with young local creative agencies and not with an international network, Ikea can hope to retain a young image, drawing on the most innovative aspects of local cultures and creative ideas at all times.

Unless care is taken, the aim of globalization can rapidly lead to the reductionist choice of the lowest common denominator, thus contributing to an overall loss of identity.

The example of L'Oréal

The L'Oréal group has a presence all over the world. However, this has not prevented the group, for all its globalizing tendencies, from appending the word 'Paris' to its brand name. This approach may seem illogical, suggesting as it does an extremely restricted geographical origin. Yet the ploy is strategically a very appropriate one. Simply put, the L'Oréal Paris identity is without doubt stronger than just L'Oréal – especially in the business sector it has made its own, and taking into consideration the fashion, beauty and luxury connotations traditionally associated with the French capital.

Reconciling evolution and innovation to avoid ageing

Not all innovations are intended to generate results over the same period of time. It depends on the product concerned, the company's business sector, the nature and origin of the innovation, etc. Furthermore, we should not confuse groundbreaking innovations and simple product evolution. Both are, of course, likely to contribute to the brand's dynamism as they constantly adapt, renew and perfect the offer made to the consumer. However, they are not managed in the same way. The growth of a brand's assets is now expected by a difficult and demanding target market; its management must therefore be a part of the normal life of the brand, and not some sort of exceptional occurrence. It combines a number of small modifications to the offer, no more or less than the illustration of the attention phase mentioned during the presentation of the OCARA principle (see page 12). Regardless of the care taken over the design and manufacture of goods or the specification and implementation of a service, the total satisfaction of the target market will always be observed to be a partly iterative process. This is simply because the real world cannot be perfectly modelled, and the consumption of the product and/or the use of the service will always reveal small, unnoticed imperfections during the creation phase. Constant attentiveness and vigilance is therefore required when bringing goods or services to market, in order to make the handful of corrections that may potentially be required, or may simply appear a wise move. All these little developments in the goods or services allow their parent brand to remain utterly contemporary and in perfect step with its target market and its conscious and subconscious expectations. The strategy may seem logical, or even self-evident, but observation forces us to conclude that it has not yet been adopted universally. In addition, the vast majority of these developments are not advertised by the brand. However, this does not mean that consumers do not include such factors in their evaluation processes. Just like the use of technical wizardry in a science fiction film, the public may end up being convinced by the practically life-like special effects, which thus start to seem almost normal.

Innovation, for its own part, represents a sort of rupture as a result of the change it proposes. It is therefore a major evolution that needs to be fully justified. We should consider the damage it can do to the brand when it is not used strategically. However, we should also bear in mind the example of pseudo-innovation, which will not hold consumers' attention for long and/or will even disappoint them. Ultimately, to present a simple evolution as a genuine innovation in the simple aim of revitalizing the brand is to bet on an assumption of naïvety the vast majority of consumers lost a very long time ago.

The example of American Express Blue

In 1999, American Express launched its Blue card. Only a few months later, the threshold of one million carriers had already been crossed. The product was a genuine innovation the added value of which was immediately perceptible. Unlike most US cards – and particularly the famous American Express green card – the Blue card contained an electronic chip allowing the card to be used safely. In addition, American Express supplied its new carriers with a kit allowing them to make internet purchases in total security. Launched with a free annual subscription and a free revolving credit system for the first six months, accompanied by attractive rates, Blue represented profound innovation compared to what the rest of the sector was offering. With Blue, AmEx was also aiming to attract a clientèle in the 25–40 age band, younger than its usual core target market.

The Ogilvy & Mather Momentum agency offered music for the launch strategy. The name of the operation was: 'Central Park in Blue'. Such singers and musicians as Sheryl Crow, Keith Richards, the Dixie Chicks, Eric Clapton, Chrissie Hynde and Stevie Nicks were invited to take part. During the event, professional photographers took digital photographs of the concert and the audience; these were downloaded to a website on which – of course – it was possible to order a Blue card. Afterwards, a CD was produced and sold. Not surprisingly, the CD contained an American Express application form for the Blue card. AmEx had suddenly become a much 'cooler' brand. In concrete terms, a study conducted among consumers attending the concert remembered that AmEx was the event sponsor, and spontaneous recognition for the Blue brand rose from 5 per cent to 31 per cent. Mission accomplished!

Fashion effects: misleading rejuvenation effects

Ignoring certain trends can damage a brand, and therefore potentially unfurl a luxurious red carpet towards multiple causes of ageing. However, of all the fashion effects bursting into our lives on an almost daily basis, very few will survive time themselves and thus attain the status of trends that have taken a firm root in our consumer society. Jumping on the bandwagon in too obvious a manner can then put the brand in a dangerous situation when the effect disappears, changes or undergoes a brutal metamorphosis. The decline may be as fast as the original launch was. The clothing brand Tommy Hilfiger learned this lesson the hard way in the late 1990s, when tastes changed and young consumers who had been attracted by the brand switched their allegiances to other labels.

The example of Aqua Velva

In the 1970s, the Aqua Velva lotion was tempted to follow new entrants into its sector from the world of design and perfume, a move that would have appeared attractive from the point of view of a number of consumers. The brand progressively lost its identity in the process, and began to experience an inevitable ageing process, which penalized it for a number of years. It was only after a rigorous rejuvenation plan accompanied by coherent repositioning in the early 1990s that the brand was able to rediscover the dynamism and advantages of a positive image. By producing complementary products such as Ice Sport and Ice Blue – versions with more dynamic positioning – it was able to expand its market while at the same time maintaining the respective identities of the various target markets using the lotion.

Most of the time, fashion effects go hand in hand with a significant youth effect for the beneficiary brand. The brand then enjoys heavy – and usually free – media coverage, and naturally ends up appearing to be fully in step with its time. At the most basic level, these fashion effects are not actually fashions, and certainly not trends, but they pose a serious problem for even the most seasoned marketer. There appears to be every reason to follow them, as they seem to offer unlimited turnover in the short term. The press talks incessantly about them, and their (often self-fuelled) media coverage gives birth to a target market that seems to grow bigger every day. In many cases, one or more competitors have already made an initial step in this direction, which inevitably generates additional pressure. So is the solution to follow the crowd in pursuit of the fashion effect with all of its attendant advantages and risks? There is no simple answer to this. It is, however, useful to try and shift the basis of the analysis, concentrating not on the effect but rather the probable factors – or lack of them – supporting longevity. The modern consumer puts too much emphasis on new opportunities for most of these effects to become trends of any lasting significance. Here, trend advisers can prove useful. Not all are professional – far from it – but a number of agencies with a reputation for high-quality trend information may be contacted to validate specific effects, or, as part of a prospective study, to try to uncover future trends in order to incorporate them at an early date and as far upstream as possible. The use of a trends agency supplies not only a professional view but, more importantly, an often more objective view than the one the brand may have of itself.

In a case where the fashion effect has been started by the company itself, either intentionally or unintentionally, a similar analysis is needed. How many products, basking in the glory of quick fame yesterday, have now returned just as rapidly to anonymity? The rejuvenation of a brand is a strategic approach, and not an operational tactic. In other words, we must manage not only the fashion effect itself, but also what happens afterwards. The fashion effect operates along parallel lines in several potential areas. The first of these may be legal, in order to protect the company as quickly as possible from parasitic competitors. However, protection is not always an entirely achievable goal, unless other parasitic actions end up collapsing under the sheer cost of the counterfeiting process. The second area is advertising. With the exception of a product with a life span decreed to fall into the 'gadget' category from the start, the aim here is to stretch out advertising as much as possible over time in order to achieve gradual recognition in the maximum number of segments. This is a difficult task, since it is extremely difficult – or even impossible – to control the media.

Many brands have undulating life patterns simply because their managers allowed themselves a break after undertaking major work. Markets, however, do not take breaks. The interconnected nature of these markets, born of or amplified by globalization, along with the advent of the information society encouraged by the explosion of the media and the support of the internet, means that brands no longer have the luxury of taking a short rest following a success – unless they want to see all their hard work rapidly compromised. For this reason, L'Oréal is constantly investing in cutting-edge research for its sector, innovates as a matter of course and is always changing. Success is a notion that, for the wise brand manager, should be evaluated either in the past or in the future, but never in the present. The past belongs to old, declining brands whose glory days have come and gone. The future is for young, dynamic brands that are constantly setting themselves new goals in order to retain their gains and, more importantly, to build on them. This approach may seem a stimulating exercise. In fact, it is exhausting, demanding and uncompromising! The former CEO of Intel, Andy Grove, has written a book entitled *Only The Paranoid Survive*. The truth of this statement is beyond doubt. However, even then, they will only survive if they never sleep!

Innovation in the use and/or contents of the product

An original way of keeping the brand young, dynamic and at the forefront of consumers' minds can consist of new ways of using the product that bears the brand identity. Indeed, some brands have built all of their present success on this innovation in their use. The basic objective is always to retain the brand's identity. Once incorporated, however, the marketing possibilities presented to the imagination seem limitless.

The example of Oil of Olaz

During the Second World War, a South African chemist, Graham Gordon Wulff, developed an anti-dehydration treatment for burns sustained by RAF pilots. At the end of the war, the product's explicit positioning seemed unlikely to destine it for widespread fame and glory. Graham Wulff then had the idea of refining it a little more to find another use for the product in the feminine cosmetics market. He combined forces with Adam Lowe to sell the product and they opted for the name Oil of Ulan; the name 'Ulan' was intended to suggest a rare exotic plant from which the essence of the product could be imagined to derive. No such plant ever existed. And with a clear marketing strategy in mind, the two associates took care to modify the name for each country of sale, on the basis of the most appropriate-sounding effect on the local ear. Thus it was that Oil of Ulan in South Africa was christened Oil of Ulay in the UK, Oil of Olay in the United States and Oil of Olaz in most other European countries. Although globalization issues were clearly not the main concern underlying this approach, innovation in terms of the product's use has made it (and kept it) the best-selling hydration product in the world.

(*Note:* The Oil of Olaz brand now belongs to the Procter & Gamble group.)

Professor Brian Wansink, of the University of Urbana-Champaign in Illinois, is also a manager of the Brand Revitalization Consumer Panel, a consumer panel whose work is devoted to the process aimed at redynamizing a brand. The results of the various different initiatives conducted over recent years provide us with information that can be put to judicious use by an anti-ageing strategy. We know, for example, that the more a brand's frequency of use is maintained, the more chance it will have of remaining in the consumer's memory and thus continuing to benefit from a positive image. Brian Wansink starts from the simple observation that a brand that simply manages to increase its buyers' consumption by between four and five units per year will be earning itself an extra 25 per cent in turnover without even having recruited a single extra buyer. This is no mean achievement. To do this, it is possible to imagine new uses for the product that will allow greater consumption and a higher degree of exposure to the brand. This aim may seem a simple one, yet it requires a degree of prudence. The essential precondition, revealed by various studies, suggests that the proposed new uses must not be too far removed from, or indeed contradictory to, those already adopted by consumers. For example, the de-structuring of meal times has created new consumption opportunities in the form of 'grazing' throughout the day. Many brands have thus simply produced miniature, portable versions of their existing products, ensuring that the promise of satisfaction remains the same. However, the approach may also consist of promoting a new consumption opportunity for the same product. In the United States, Philadelphia cream cheese was wisely advertised on the basis that Philadelphia cream could also be used as a replacement for butter. Wansink also cites the example of Orville Redenbacker popcorn, which used advertising to explain to consumers that it could be fun, original and healthy to offer popcorn as an apéritif or at ceremonial events in place of the traditional peanuts and crisps. This is not a question of repositioning the brand, but rather a new consumption opportunity. However, when Heinz noticed that its vinegar was also regularly being used for cleaning windows and carpets, there was no easy way of advertising both uses simultaneously.

In a similar spirit, it is also possible to a certain extent to 'play' on the product's packaging. Highly innovative companies can now exploit their ability to use colour to create products that would previously have been unimaginable. Consider, for example, Michelin, whose Colorado tyre is available in yellow, red, blue, green, etc, as a colourful alternative to the usual black. Not to be outdone, the automobile sector has adopted colour nuances as a way of creating individual identities for each of the models of a brand. The phenomenon is not hard to understand. Modernity and youth, by nature, require diversity. The colour spectrum, although limited, offers virtually unrestricted possibilities for variation. The attraction of such a packaging innovation is easy enough to see when the goal is to renew and dynamize the brand through its products. No doubt this would cause the august Henry Ford, with his dogged adherence to black, to spin in his grave – and the war of the pigments is only just beginning! As a tool for differentiation, its result is sure to be a series of battles against opposition troops armed with increasingly thick colour swatch books. The universe of colours has now been completely opened up, and cultural assumptions are falling one by one. The cosmetics industry has thoroughly understood this fact, and is now taking on the bold task of rejuvenating its ranges with extraordinary colour ranges that lend each product its originality, differentiation and/or pleasure aspect. Some may remember that in 1990, via its Lancôme brand, L'Oréal was the first to innovate in this direction with its Maquimèche hair mascara. Like the launch of a rocket – and irrespective of its quality – innovation requires an *ad hoc* launch window if it is to achieve its objective in full. Too early, and the result could be a failure to rendezvous with the target market.

Brands with packaged products have a certain advantage. Packaging design is in a state of constant change, allowing the brand to be revitalized with the assistance of a renewed product image. The advantage of this approach is that the brand can be redynamized without losing its own identity in the process. Nowadays, although colours and shapes can supply the brand with aesthetic evolution almost indefinitely and lend it a permanently contemporary image, we can take advantage of the technical functions of the product packaging. Much more economical packaging for a larger volume would constitute a clear invitation to consume more. The measures implemented on 47 products from different categories by the Brand Revitalization Consumer Panel clearly showed that, for products packaged in larger sizes than usual, the frequency of use can be increased by between 19 per cent and 152 per cent, with an average increase of 32 per cent. The main reason is related to the removal of price-based guilt, as the product's large size suggests a relatively lower price. It must, however, be pointed out that there is, of course, a limit to this size effect. A saturation effect (which varies according to the nature of the products) is observed. The fact that salt cellars now contain 300 g of salt instead of the usual 200 g does not mean that consumers are about to start ramping up their salt intake. It has, however, been observed that a large packet of M&Ms prompted cinemagoers to consume more during the showing of a film.

This mass effect also takes account of the fact that the product is being stored in the consumer's home. Brand managers often worry about the results of brands' special promotions, fearing that once the positive effect of the promotion has passed, sales will fall back to their average volume for the year. A number of research studies have shown that, apart from the outcome of temporarily boosting sales that such promotions generally achieve, the result may also be an increase in overall volumes. This stems from the fact that a product stored in large numbers in a consumer's home will have a mass effect similar to that created by a brand on store shelves when its shelf frontage area is increased. In other words, the product will tend to be consumed in greater quantities. If you can ensure, in a controlled way, that the brand has adequate visibility in the world of consumer consumption, there is every chance that your brand will be consumed. Renew its appearance regularly, and it will increase its own chances of appearing young.

14 Formulae and models vs analysis and creativity

Is there any hope that one day, inspired by the goals of medical researchers at the University of Illinois in Chicago in the field of human medicine, we might one day find the FoxM1B gene for brands – that is, the gene for eternal youth? How simple the world of economics would be if we could break it down to a handful of formulae and models that, when applied to the letter, would churn out guaranteed results every time. Although the subjective age of a brand can be determined fairly accurately by means of an equation, it has still been impossible (at the time of writing) to produce an exact model for the way this age changes over time. Even so, we may be permitted to believe that in cases where strategic analysis is needed, the marketer has a chance of stealing a glimpse into the legendary book of spells that holds the key to the great hourglass of time, and can thereby aspire to gain some control over a few grains of sand. Would this mean that our marketer would have to renounce the creative urges of his or her own imagination? Certainly not: the ageing phenomenon is so complex that we must take any possible means of retarding its advance into consideration. True, the result in some cases may be a variety of highly original solutions; but who ever said that marketing was founded on principles set in stone?

The example of Valda

The case of the Valda factory in Rio de Janeiro in Brazil is probably one of the more representative examples of an unorthodox solution to a problem. However, provided that the objective is achieved, who cares about the method, as long as it remains ethically appropriate? Many countries are familiar with Valda pastille confectionery, a little green sugar-coated cone scented with the delicate fragrances of eucalyptus and mint. The sweets owe their origin to the French chemist Henri Canonne, who created them in 1904 as a remedy for respiratory diseases. Today, the Valda pastille is using advertising to distance itself from a rather old-fashioned image derived from a core consumer base often depicted as consisting of homely grandmothers. To rejuvenate the brand's image, the manager of the Rio de Janeiro plant, Hugues Ferté, came up with the original idea of lending support to young local musicians. The factory thus installed its own on-site recording studio, and for a number of years even financed a music production company. Today, it is still a partner in Festvalda, an annual festival which celebrates young Brazilian musical talent. Needless to say, the combination of these young musicians and the factory workers may appear somewhat unorthodox; but today, virtually all young Brazilians know who Valda is. From an image point of view, then, the message has been 'Goodbye Grandma' (unless that grandmother happens to be a star such as Tina Turner).

The rejuvenation of a brand cannot be summed up as a series of equations (linear or non-linear), lined up side by side, that will invariably result in a young brand once fully resolved. Each case is distinct, specific and unique. Certainly, a strategically thorough approach is a good idea. However, it must leave room for creative strategies that match the specific imagination and identity of the brand in question.

The example of New Balance

All leaders, regardless of whether their name is Reebok, Nike, Adidas, Puma, New Balance, Asics or whatever else, are constantly vying with one another to introduce technological innovations and new designs. However, when repeated ad infinitum, such innovation limits mass production and thus reduces the opportunity for economies of scale.

And the lower the economies of scale, the harder it is to keep margins high. This partly explains why nearly all of the key players in this market have relocated their production to Asia. A worker in the United States earns around US $14 an hour, whereas in China this figure rarely exceeds 40 cents. Putting the issues of quality and productivity aside, the calculation results in a fairly straightforward decision even for the less intelligent manager.

How, then, can we explain the fact that the New Balance brand stubbornly insists on producing shoes 'Made in America'? The brand's products, which are renowned for their quality, are not significantly more expensive than others made outside the United States. Firstly, New Balance exercises its creativity not only on the designs of its footwear lines, but also on the tools required to make them. As it adapts its machine tools to the specific requirements of New Balance shoe production – for example, by developing its own patterns – constantly taking advantage of technological innovations developed in the sports shoe sector or in other associated sectors, and makes use of the IT capabilities of modern production management, New Balance is always on the lookout for technological improvements that will allow it to achieve productivity gains.

The second factor is human capital. The cost of labour in Asia is so low that not only is there no point in investing in training, but it is also virtually impossible to do so without increasing costs dramatically. By contrast, New Balance employee training is a key part of the company's business strategy. It is systematic and forward looking, every day expanding the abilities of individuals who become increasingly multi-skilled and competent in their jobs, and used to working in small, dynamic, flexible teams of five or six. Whereas it takes around 3 hours to manufacture a pair of shoes in Guangdong, the same job only takes an employee at the Norridgewock plant in Maine 24 minutes. As a result, a pair of shoes that used to cost more than US $40 to make can now be produced for a mere US $4. Of course, at US $1.30, the Chinese-made shoes are still competitive. However, in a market like the sports shoe market, a difference of this order remains feasible in view of the final sale price of a pair of shoes, not least because of the enormous logistical advantage. By running its manufacturing operation at the geographical heart of its market, right among its consumers, the responsiveness that is so important to increasing production is improved enormously, and the replenishment of sales points is made much easier – and much faster. In 1972, when Jim Davis acquired the company, sales were barely making

US $100,000 a year. Today, its annual sales are US $1.1 billion. Paradoxically, the company's success has been so complete and so rapid that today, New Balance too has some of its production sourced in Asia. One of the secrets of the study-creativity combination is never to reject any idea, but instead to know objectively where, when and how to use it.

Avoiding ageing through complementary physical brand manifestations

To avoid ageing, the brand has to create a presence in the minds of its consumers and, of course, generate the right environment for remaining there. To do this, the relationship it forms with its consumer must be constantly maintained and renewed. To this end, a number of manufacturing companies have attempted to create an element of theatre around their offer. As we have seen, some have been quick to assume total or partial control for their own distribution. Others have gone further still, creating temples dedicated entirely to their products. By introducing the Niketown store, the footwear and sports items manufacturer Nike gave itself a stage on which to exhibit each of its products in a sales and advertising environment that it not only controlled totally but that could also be renewed over time. In addition to its products, the brand is thus given a physical form through one or more actual locations that make contact with consumers easier as well as providing an opportunity for renewing the nature of this contact. Nike's aim was not to become the sole distributor of its own products by taking the place of its existing distributors. It simply wanted to confirm the brand's identity within an environment entirely under its own control. This identity can take on a rather more concrete form in areas such as positioning, codes of expression, projected image, attitude towards its customers and individual character. When it established its Cité de la Femme in Paris, Etam did the same thing. The brand gained a fantastic exclusive shop window and an enormous laboratory for testing out new concepts.

Others go further still, aiming for manifestations of the brand not only where their products are sold, but also where they are consumed. The attempt is a more ambitious one, and cannot be transferred systematically from one area of business to another. However, in cases where it is possible, it provides a certain advantage for a mass-retail product brand, allowing it to get closer to its consumers. After all, it is a well-known fact that the closer we are to a particular person, the less we notice any symptoms of ageing in them. The main aim, therefore, is to acquire for oneself an original communication vehicle that expresses a dynamic physical manifestation of the brand more in touch with its consumers. However, although advertising is essential, such brands do not commit themselves to this approach without the question of profitability in the back of managers' minds. This is all the more true in cases where the points of contact appear in large numbers, such as Johnny Walker bars, or Nescafé coffee bars that Nestlé is gradually introducing all over the world. In the coffee sector, other producers – such as Segafredo, for example – are also opening expresso bars for the same reasons.

Rejuvenation through globalization

Globalization is an oft-decried model. However, its purpose was to bestow glory and profitability, and great hope was placed in its use. Globalization probably constitutes one of the most difficult traps to avoid when it comes to the possible ageing of the brand. The basic principle of globalization suggests that the same theory be applied to the brand in all places where that brand operates. However, with all respect to Theodore Levitt, the only place where the global village truly exists is in the plans of those who aspire to it. The markets in question, even as part of a fairly homogenous economic area, still remain very different from one another at present. This means that the ageing factors with which the brand could be confronted may vary considerably from one market to another. This is where the trap of globalization suddenly snaps shut on its prey. When fighting against ageing, it is impossible to adjust one variable in one market without doing the same in the other markets, as required in the name of coherence and globalization. However, there is no guarantee in such a case that the same adjustment will produce the same effects again. Even worse, there is no guarantee that it will not have entirely the opposite effects. Even Coca-Cola and Procter & Gamble, both proponents (and often successful ones at that) of all-out globalization, have now had to accept the fact that it is not possible simply to impose any chosen brand, one standard packaging or a single uniform marketing strategy on consumers in any given country. Ultimately, brands that attempt to do so run the risk of incurring overall costs considerably higher than the accrued benefits.

The example of Zara

This brand could easily be described as young, dynamic and fashionable. It does, however, inhabit one of the most fiercely-contested market sectors – clothing. Zara accounts for more than three-quarters of the business of the Spanish group Inditex, a little-known company which has nonetheless achieved remarkable success. At the head of the company is a talented captain of industry in his sixties with something of an aversion to the spotlight, yet blessed with a mastery of company strategy that equals his excellence in the creative art of design: Amancio Ortega. It is natural to compare Zara with New Balance (see page 182) – firstly, because the sector is just as prone to the vagaries of fashion, and is thus subject to brutal market reverses in response to the slightest fashion effect; and secondly, because the strategic approach adopted by Inditex (and by Zara in particular) is similar to that of New Balance, and clearly diverges from the strategies implemented by most of its competitors. As paradoxical as Zara's strategic approach may seem, it deserves our admiration: not only has it allowed Zara to retain the extremely youthful image that has won over the immense majority of its clients, but it has managed to remain just as profitable in the process. Indeed, Inditex regularly comes close to achieving 20 per cent net margins, while larger competitors such as H&M and Gap turn in figures of 8.4 per cent and 6.4 per cent respectively. However, to achieve such profits, the brand has to navigate a veritable logistical minefield. A traditional Zara store measures 1,200 square metres and every years offers its male, female and child clientèle around 10,000 different products devised by Arteixo La Coruña in Spain, under the watchful and benevolent gaze of Amancio Ortega. Unlike its competitors, Inditex uses a network of small local subcontractors.

Pre-cut pieces are delivered with simple but thorough instructions which must be followed to the letter. The information chain for raw materials, labour and finished goods is stretched to its limits in real time and given an impressive logistics and distribution platform. Inditex relies on the differentiating advantage created by its flexibility and responsiveness. It often takes more than four months for a new design from Gap or H&M to work its way through the various stages from production to distribution. In barely three weeks, Inditex is able to react to the slightest change in the market. In short, it adopts a genuine marketing approach in near-real time, turning fashion into a constant ally rather than a perpetual restriction.

As a result, it is rare indeed to find any given design remaining on store shelves for more than four or five weeks. Such dynamism also has a further by-product, generating much more regular point-of-sale traffic than purely seasonal collections are capable of achieving. It is true that there may be a question mark over what the future will hold for the Zara system in a modern Spain that is becoming increasingly European. At present, however, Zara – whose first store opened in 1975 at Arteixo La Coruña – has the same perceived age as that of its customers, regardless of whether that customer is a child, a teenager, a young woman or an adult. This is probably one of the greatest demonstrations of the brand's success. Perpetual renewal, clever style choices, consistently modern designs, a fully strategic price positioning in each country, strict quality checks on manufacturing, tightly controlled distribution, an unequalled response time to the slightest changes in the market – all of these factors have prepared Zara well to face the ageing process, making it a brand that is truly of its time and always able to meet both the conscious and subconscious aspirations of its clientèle. All this has been achieved without spending a king's ransom on advertising: Zara's advertising is renowned for its astonishingly low-key approach.

A brand's destiny: chiefly in the hands of one person

More than just the abilities of a board of directors, more than just effective combinations of dynamic, high-performing staff, more than just skilful management of the prevailing positive or negative circumstances, the brand needs a soul if it is to live and remain young. Of course, everyone has their own interpretation of precisely what constitutes this soul. But we should agree that behind every great brand – regardless of the specific business sector – there is always, at any given time, a highly-talented man or woman. Would Coca-Cola have become Coca-Cola without Roberto Goïzueta? Or would Danone have become Danone without Antoine Riboud? Could Chrysler have continued to exist without Lee Iacocca? Without François Dalle, would L'Oréal have become No.1? Would Axa have got to where it is today without Claude Bébéar? Where would Bolloré be without Vincent Bolloré? Would Procter & Gamble's brands have been a worldwide success without Edwin Artz? Could Vivendi Universal have been born and become what it is today without Jean-Marie Messier? Would General Electric have become General Electric without Jack Welch? Would Michelin still be Michelin without François Michelin? Could Disney have been the success it is without Michael Eisner? Would Leclerc have achieved its current status as a retailer without Edouard Leclerc? Would Dell have become a leader without Michael Dell? Would L'Oréal have achieved its undeniably remarkable results and success without Lindsay Owen-Jones? Could News Corp have become the powerful media group it now is without Rupert Murdoch? These are just a few charismatic examples.

Here, of course, one is tempted to think back nostalgically to the glory days of the 1980s, when companies and brands took second place to overhyped megastar bosses. The point we are trying to make here has nothing to do with this. We simply wish to observe that a brand cannot survive without a soul; and this soul, in the noblest sense of the word, is often breathed into it by a man or woman who, at a particular time in history, has found himself or herself at the helm of the company. Regardless of the nature and quality of the marketing and strategic studies conducted, choices have to be made. Choices that benefit not the man or woman running the company, but the company itself. We should note that although we marvel – often with good reason – at the talent, dynamism and ingenuity of a particular company CEO, it would probably also be appropriate to acknowledge the vitality and soul that person attempts to bestow upon the brand from day to day while he or she is primarily in charge of it. As we know, the law defines a brand as a factor that can assume a physical manifestation. However, perhaps we may also use the additional image of a developing flower – a beautiful flower, of course, such as an orchid. Just like this flower, the brand constantly needs to obtain a large share of its nutrients from the life of the manager responsible for it. The more vitality, genius and dynamism the manager possesses, the more the brand will benefit and be able to protect itself against the potentially harmful effects of time.

These managers have only their modest time on earth to dedicate to serving the brand. And as they grow inexorably older, the brand will feed on their lives to stay young. Some will occasionally leave a more profound and noticeable imprint – a brand name given to the company by a remarkable founder, owner or manager – as an essential part of its identity. But with their full consent, the brand will draw thirstily upon their wisdom, creativity, strategic intelligence and – quite simply – on their physical strength in order to exist, derive its value and remain as young and prominent as possible in the minds of its target market. The people we refer to as the great captains of industry represent the essential sap on which the brand feeds throughout the duration of their mandate. We often deal with brand strategy by analysing marketing decisions, the results of a particular policy, directional decisions, balance sheets and other financial accounts to assess the actual value of a brand, deriving a figure that is purely economic or an overall total incorporating the brand's image and growth potential. However, in so doing, we are merely touching the tip of the iceberg: behind these facts, there are always one or more men or women whose abilities – often only fleetingly recognized – have helped to make the brand what it is today. Men and women who, in addition, have succeeded in involving, training and motivating other men and women in the process of making the brand what it now is.

We often refer to a brand as capital, and the truth of this concept is now undeniable. However, woe betide anyone who might be tempted to interpret this term in its strictly financial sense. Although it is true that the brand can have a physical manifestation (and can thus be perceived and valued in financial terms), it still retains a soul; a heart formed through the synergy of the combined efforts and wisdom of many individuals and the support given to the brand by everyone in the company. Company models are often referred to in which all management science disciplines dovetail perfectly with one another, and no doubt this is of benefit in producing the desired results. Even so, a brand is not an inert object that can be pinned down and analysed in the minutest detail. It is not merely a variable that can be easily incorporated into a chosen template. The brand is a living being and is born as one, often with difficulty. It grows as a living being does, often going through a period of teenage crisis, having to deal with difficult choices and sometimes even suffering from a number of illnesses for which a suitable cure needs to be found on each occasion. Unlike a human being, however, its allotted time-span seems limited only by the date of its origin. That is where the absolute power of its human manager lies, even if that manager is not always aware of the fact. The manager is, in a way, the master of the second time marker, and it is his or her job to place that marker on the brand's time line or, alternatively, to do his or her utmost to postpone its placement indefinitely.

It is an extraordinary power, and one that, sadly, cannot be translated into formulae (however sophisticated) and/or models (however perfect). It is a power of which only the most astute managers are aware. It is a power with multiple and varied points of origin: constant vitality, absolute dynamism, strategic intelligence, the perfect retention of knowledge, managerial pragmatism, rare perspicacity, exceptional responsiveness, unusual creativity, limitless endurance... the list goes on. However, even though the sources may be known, the alchemy that lies behind their most potent combination and manipulation remains the secret of a select few – the ones known as the great captains of industry. We should give them the recognition they deserve; only their repeated efforts to stimulate each of these sources of youth can enable the brand to survive over time and, in an ideal world, to prosper in a state of insolent youth. Lastly, it is possible that one of their qualities – a fairly understated quality, but one that is essential in terms of the strategic management of the brand – is the ability to ensure the long-term success of their efforts by preparing, assisting and supporting those who come after them. This is by no means an easy matter. It is, however, of critical importance in preserving the image and position of the brand and the results thus obtained.

However, for every handful of success stories, there are many tales of woe; and some jewels entrusted to bad alchemists can rapidly lose their sparkle and sink just as quickly into the abyss of oblivion. Naturally, the more charismatic the boss at the helm, and the greater his or her involvement in the company, the more delicate the transition is likely to be. However, the issue is more about the strategic choice of a successor, a concerted effort in handing over the baton and the provision of abundant support than the impossible pursuit of an identical replacement. Yes, the brand's personality will often experience change as a result, but this is not necessarily a bad thing. On the contrary, a rejuvenated soul can provide this brand with a fresh spirit of dynamism and open up new horizons and new opportunities. Even the finest of boats, once it has left port, is at a disadvantage unless there is an excellent captain at the helm to steer the vessel and to ensure it benefits from the slightest wave and smallest breath of wind on its sails. In contrast to received wisdom, then, we should never forget that behind a great brand there have been, still are and always will be great people; and not just a positive environment, marketing tactics, large advertising investment or, as is usually the case, luck.

15 Management of the brand equity; or, how to avoid ageing

If there are still any managers out there who need convincing of the importance of managing brand equity strategically to avoid seeing it age – or at the very least to keep ageing effects to a bare minimum – the financial logic alone should prove persuasive enough. As we have already seen, it is still possible to analyse the factors of ageing in detail in order to deploy countermeasures for the rejuvenation of the brand. However, there is no doubt that the financial and temporal cost of such an action is much greater than the cost of a strategy that anticipates the ageing phenomenon. To return to our analogy of a giant hourglass, the aim is not to stop the flow of the grains of sand or to make time run backwards. Instead, the goal is to turn the hourglass over at regular intervals to ensure that the flow of sand never stops (see Figure 15.1).

Through its constant pursuit of an anti-ageing strategy, the brand is able to change by tiny increments, sometimes without its consumers ever having noticed the change. The payback on this investment comes in the form of a brand that appears 'naturally' young and never attracts questions as to its age. This is probably the main advantage of pursuing an anti-ageing strategy. A rejuvenation remedy, since it presupposes that ageing is already evident, usually confines the brand manager's options to drastic recovery work, undertaken as a matter of urgency on several aspects of the brand simultaneously. This change, which can often be a brutal one, runs the risk not only of profoundly altering the brand's identity (as we have already seen), but also of confusing the consumer, whose points of reference are turned upside down. In the worst-case scenario, if the modification (name, packaging, advertising, positioning, etc) is too severe, there is a danger that consumers will no longer be able to discern a link between the 'before' and 'after' versions of the brand, and may ultimately turn away from it completely. By contrast, the manifestly proactive approach of the anti-ageing strategy enables it to set its sights on any aspects of the brand, and any components in the marketing mix, where work is needed. There is, however, one sizeable difference: the relative mastery of time. The phases of the chosen preventative treatment may then be carefully ordered, scheduled and coordinated to ensure that a dynamic image and a young perceived age are maintained, without actually doing away with everything the brand was and stood for in the minds of its consumers. Regardless of the effects it produces, a facelift is always bound to come as something of a shock to the friends and family of the patient, whereas the judicious regular use of skin-care products instead may slow down some of the effects of ageing without the need to resort to playing tricks on Father Time!

This is why, in an ideal world, such a strategy cannot be adopted only during a period of decline. It must be implemented from the very birth of the brand, in order to make every effort to prevent the effects of ageing from gaining any hold on the brand. In practical terms, it means that if the brand is intended to generate one or more emotions – in addition to the cognitive characteristics of its promise – it will have to work tirelessly to maintain, revive and reinforce these emotions throughout the entire life of the brand if it is to win over the consumer. It needs a process of constant renewal that remains true to the brand's profound identity and can satisfy the permanent thirst for renewal and satisfied customers in constant pursuit of something new. Although emotions have been the subject of ever-increasing volumes of research, they still conceal a large number of mysteries. As long ago as 1980, following an in-depth study, Plutchick (1980) discussed the general woolliness surrounding the actual definition of emotion. It is not hard to see, then, why the management of such emotions is no easy task. In a particularly interesting study, Richins (1997) attempted a synthesis of the major studies on the subject published up until that date, and produced a shortlist of 20 key emotions likely to be experienced by consumers: anger, dissatisfaction, worry, sadness, fear, shame, envy, loneliness, affection, love, calmness, optimism, joy, excitement, pride, satisfaction, relief, guilt, eagerness and surprise. This just goes to show how much thought and care is needed if we wish to make use of one or more of

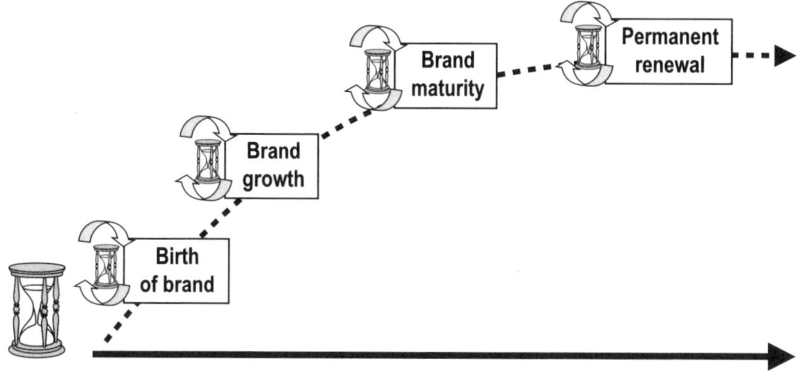

Figure 15.1 The brand anti-ageing life cycle

these emotions as part of the desired brand/consumer relationship, to contribute towards protecting the brand from ageing.

Today, brand equity management is one of the most difficult marketing tasks there is. A number of checklists provide the brand manager with a basis for taking action on the various parameters that concern the brand, such as the one proposed by Van Auken (2004). Such checklists ensure a certain coherence between the various actions undertaken; for, as discussed above, the brand's identity must remain entirely stable and coherent across all of its intangible aspects. In the United States, Burger King paid a high price for the advertising errors it made in the 1980s. From management staff changes to advertising agency changes, the brand ended up losing its internal coherence, while at the same time McDonald's was continuing to grow as it retained the equity it had been able to create. The brand needs this stability to provide reassurance and assist identification and location by its target market. At the same time, however – and just as importantly – the brand has to change, adapt and modernize. The central core of the brand must be protected at all costs, but it must not prompt the brand manager to consider it as some sort of megalithic monument frozen in time and space. This is where brand strategy comes in – a brand strategy constantly supported by the fullest possible analysis of the existing competition and environment. The factors that cause the brand to age are not innate ones likely to occur at a specific time without any possibility of controlling their growth. The ageing process is brought on by a contamination effect created by the brand's environment. As we have seen, this contamination may primarily affect its products, its advertising and/or its target market as the brand is compared with other points of reference that are newer (and thus naturally younger), or at the very least create a younger image in consumers' minds.

This is where brand equity management comes into its own. Not ageing is not the same thing as halting the course of time (brand life cycle management – BLM) – a feat that surely no-one in their right mind could harbour even the slightest ambition of achieving. Not ageing implies identifying the attacks of time, locating them and, as far as possible, limiting their effects in order to adapt the brand accordingly. This gives us an idea not only of the thoroughness required by such a goal, but also of the creativity expected of our brand manager. After all, there are of course no simple, standardized solutions in this area. The brand is by its very nature unique. Even in cases where issues of territorial scope and specialism have unintentionally provided it with similarly named contemporaries, it remains unique. We must therefore take note of its specific characteristics so that we can identify the reactions and actions that will improve our management of the capital it constitutes.

Bernard Arnault, CEO of the LVMH group, interviewed by Suzy Wetlaufer, editor of the* Harvard Business Review*, discussing the meaning of a timeless brand

It means that the brand is built, if you like, to last for eternity. It has already existed for a long time; it has become an institution. [...] The problem is that timelessness is a quality which takes years – even decades – of development to achieve. You can't simply wish it into existence. The brand has to pay its dues; it must reach a point where it represents something in the eyes of the world. However, as a brand manager, you can lend this timelessness a helping hand – by which I mean that you can create the impression of timelessness sooner rather than later. The way to do this is through uncompromising quality. Many companies pay lip service to quality, but if you really want your brand to become timeless, you have to be absolutely fanatical about it.

Remember that the brand performs 10 key functions (see Table 15.1) which proves just how important it is to protect, maintain and nurture this equity. The very fact that the brand enjoys the benefit of this equity explains how it can perform all of these functions and constitute the most strategic of all variables in the mix. Indeed, Carpenter, Glazer and Nakamoto (1994) showed that the capital could even influence purchasing decisions in cases where it merely identified the component parts. In other words, the consumer was willing to pay extra for goods in cases where intermediary products of an identified brand had been used in their manufacture. The

Table 15.1 The 10 key functions of a brand

1. **The brand attracts.** It draws the consumer's attention to the product and enables it to exist in an increasingly competitive world.
2. **The brand informs.** It informs the potential buyer about its own characteristics and the characteristics of its products.
3. **The brand positions.** Explicitly or implicitly, it delivers information assisting its own positioning and that of its products.
4. **The brand distinguishes.** It is increasingly becoming the factor of absolute differentiation between two products with similar characteristics.
5. **The brand endorses.** It reassures the consumer about the promise made for a product with which he or she is not yet familiar.
6. **The brand communicates.** It builds and nurtures an affinity- based capital around the company and/ or its products.
7. **The brand simplifies.** The establishment of a relationship built on confidence and loyalty assists the process of choice for the consumer.
8. **The brand satisfies.** It wins over the consumer by satisfying his or her expectations and sharing his or her values.
9. **The brand defines.** It creates the impression of belonging to a defined group.
10. **The brand adds value.** It promotes a transfer of image and of status towards the buyer, who feels enriched as a result.

Source: Lehu, J-M (2001) *strategiesdemarque.com*, Éditions d'Organisation, Paris

brand can become a powerful beacon for guiding the consumer. It constitutes a benchmark that has evaluation criteria chosen by the consumer. From that point, regardless of the cost, it is possible to link it to the profit the brand is able to generate for the products and services sold under its name. In 2001, Alain de Pouzilhac was quick to invest 4.5 million euros in his Havas Advertising group so that it could buy the Havas brand from the Vivendi group. Back in 1832, when Charles-Louis Havas founded his press agency, he would surely never have believed, imagined or feared that a day would come when his name alone would be worth such a sum. And yet the price paid by the CEO of the Havas Advertising group was far from exorbitant. It was an extremely wise strategic choice in view of the equity – both in France and the rest of the world – vested in the Havas name.

It is the responsibility of the brand manager to identify the constituent components of the brand that contribute to its image and must endure. Failure to achieve this may damage the perception of the brand by its consumers; hence the need for a strategic approach. In cases where this strategy acts as a guarantee of coherence, operational tactics will enable the brand to demonstrate its innovative nature and dynamism. Today, Procter & Gamble probably takes more care than almost any other company to protect this brand coherence – and yet no-one could accuse the

...d group of a failure to innovate. However, the fact that ...up's brands are also old ones is probably not an accident. ... philanthropic about this. Maintaining a coherent, positive ...y backed up by powerful brand equity is a source of revenue for ...e brand – even if only in terms of savings in the advertising budget.

The example of the Mini

The little car was officially born on 26 August 1959, under two different names belonging to two different brands: the Seven, under the Austin brand; and the Mini-Minor, under the Morris brand. The two cars were utterly identical apart from their badges. The reason for this dual identity was that Austin and Morris had merged in 1952 to form BMC (British Motor Company), but without giving up their respective brands. The car was born in the heart of the UK, and was conceived by the imagination of Alexander Arnold Constantine Issigonis.

Considering that on the Continent, Seven and Minor did not command the recognition they had been able to acquire in the UK as a result of the brands' previous cars, it was decided to rename them the Morris 850 and Austin 850. Bought out by Rover, the Mini naturally became the Mini Rover. Rover was then itself bought out by BMW, which ultimately only kept the Mini branch of the company. In 1997, the idea of relaunching the Mini was put forward: it was not until 2001 that the idea became a reality. Two versions were initially launched: the Mini One and a new Mini Cooper. It is worth noting in passing that BMW chose to keep a low profile as the parent brand. True, all advertising did bear the discreet caption, 'Mini, a BMW Group brand', but there was no BMW emblem on the vehicle's radiator grille, and no flashy claims of origin. With a rejuvenated logo, the Mini had become an entire brand in itself, and deserved to exist as one. This was a genuine gamble: even though the brand was a fairly recognizable one, it was old, and its capital naturally needed to be increased by focusing heavily on the 'friendly' image of the car, although this notion was not necessarily one already present in the minds of the new, younger customers the brand hoped to reach.

The fight against the grey market and counterfeiting

One crucial decision to be taken in order to avoid being left at the mercy of a downturn in the market concerns the eradication of counterfeit and grey-market products – a task that becomes trickier every day. Previously, counterfeiting was usually a crude operation that could be easily spotted by even the lowliest customs officer. Today, freer circulation of merchandise, combined with increased skilfulness on the part of the counterfeiters, in terms of both production techniques and distribution networks, have made it much more difficult – and therefore more costly – to combat this phenomenon; especially since the actual quality of the counterfeit items is rising constantly, particularly in the luxury sector. Only the prospect of government action in countries that still tolerate this practice has any hope of creating a genuine obstacle to the serious threat it poses to the income of official brands. In 2000, the Burberry brand was quick to launch a major press campaign to point out that Burberry tartan – like the brand itself – was a registered mark, and that legal action would be taken against counterfeiters. In 1917, Thomas Burberry, who had trademarked the name 'gabardine' a few years previously, abandoned this legal protection, as part of the war effort. In 2000, the war was now being fought on an entirely different front; and Burberry had no intention of giving the illegal counterfeiters any advantage. Furthermore, even though counterfeiting is listed as one of the World Trade Organization (WTO)'s main concerns, it now affects not only luxury brands, but any product that can be profitably counterfeited and sold. In 1950, the United States extended protection on goods through a decision of the Supreme Court known as the 'Doctrine of Equivalents'. Any organization with a product that was, to within a few details, the same as another could be subject to prosecution for counterfeiting. However, in November 2000, the Festo judgment by the US Court of Appeal overturned the previous decision. Despite the curious fact that it passed virtually unnoticed by the media, the decision is likely to have a considerable economic impact. A number of companies immediately rejoiced, believing that the gates of innovation had just swung wide open. Others, more circumspect, were quick to start pondering the counterfeiting opportunities that such a decision was sure to create.

In general, the grey market operates on the basis of a differential in taxation or manufacturing costs. The brand then watches helplessly as its exported products return to the country of origin via channels generally outside its control. Depending on the precise nature of the product and the respective legislation in force in the countries of the economic zones involved, it can also often be difficult to fight against such practices. Counterfeiting and grey imports are two major preoccupations of a business in the management of its brand equity because they both represent a potential loss of control over the brand. In the worst case, the quality of the brand will not be maintained; and deceived consumers will hold the brand itself responsible. In most cases, the sale of such products disturbs the whole set of variables in the mix established by the company and ends up altering the brand's positioning and image. Ultimately, of course, such a disturbance can become a source of premature ageing for the brand, resulting in the type of consequences already described above.

This battle against counterfeiters is not an easy one. The brand must be capable of remaining in close contact with its market and of protecting its creation to the maximum extent permitted by law. Such an approach is easier for companies that have implemented direct or exclusive distribution strategies, or for those that have chosen to pursue selective, controlled distribution policies. However, for the vast majority of companies producing retail goods, this task is almost impossible. Given that a fairly long distribution chain is usually necessary in order to be able to make use of specialist providers, the traceability systems presently in use are not yet able to offer total control over all products sold throughout the entire supply chain. A willingness to fight also implies a protection cost, and this can be considerable if the range of products sold is a wide one and/or the geographical sales area is large. A few years ago, the more reckless companies gambled on innovation, putting their faith in the fact that counterfeiters would struggle to keep up. Today, this is no longer enough. The speed at which information travels, combined with the speed at which counterfeiters are able to adapt their manufacturing processes, is such that legitimate companies can no longer rely on making the return on investment they need to cover the cost of their constant innovation.

Sometimes, however, a point in favour of the enemy can be turned to the advantage of the honest competitor. Nowadays, the incredible advances in the field of information systems – in the way this information is both stored and managed – hold out hope that there will be similar vast improvements in traceability throughout the supply chain, from raw materials to the end consumer. For the company, this opens a door to a marketing resource currently only in its infancy. As an additional advantage, the constant reduction of the cost of the technology that provides such traceability makes it likely that, in the near future, such technology may also become accessible to mass-retail goods, and not only to luxury products. Whether the technology involved is an encrypted bidimensional barcode, a high-tech permanent hologram, a secure electronic microchip, a coded magnetic strip or a DNA signature, improved traceability techniques that are both effective and affordable are on the way, ensuring greater protection for the brand and its products. As it gains a little more control over one of the parasitic factors contributing to its ageing, the brand will make a small improvement in the partial control it can hope to exercise over its perceived age.

Be quick to capture new markets

Some domestic markets may be protected in one way or another. In such cases, there is a great temptation to fashion a cosy existence for the brand there, far from the cut-throat environments of foreign markets. However, such an attitude can quickly become a synonym for immobility. Certainly, foreign markets – particularly those which are very different from the domestic market – impose considerable restrictions in terms of the need to adapt. However, these restrictions may also be viewed as stimulants that allow the brand to retain a vital dynamism.

The example of Haier

When asked about its various appliances, the Western white-goods supplier Haier spoke of brands that vary a little from one country to another or from one geographical area to another. However, as the number of mergers increases and brands are bought out one by one, manufacturing groups of any size are becoming increasingly rare. At the head of the pack is the incontestable leader, the US firm Whirlpool. There is no clear No.2 in the market: positions vary depending on which evaluation criterion is used (turnover, margin, number of units sold, range, etc). However, the names of the leading groups are the usual familiar household ones, including Electrolux, General Electric, Bosch, Siemens and Samsung. Where is Haier among all these?

The brand is Chinese. Despite the fact that it is still unknown to the vast majority of Western housewives, this is no outfit run by some small-time Beijing operator putting domestic appliances together from salvaged parts in his or her garage. Such a stereotypical developing country image does Haier no favours. In reality, the firm sells more domestic appliances than Philips, Sharp, Moulinex or Matsushita. Of course, cynics will say that after all, with more than 1.2 billion potential customers in its own domestic market, Haier's sixth-place ranking in the world is no great achievement! However, this would be not only a rather simplistic view, but also largely wrong. Firstly, the company's factories in 13 different countries exist not to satisfy Chinese demand, but rather to extend its own production to cover more than 160 countries; nearly one small fridge out of every three sold in the United States is a Haier product. And of course, this result was achieved before China even joined the WTO.

Although Haier's chairman, Zhang Ruimin, claims to draw the inspiration for his management principles from the abundant and rich corpus of traditional Chinese philosophy, this is not to say that he has neglected the precepts of modern management sciences. Of course, cynics may take issue with the often rather paternalistic approach of the company, which is somewhat reminiscent of the attitudes of Western companies at the end of the 19th century. However, the company is just one small tree supplying oxygen to its economic and social environment; a small tree with an enormous forest behind it. Haier's strength lies in the fact that it has not adopted the traditional approach of its industrialist compatriots who have positioned themselves mainly on price, who take advantage of – not to say abuse – a relatively undemanding domestic demand, and who venture into foreign markets at the same economic level as China or perhaps even lower. Haier was very quick to appreciate the role, importance and potential value of a brand if, in association with a genuine strategy, it was supported by quality products that satisfied customer expectations. This may appear paradoxical or even outrageous to the stereotypically doctrine-loving Chinese observer, but it is nonetheless one of the facets of modern China. Haier does not produce the same products for the US market that it does for the Chinese market. Maybe one day it will. Today, however, the most important thing is to stay as close as possible to consumer demand. Haier identified the increasing popularity of fine wines in the United States as the key to a high-yield consumer segment in that market. The firm therefore produced a tailor-made refrigerated cellar, which is now one of the star products in the range. These 'Western capitalists' are no longer seen as enemies of the doctrine, but potential partners – even if only for a short time – with whom to develop additional and/or complementary areas of business. By growing constantly and even opting for a gradual outsourcing of its production, Haier is nurturing its brand, constantly renewing it and introducing it to new consumers; in this way, it is preventing it from ageing. Its inspirations: General Electric, Nike, Whirlpool and Dell. Somehow, it is hard to imagine names such as these appearing in the index of the Little Red Book.

Leadership: a potential booby trap

It is interesting to observe just how many economic ideas appear intrinsically linked to a cyclical effect. The phenomenon is an interesting one because, whichever trend one chooses, there are always passionate adherents to be found on both sides of the fence, all convinced that their own opinion is the right one. No doubt if the readers of this book were to be polled, many would maintain that 'small is beautiful', while others would more happily associate themselves with the opposite position. Such thinking is also subject to the cyclical effect; and we are regularly presented with thinkers and doers who try to convince us that power is strength and it is best to be the biggest company in the sector, while conversely, others will maintain that it is actually a better idea to be small, mainly to be able to adapt to changes in the market.

Of course, our aim is neither to fuel this debate nor to take a firm stand in favour of either position. However, it has to be admitted that the laudable pursuit of power is often accompanied by a hidden trap: lethargy. A company that, by luck and/or through its own efforts, has managed to make it to the top step of the podium and assume the position of leader, often succumbs to the temptation of resting on its laurels. It may do this consciously, believing it to be a part of the reward for its efforts. Sometimes it happens against the company's will, because its structure has become too ponderous and is preventing the company from reacting as promptly as before to changes in the market in the way that a smaller, more dynamic and responsive company would be able to. Are analogies not sometimes made between sleep and death? It is a valid comparison here. A brand that sleeps is a brand that ages faster than its competitors – and if the objective of this book is to urge the professional to pursue a preventative anti-ageing strategy, it is simply because it is easier to check the rate of ageing than it is to hope to effect an easy overnight rejuvenation.

Leadership is not some sort of reward. It is an opportunity. An economic, financial, technological and human opportunity, offering the ability to move forward. It is true that a company often needs to reinvent itself to achieve this goal. However, risks of this kind have always been a possibility from the start. In such a case, there is no doubt that the worst error the brand could make would be to isolate itself from the market, whether intentionally or unintentionally. In a free and increasingly globalized economy, the market in question no longer follows the predictable patterns of the earth's rotation; it lives, grows and changes 24 hours a day, 365 days a year. There is no longer any point in talking about consumer satisfaction. Consumers will never be satisfied, except temporarily, for brief, ever-shortening periods of time. It may have been that a century ago, a company launching itself in a market – any market – would still have had time to limber up at the starting line, maybe take the opportunity to get comfortable in its blocks and, in its own time, set off towards the finishing line at the end of a track it had mapped out itself. If it finished in first place, then it was generally given time to savour its victory and maybe even a little more time to prepare for another race. Supply was king. Demand took second place. Today, nobody knows when the race actually started, but there is no doubt that it has. Worse, no sooner does the company set foot on the track than the starting line disappears. The aim is therefore no longer to reach some theoretical end point, but simply to check constantly that the other competitors are all still in sight; ideally, without having to turn around to look behind. This endless race consists only of split times and parallel tracks of varying speed. The success of the company's strategy depends on the quality of its race, its speed, endurance and its choice of track. Any company spending its entire life on the same track and/or stopping to catch its breath would be left with only one advantage: it would no longer have to turn around to see where its competitors were.

The search for integration: an essential quality in the anti-ageing strategy

Good brand equity management cannot be provided by the brand manager and/or owner alone. The brand is now omnipresent. It exists within the company, at the retailer and among consumers. Any attempt to manage brand equity merely by using external advertising will usually, as is often the case, be doomed to failure.

The big issue in this respect is integration. It is essential to check that the anti-ageing strategy is not merely an external remedy. Taking the example of an anti-ageing cream that aspires to delay the effects of ageing as much as possible, the cream is merely one aspect of the battle plan against time. Cigarettes, drastic and prolonged exposure to the sun or an unhealthy diet that would prompt even the most stoic of nutritionists to contemplate suicide – each of these would rapidly reduce the effectiveness of any new 'wonder ingredient' in the anti-ageing cream. The same is true of the brand. This is without doubt an area in which the genius of the brand manager is needed. Once that manager has finished reading this book, he or she will know which causes of ageing are threatening the brand, as well as which rejuvenation factors he or she can implement to remedy this situation. The brand manager will also be aware of the fact that proactively pursuing an anti-ageing strategy will be more relevant, less costly and generally more effective than implementing a reactive rejuvenation remedy only once ageing has been observed. However, as we have already said, the battle against time is not simply a series of techniques and methods that merely need to be combined to form a model that, when put into action, will guarantee that the brand will be rejuvenated; or better still, will not age in the first place.

The example of Coca-Cola

The Coca-Cola brand is now more than a century old: the famous soft drink was created in 1886 by John S Pemberton. Despite this fact, it remains a very youthful drink to this day, thanks to its positioning and image, but also because of its production techniques, distribution networks and, of course, its advertising. The Atlanta-based group derives its manifest youth largely from its integrated marketing. All the pieces in Coca-Cola's strategic jigsaw appear to fit together perfectly. From design right through to consumption, and including production, distribution and advertising, the overall package is perfectly coherent, beautifully executed and strategically thought out. For advertising alone, which is essential for a brand such as Coca-Cola, every component part – packaging, advertising, promotion, point-of-sale display stands, in-store events, interactive publicity materials – appears logically linked to all the others to produce an effect of synergy that promotes the brand and thus its products.

Integration is a difficult strategic objective to achieve, because it operates horizontally right across the company. It does not apply only to the marketing department, but to all departments which, because they are all part of the same entity, can each hope to make a contribution in managing the brand equity. It is not difficult to imagine how much coordination this implies between the various divisions of the company. However, this coordination is essential; after all, the brand is being judged on the basis of each of its points of visibility. This may be – at the most obvious level – the product or service representing the brand; it may be the points of sale where the brand is sold; or indeed it may be the various internal and external advertising campaigns promoting the brand. Regardless of which direct or indirect point of contact between the consumer and the brand we look at, the brand must always be capable of remaining faithful to the positioning and image to which it aspires. Not a single detail must be overlooked.

The example of Littlewoods

Restructuring a brand is a very difficult operation that calls for both genius and courage. In 1998, when the UK retailer Littlewoods – founded in 1923 by Sir John Moores – decided to rejuvenate its brand, it did not start with an advertising campaign. There would have been no point in doing so: even if it had achieved its goal in the short term by generating new traffic to the stores, any customer walking through the door would have been disappointed to realize that nothing had changed. Given the business sector involved, Littlewoods' first decision was to rethink the internal décor and merchandising in its stores, in line with the rejuvenation plan that had been determined. However, the measures were insufficient, and the brand failed to recover its former dynamism. It was sold in 2002 and further restructuring work was undertaken. Yet in 2005, Index – its catalogue branch – was still making heavy losses, a fact which forced the retailer to attempt a new restructuring initiative involving the disposal of its last Index stores and the closure of Index departments in its Littlewoods branches. Well-established Western retailers have considerable difficulty in reinventing themselves, having avoided making any changes until they were ultimately forced to do so. Most of them have used up all of their brand equity and now find themselves fatally short of options when there is no choice left but to take action. Too late!

The strategic solution of the anti-ageing wheel

The battle against time is difficult; but more importantly, it is never-ending. If the brand's ambition is to take control over some of the effects of time that are apparent in its image, its brand manager will need to wage war on several different fronts. There are seven of these in total, each of which must be strategically managed. An analogy might be made with the enormous wheel representing the brand's image equity. The brand manager must attempt to keep this wheel in constant rotation in the hope of avoiding one or two of the perfidious attacks of time.

This symbolic wheel (illustrated in Figure 15.2 on p 214) thus consists of seven main segments, representing the main fronts on which the brand manager must fight. There is no doubt that first and foremost, the offer made by the brand has to provide real added value, as has been clearly shown in the work of Maklan and Knox (1998). If one of these segments is missing – or in other words, if, through the marketer's own negligence, the battlefield it represents is deserted – the wheel is left unable to function properly, and the partially or fully immobilized brand will then become an easy target for the enemy to pick off. Whatever the reasons and circumstances underlying such negligence and immobility, its rapid outcome is the opportunity the enemy has been waiting for to recommence its assaults with renewed vigour. In this way, before it has even had time to become aware of the fact, the brand has started to age at a fearsome and often unstoppable pace. At the centre of this wheel is an 'axle of time', containing the image of the great hourglass representing the perceived passage of time. Clearly, for as long as the wheel continues to turn, the grains of sand will move continuously from one chamber to the next without ever fully emptying one or filling the other. The brand is thus able to defy time; and, regardless of its advancing years in chronological terms, its image reflects a carefully-controlled perceived age.

What remains is for the seven main fronts in this endless battle to be managed efficiently. Their respectively equidistant positions from the central hourglass symbolize the fact that no single one of them is any more important than the other. Each has the same weighting. However, they are all interlinked, and must be managed simultaneously and with unity if a coherent approach is to be developed that corresponds to the appropriate anti-ageing strategy.

An expected promise that is fully satisfied

A brand that starts a fight against the effects of time on its perceived image is, first and foremost, a brand that has implemented a rigorous marketing strategy; it is also a brand perfectly aware of the fact that its products and/or services constitute, most importantly, a promise of satisfaction, the basis of which derives from a detailed marketing study into the characteristics of the target market. By undertaking an anti-ageing strategy, the brand's aim is that a positive image of itself will be indelibly stamped in the minds of its target market. The BrandAsset Valuator tool, developed by Young & Rubicam to measure a brand's equity, is centred on four different axes: differentiation, relevance, esteem and knowledge. In short, differentiation is based on the brand's ability to distinguish itself from its competitors. Relevance refers to the fact that the brand should seem appropriate to what it stands for, while esteem is linked to a combination of notions of the brand's popularity and the quality of its products. Ultimately, however, the key factor is knowledge of the brand. This knowledge must not be confused with mere recognition of the brand; instead, it represents a full, deep understanding of the brand. Its equity is most perfectly founded on the promises it has made and then kept. Does this mean that the battle can be fought only by companies conducting demand-based marketing, obtaining the raw material for such promises by analysing demand? No. For this reason, let us once again state the basic notion that constitutes the promise of satisfaction. The fact that the company involved may operate a supply-based marketing policy does not mean that it has chosen to forego such a promise to its consumers (or customers). The promise is merely lent a tangible form by its products and services, which have been devised and created for this purpose. It represents much more to the consumer. It incorporates not only the quality of the good in question, but also the quality of the point of sale, the behaviour and status of the company, and so on. It is therefore important that this promise should meet all these requirements of the target market; and that, ultimately, this promise should be fulfilled completely by the brand. The time has long since gone when such a promise acted simply as a lure to attract and trap naïve customers. Such naïvety can now be found only in a handful of marginal segments. This should, therefore, serve as a warning to unthinking manipulators who still believe they can get away with making fine promises they will never have to keep.

The example of Avon

In 1886, David H McConnell founded his own company, The California Perfume Company, with the aim of selling perfume in an original way: through door-to-door sales. The concept was accompanied by a promise of satisfaction that committed the brand to refunding dissatisfied customers – a marketing strategy before the fact. In 1896, harbouring nostalgic memories of the town of Suffern, which reminded him of Shakespeare's Stratford-upon-Avon, David H McConnell started using the Avon brand name on his products. The company adopted the name in 1939, and it is still in use today.

An innovative marketing-based offer

We learn through operating a proper loyalty strategy that although satisfying a customer or client is a necessary first step, it is no longer sufficient on its own. Many brands have had satisfied clients who have later become the clients of those brands' competitors. The reason was simply that, in addition to wanting satisfaction, these clients just felt like a change. Permanent innovation is of key importance because its absence quickly generates listlessness, regardless of the quality of the products. Permanent innovation stands for renewal, change, evolution, the fun of new experiences, and so on. The incredible explosion of the media over the past few years, boosted yet further by the advent of the world wide web, has introduced consumers of all ages to opportunities for discovery and an almost limitless palette of experiences that just one short life on this earth could never be enough to satisfy. Monotony, even of the top-quality variety, provides an implicit foundation for this underlying dissatisfaction, which then emerges to contradict what the consumer had hitherto assumed to be total satisfaction.

However, be warned: this is not about pulling some pseudo-innovation out of a magician's hat! As we have already said, the aim is not to produce something new at any price: such an approach is only likely to capture the consumer's attention for too short a period of time to make the effort financially worthwhile. Marketing research is not some temporary resource to be resorted to while the product is still on the drawing board; it should also form the shield that steadfastly enables the brand to protect itself against its constantly shifting environment. However strong the fortress built by the brand at the time of its launch, the inevitable invading hordes will only be driven back by genuine and constant innovations in its defences.

The example of Levi's

Having suffered from the accelerated ageing of its image up to the early 2000s as a result of products that maintained a high level of quality but had no real innovation behind them, Levi's took firm action, including the development of Sta Prest: clothing with a permanent crease; Engineered: jeans with a twisted cut flowing around the contours of the body; the Type 1, revisiting the original jeans cut; and also the increased use of collections (Girls Only, Red Tab, Vintage Clothing, Blue, etc). Levi-Strauss also devised the entry-level Signature brand as a means of taking a firm step into the retail market and thus meeting the price expectations of a part of this target market. In 2005, the company finally returned to profitability.

Clear, coherent and well-supported positioning

Where exactly is the brand located in its own market, along its own life path, on the scale of values of its target market, relative to other innovative trends? If we are to have any hope of managing the perceived age of the brand, we have to locate it clearly in the minds of its consumers for all facets of its positioning, both in terms of absolute positioning (in comparison to the objective qualities of the offer) and relative positioning (in comparison to the brand's competitors). This positioning is at the heart of the promise. It must not only allow the brand to be easily identified, but also contribute to its evaluation. Once again, there must be no tricks here. This positioning must be perfectly consistent with the nature and quality of the promise made by the company. On the same note, it should never be forgotten that although the company may aspire to a specific positioning, the only positioning that ultimately matters is the one determined by the target market. If the signals (products, prices, sales point type, innovation, advertising, etc) sent out at the same time by the brand do not appear totally consistent with the positioning to which the brand aspires, the target market will not lend its support to that positioning. Even worse, it may – in extreme cases – acquire a feeling of suspicion towards this brand, as it makes statements that do not match up with its actions. Lastly, positioning is not a winner's medal to be pinned onto the brand's chest and kept for ever. It is a position that will, of course, be directly or indirectly attacked by the competition. It is a position that will be consciously or subconsciously re-evaluated by the target market as the environment changes. It is a position that may be altered or confirmed by the various different actions taken by the brand. In other words, it is a fragile position that must be permanently protected. Although innovation is necessary to allow the brand to retain its dynamism and youth in the eyes of its consumers, some brands treat it as though it constituted positioning all on its own.

The example of Rover

The UK car brand Rover went bankrupt in 2005. It would be extremely glib to claim to be able to explain the reasons for this failure in a few short lines. However, in retrospect, it is possible to add the following point to any list of reasons: during its final years of existence, the brand had lost its positioning. By attempting to offer both entry-level and mid-range products, and even sometimes claiming certain high-end qualities as its own, Rover ended up confusing its own image. A change of hands into the ownership of another brand (BMW during 1994/2000) – which decided to retain only the legendary Mini – then the possibility of an alliance with the Chinese manufacturer China Brilliance in 2002 for the development of a new model, and then the 2004 'agreement' with another Chinese industrial firm, Automotive Industrial Corp.; all of these ultimately hindered any clear perception of the brand's identity. At the same time, its ability to innovate was shrinking year on year. The final analysis: a chaotic but fatal ageing process.

A target market renewed over time

A brand cannot survive without renewing its customers. A brand that officially targets one or more segments of the senior citizen population is not necessarily considered as old. However, a brand with a consumer base that ages over time will itself end up ageing. Clearly, such renewal naturally takes the form of attracting new customers whose attitudes to the brand and purchasing behaviour in terms of its products and services may be very different from those of the customers the brand was formerly used to serving. However, is marketing not primarily notable for the fact that it does indeed allow the brand to adapt constantly to a perpetually moving environment?

The example of Lacoste

Sometimes the target market renews itself, and not necessarily in the way the brand would ideally have wished. This is what happened to Lacoste which, in the late 1990s would perhaps not have chosen to have its brand label adopted in France by sections of the public sweepingly and hastily described as *jeunes de banlieue* ('suburban youth'), whose social behaviour was admittedly not generally commensurate with the traditional values of the brand's urban, well-heeled, older target market, which was ageing slowly but surely. This untimely underground regeneration of the target market thus created a situation of genuinely parasitic publicity from which Lacoste attempted to bounce back in the early 2000s. It was a risky strategy, but this parasitism constituted a constraint the brand was obliged to deal with. Firstly, the brand's advertising was rejuvenated to allow it partly to reflect this change. The new young style designer Christophe Lemaire saw his remit expanded to cover the entire brand – a brand which, in 2002, also benefited from a facelift to its famous logo, with lighter typography and a more discreet and slightly slimmed-down crocodile.

For nearly two generations until the end of the 1990s, Lacoste seemed not to have worried too much about the life of its brand, mainly because life was good for the company. But all brand managers worth their salt know that it is precisely when everything is going well that a proactive approach should be adopted to move the brand forward. It is true that Lacoste was conducting a rigorous and justified battle against its innumerable counterfeiters worldwide. But its marketing strategy, particularly in France, seemed to be lacking something in terms of innovation and anticipation. Some observers felt it necessary to issue a warning to the brand regarding the danger of overly drastic rejuvenation attempts, such as trying on the one hand to spread itself too thinly between generations far removed from one another; and on the other hand, attributing too much value to these marginal target markets, which had an indirect prescribing function, but nonetheless exercised a parasitic effect on the brand's image.

> Firstly, an excessively ostentatious promotion strategy could cut the brand off from its traditional core market, which would be unwilling to be assimilated. Secondly, the bulk of these young consumers belonged to 'Generation Y', which was known in particular for its extreme volatility. Although Lacoste is now an ostentatious symbol of existence, accessing the well-off consumer society, it could just as easily be suddenly replaced overnight by another top-of-the-range brand with its original identity intact. Another current need is to reduce the parasitic effect on the brand's image, which still remains a predominantly French phenomenon: after all, France represents no less than a quarter of the turnover of the Devanlay group's Lacoste business.

Dynamic and renewed advertising

The brand is *helpful* for differentiating between several goods in the same category. It is *useful* in assisting the consumer's choice. It is increasingly *necessary* in cases where that consumer perceives a high level of risk. It is *vital* as a means of identification, location and favourable evaluation during a purchase. This clearly shows just how much it needs to demonstrate its existence in as strategic a way as possible. Over the course of just half a century, advertising has become an almost indispensable element of the marketing mix. There is no doubt that first and foremost, the offer made by the brand has to provide real added value, as has been clearly shown in the work of Maklan and Knox (1998). If not, the brand's advertising might succeed in securing an initial sale, but certainly not any repeat business. This is, incidentally, one of the main criticisms levelled at multiple rejuvenation 'plans' that immediately seize upon the advertising variable alone as a means of saving the brand and fall over themselves to appoint a new advertising agency; after all, if the brand has found itself in such a mess, it can surely only be the fault of poor advertising, since the entire product range is beyond reproach! When a preventative anti-ageing strategy is implemented, advertising – perhaps more than any other variable in the mix – must demonstrate the brand's dynamism and its daily efforts to renew itself and confirm the promise of satisfaction it makes to its consumers. This dynamism must also be a reflection of a coherent long-term approach that brings together brand advertising, product advertising and human-based advertising. Some sociologists are quick to advance the point of view that advertising is a faithful reflection of society. In such a situation, it would be foolish to risk reflecting an image of a society belonging to the past. The idea is a simple one in theory, but, as everyone knows, difficult in practice. After all, we must naturally avoid falling into the numerous traps laid by fashion effects that, for a (usually short) period of time, propel the brand into a position of ultra-modernity, but can subsequently push it back towards an out-of-date image with highly damaging consequences. Once again, advertising must *serve* the brand. To this end, it must first and foremost respect the brand's profound identity and find its place within an overall strategy, all the while renewing its codes of expression. The aim is to ensure that advertising can be used to assist in managing the brand equity of the present and the future, and not just the cash till at the end of the month.

The example of Bodum

House and home are gradually becoming a major area of interest to the Western consumer. After more than a generation of fighting against materialism and moving away from the nuclear family model, the trend is now discernibly swinging back again. As a result, our daily environment is becoming more and more luxurious, and the accessories contributing to it are becoming more and more prominent. US brands such as Bed Bath and Beyond and the ubiquitous Crate & Barrel have understood this fact. In Europe, Habitat, Resonances and even Ikea are good examples.

The Bodum brand may have a lower media profile than other brands, but it is just as indicative of the success in this area. It appears rooted in a constant drive for innovative design, with seemingly fresh advertising for each of its successive collections. It has, however, been more than a quarter of a century since the Dane Jörgen Bodum took over the business his father Peter had founded in 1944. Today, guided by a marketing approach as rigorous as it is creative, the design of Bodum products makes them welcome in stores all around the world. An international team of designer-architects provide a rich advertising mixture suitable for illustrating and/or revealing the next trend. The brand has its own chain of retail outlets, but it can also count names such as Muji and even Procter & Gamble among its clients. Like its designers and chairman, Bodum's advertising is low key, but its ranges are constantly renewed and modified to suit the tastes and expectations of its customers.

Informed, involved and motivated employees

In 2001, in an interview with *Le Figaro*, Herbert Hainer, the chairman of Adidas-Salomon, told Jean-Yves Guérin that his three principles of management were: 'Stay in touch with consumers, keep a secret garden for yourself, and communicate with your employees.' Regardless of the dynamism of the spirit at any given time, as the saying goes, you're always the same age as your arteries. It is therefore crucial that these arteries always work properly.

A brand belonging to a company that paid no attention to its employees would seriously compromise its own efforts at brand equity management. A failure to take staff into consideration could ultimately generate an attitude and behaviour that would damage the brand equity; and contamination effects can rapidly spread this damage to all of the brand's business clients and retailers. Then, just as quickly, secondary contamination effects may carry it from business clients to the brand's consumers. Once the entire chain has been contaminated, there is no doubt that the brand will age quickly – often fatally so.

A company's human capital and its brand equity cannot be separated. Quite the opposite: human capital plays a direct part in feeding, promoting and protecting the brand. A lack of sensitivity to the slightest weakness in the building will jeopardize the entire anti-ageing strategy. Worse still, the excessive churn among staff – regardless of the underlying reasons – experienced by some companies and/or sectors is itself likely to result in work on the brand that is often motivated by a desire to make the brand manager look good in the short term, regardless of the ultimate cost to the brand. Clearly, the task of steering the ship is not made any easier if the captain is replaced too often. The brand must not be put out to pasture in a spirit of ignorance and/or indifference, to be left at the mercy of a manager's CV or ego. It constitutes far too precious an equity for such a risk to be permissible.

However, ensuring that all staff – regardless of their level – are kept informed, in the interests of keeping them involved and motivating them to work for the brand, is neither a foregone conclusion nor a simple matter. But just how much should we expect from a company in terms of brand equity management if it has already proved itself incompetent when it comes to managing its human capital? At Brioche Pasquier, staff are given as much responsibility as possible, because Serge Pasquier can clearly see the potential pitfalls of a top-heavy management structure squatting atop a pyramid with no signposted entry door. The brand's factories each have a display board on which the results of the various production lines in terms of performance are regularly written. However, the same board is also home to letters of complaint from dissatisfied customers. This transparency, and feedback of communication, means that staff are kept informed with the aim of involving them as far as possible in their work.

The example of JC Penney

In the late 1980s, in the United States, the JC Penney store chain recognized that its positioning was no longer suited to the competitive environment in which it operated. For more than 20 years it had been possible to describe the company's product range as generalized and aimed at US blue-collar workers. However, a growth rate that was steadily falling every year prompted the company to consider rejuvenating the brand. There were three key aspects to the strategy. In the first place, the company's product range was to be redefined. Following an audit of the brand itself, many departments (electrical household goods, electronics, photography, etc) in which the brand was not competitive were simply axed, as there was now too much competition from specialists.

The second aspect was the decision to restructure, allowing the recovery of floorspace that could be reallocated to the surviving shelves, and provided an opportunity for the modernization and more aspirational refitting of the stores' points of sale. This strategy was accompanied by considerable work on the nature of the products to be stocked. Higher-end brands known for their quality (Vanity Fair, Healthtex, Van Heusen, Haggar, Henry Grethel, etc) replaced several brands sold until that point, with the new strategy even going as far as to follow the recommendations of the marketing research to establish a range suited to the actual town in which a store was located.

The third aspect, however, was by far the most important. JC Penney undertook an enormous programme of informing and training its staff regarding the company's new ambitions. Plans for rewards and results-driven profits were developed in order to give JC Penney one of the best customer service departments in the country. The aim was for the group's entire institutional image to be visible at each point of contact with the customer. Staff thus became the essential key to the success of the project. Considerable effort was expended. The results were impressive, but had to be repeated in the late 1990s, because the competitive environment had changed once again.

Positive, maintained and consolidated value

Time is pitiless because it has the advantage of having strength on its side. Perceived value illustrates the benefit to the consumer of choosing one brand in favour of another. In a way, it represents the physical manifestation of the entire brand image in the mind of the consumer. It is thus of crucial importance to maintain it over time, to consolidate it at each opportunity either for contact with, or simply the expression of, the brand.

The example of Jaguar

In 2005, the Jaguar car brand approached its advertising agencies over the issue of rejuvenation. This is no easy task for a brand such as Jaguar, which has historically benefited from a top-of-the-range brand image but now, by expanding its range and offering models at more accessible prices than the XK or even XJ ranges, is in danger of seeing its positioning become more uncertain and its image blurred in the minds of its traditional core market. Rejuvenation must therefore be implemented with the assistance of strategic planning, which can be disrupted by short-term sales objectives.

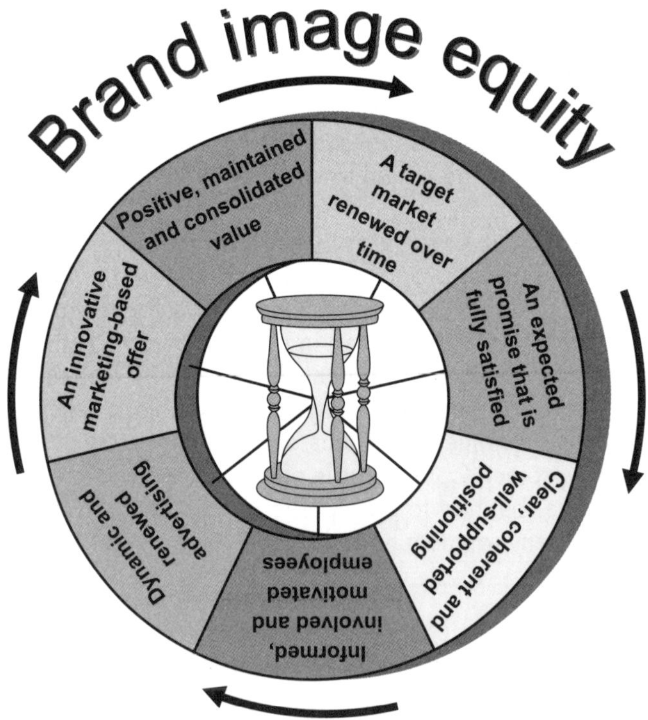

Figure 15.2 The brand anti-ageing wheel

The very fact that it is difficult to obtain a perfect 20:20 marketing view of a brand to spot the symptoms of ageing should on its own be sufficient to persuade the brand manager to implement an anti-ageing strategy. It necessarily implies constantly monitoring the competition, the environment, consumers, innovations and trends. Irrespective of the volume of upstream marketing research that has been conducted, a brand is never safe from errors detected after the fact, once it has already entered the market. Such vigilance, made possible by the deployment of an anti-ageing strategy, allows the brand to react to such oversights as soon as they become apparent, taking action against any potential degradation in the brand's image as soon as possible.

We must, however, emphasize the obstacle facing the brand manager in most modern companies: the constant insistence on short-term results. Some may be quick to take offence at any criticism made in this area; after all, the notion seems so intimately and naturally linked to the very heart of the company's business. The obstacle arises from the fact that such an insistence is, practically and systematically speaking, a short-sighted, short-term requirement in the vast majority of cases. Its result is to transform most brand managers into mere tacticians stymied by the consequences of a lack of vision that usually overlooks their strategic objectives. However, it is true that such behaviour does produce results. Fed on constant knee-jerk reactions to competition and repeated promotional work to stimulate sales, and stumbling from one corrective advertising campaign to the next, the brand is kept alive like a patient on a drip and artificial respiration. In many cases, though, the main problems of ageing continue to take hold. They may be masked by the cortège of tactics employed by the attendant doctors, but they are nonetheless entirely real; until at last the day comes when the age-induced terminal decline begins and nothing seems to have any effect any more. All it takes is for any one of these tactics to fail, and the ageing, which has until now been kept at bay, takes the upper hand in this already-lost game of hide-and-seek. Perhaps a magician would be capable of some amazing feat even at this late stage, but we do not expect magic from strategists – only strategy.

Such irresponsible behaviour is what Lewis Gediman, CEO of The Gediman Research Group describes as 'frenetic brand management'. He sees this as one of the three main factors (along with a lack of a clearly-implemented strategy and a decline in enthusiasm for the brand) that cause the brand to age. Day after day, the brand writes its own history. This history is a part of its identity. By protecting and promoting this identity, the brand has now become an essential point of reference, a seal of quality, a signature promoting confidence, and a guarantee of stability to consumers who every day become more aware of the highly unstable world in which they live. A failure to take account of this – either consciously or subconsciously – amounts to taking a serious gamble with the brand, running the risk of creating inconsistency in the messages it gives out and/or bringing about such a violent change that it will frighten off even the most faithful among the core target market. Even worse, as the results of work by Wernerfelt (1988) and Wernerfelt and Montgomery (1992) have shown, some consumers could end up blaming the brand for having abused their confidence in it.

A good brand manager is neither an extraordinarily gifted tactician nor an exceptional strategist. Rather, a good brand manager is one who is able to combine both exceptional strategy *and* inspired tactics to form a single coherent, synergistic and potent whole. This implies a long-term view of the brand equity, and therefore requires the support of the company managers to make this possible. Good strategic management of this brand equity therefore presupposes that it is possible to protect this vision on a daily basis, using operational tactics that are relevant, regularly updated and appropriate for handling the vagaries of fate, without damaging the basic foundations of the brand's identity. It is a perpetual tightrope; a constant challenge; an unequal fight. And yet the brand represents the most powerful lever of potential growth available to the marketer. Protecting it is a duty. Controlling it is an urgent need. The reward for constant effort will be its mastery.

Sitting side by side in the proposed anti-ageing wheel for the brand, the key elements of the anti-ageing strategy to be followed should be viewed as a basic minimum set of necessary parallel objectives the exact nature of which will naturally vary depending on the type of company, the nature of its business, its environment and each of the brand's individual characteristics. These objectives must therefore be considered as warning signs to be monitored tirelessly, in a way which is best suited to the specific case of the brand involved. All that matters is to remember that when united, they form the brand's main shield against the ravages of time. If any one of them is forgotten or neglected, then the brand's entire protection against the effects of ageing is in danger of being compromised. It is up to the brand manager impartially to determine the appropriate weighting and order for these objectives, depending on the specific case in question. However, it should be remembered that ultimately, this order cannot be separated from any of these objectives; attempting to do so could risk ruining all the good work carried out thus far. As we have already pointed out, the battle against the effects of time pits us against adversaries of extremely unequal power. Time will always have the advantage. The brand manager must do everything possible to compensate for his or her natural weakness by implementing initiatives that have objective goals, and also closely adhere to a coherent, exhaustive, basic plan of action. Only once the basic framework of this primary shield has been securely defended can there be any hope of overall protection, in which the vigilance of the brand manager can ultimately enable the brand to make its way through time without suffering time's negative effects.

Danielle Rapoport, psycho-sociologist, DRC Manager, Paris

By its very nature, a brand – which is a symptom of the point of meeting between the company which creates it and the consumer who buys it – changes, and such a living organism creates an imprint of its place and time and expresses what makes it different. A brand can age if it fails to adapt to the requirements of individual consumers and has lost its ability to be chosen and to provide 'intangible added value' because it has become less desirable and less differentiated. A brand ages if it no longer has anything to say or any ability to inspire dreams, or if its intangible capital – which provides the true point of emotional and pragmatic contact with a product and a company – has disappeared. However, a brand which has 'aged' is not necessarily doomed. It needs to be energized in a way which is consistent with the historical values of the brand...

A brand should be thought of as the need to mark out an individual, exclusive territory, which is to be protected as such, knowing that it can only exist through a recognition of another party (the consumer). Every brand must therefore clearly state the 'metaconcept' interwoven with its history, and the factors which differentiate it, and express the above through the coherent overall use of its signs. To manage brand equity – at least at a symbolic and imaginative level – you must be attentive, vigilant, prepared to give the brand mobility and to create opportunities for it, and ready to engage the consumer in a meaningful way by creating a space in which that consumer can experience pleasure, effectiveness and confidence.

Because its vocation is to exist indefinitely, a brand deserves the same respect and attention which it must itself show to the consumers who give it life. 'Brand equity' refers to the brand's ability to garner consumer loyalty, acting as a 'gift to the brand', allowing it to assume an indefinite lifespan, provided that the brand has implemented a relationship based on appropriate proximity.

A badly-implemented facelift – one which does not take the brand's profound character into consideration – would be just as disastrous as doing nothing. With regard to ageing, we should be asking ourselves: compared to what? We should analyse the causes of ageing and play our trump cards of creativity, daring and innovation within the limits laid down by the profound structure of the brand's character. 'Rejuvenation' stems both from the signals issued by the brand and the reception they are given by consumers… who, in some cases, may lament the fact that their faithful old points of reference have changed! Indeed, the risk for the rejuvenated brand is that it may lose its 'soul', its personality and the confidence of its consumers. Every brand should be asking itself questions about the purpose – as well as the direction – of its 'rejuvenation'; this will be different in each case.

A real brand is not a clone!

Conclusion

Qu'as-tu fait, ô toi que voilà
Pleurant sans cesse,
Dis, qu'as-tu fait, toi que voilà
De ta jeunesse?

[What have you done, O you that stand
Weeping without end,
Tell me, O you that weep, what have you done
With your youth?]
Paul Verlaine
Sagesse, III, 6; 1874, 1880

This book does not claim to be the ultimate collection of anti-ageing recipes for the brand, each guaranteed to be 100 per cent effective. It is simply intended as a wake-up call for the brand manager with regard to the potential ravages of time on the brand, the nature of the main ageing factors lying in wait to attack, the appropriate rejuvenation strategies to combat these attacks and the basic principles for implementing a preventative anti-ageing strategy. Effective marketing will never be satisfied with the mechanical implementation of standard solutions. It is therefore the brand manager's responsibility to take full account of the danger that threatens the brand, and to make use of the available fruits of experience and the ideas offered here, to devise a suitable battle plan applicable to his or her own situation, providing the best possible protection for the brand and the priceless capital it represents.

It is overly optimistic to expect to be able – now or in the future – to avoid all the perils associated with a brand's ageing, even if Professor Ronald Mallett of the University of Connecticut believes that the key to time travel is to acquire the ability to slow down light itself. Indeed, theoretically speaking, there would seem to be no reason why we could not adopt such an approach to the problem, and maybe one day we will be able to twist space to such an extent that we really can travel through time, with all the chaotic potential consequences that such progress implies. However, as mysterious and captivating as that may appear, is it truly desirable? At present, we have no means of stopping time or turning the clock back. And so, for our brand, the solution must be sought elsewhere – and sought with even more devoted application, given that no miracle hormone cocktail can be bought and added to the armoury of the perfect small-scale marketer. We can only dream of sales melatonin, advertising Viagra and marketing DHEA superhormones, particularly since we are still unable to identify the brand's own legendary Chromosome 4 region, if indeed we ever will. On a more serious note, we can look at the problem in a different way, attempting to do everything possible to allow the brand to 'dodge' a factor the power and inevitability of which have been implicitly recognized. However, we are forced to note that just like humans, not all brands seem to be naturally protected against ageing in the same way; especially since it is clear that the understanding of this issue varies considerably from one brand to another.

There is no secret formula that will procure eternal youth for a brand; only the easy (and yet difficult) prescriptions of vigilance and hard work. How many brand managers have been guilty, with no mitigating circumstances in their favour, of allowing their brands to age – sometimes all the way to the bitter and now inevitable end? Calines was once a fine name for a brand of nappies. Radiola had not only the legitimacy of its own history but also a meaningful name with great potential for international use. Was the toothpaste brand Signal, chosen by Unilever, more effective than Très-Près, Gibbs or Pepsodent? Would it have been fun to listen to a CD on a player made by Teppaz, a famous record player brand of yesteryear? Felix Potin was famous in France for having been the inventor of home deliveries. If it had not disappeared a few years too early, could its network of small stores not have provided a very useful service for the 'last mile' aspect of the e-commerce industry? On paper, why should Apricot have stood less chance than Apple of becoming a famous computer brand? It is true that brands such as Maypo oatmeal, Nervine sedatives, Talbot and Datsun cars, Burma Shave shaving foam, Rinso washing powder, Postum coffee, the Bon Ami cleaner, and Goupil and Victor computers have now totally or virtually vanished. Some of these would optimistically claim that they are merely in a very deep hibernation, awaiting their fabulous resurrection. The choice of extinction, even after very careful analysis, is never a simple one because, as we have seen, it is rare that ageing can be attributed to just one factor. If this was the case, the rejuvenation remedy would then be readily identifiable and easy to implement in most cases. However, this is not the case; and some brands disappear from the shelves or are pushed into oblivion by a brand manager powerless to halt their ageing. Fortunately, though, a brand only really dies when it finally disappears from the collective memory – and this effectively never happens in a now-global market, despite what Naomi Klein may have to say on this matter.

The globalization of markets has made some brands omnipresent, and – rightly or wrongly – some of these have been rejected by consumers who are worried or frustrated by their deliberately or inadvertently imperialistic tendencies. This creates a gap that could increasingly be filled by small brands wishing to attract those same consumers by appearing to be closer, more accessible and more responsible. There would then be nothing surprising in the fact that many old brands have been rejuvenated to occupy markets – even if they are only niche markets – in which consumers are looking for diversity, renewal, nostalgia and closeness. Such brands may therefore one day hope to emerge once again from the dusty folders in which they have often been lovingly stored away or simply left to languish. For thousands of others, their sad fate will be depressingly confirmed year upon year, in many cases never even having been given a chance to defend themselves. When a brand grows old, there is often a strong temptation to hand the responsibility for its management over to the less talented employees of the company, so as not to 'waste' precious resources on suicide missions. In addition, this decision is usually accompanied by a cap on the resources for managing this declining brand. This is a serious error that unconsciously distances the brand from the often significant investments it enjoyed throughout its former life. Rejuvenating a brand calls for much greater talent than launching a new one; for in the latter case, the brand manager has a licence to invent freely.

In October 1990, thanks to Tim Berners-Lee, the internet assumed a new dimension as the world wide web spread to cover the whole planet. It thus entered Year 1, following on from the Year 0 of scientific and military use. The DNS (Domain Name System) naming register allowed electronic addresses identifying the hosting location of an internet site to be given a genuine name in addition to a series of identifying numbers and dots. Millions of names were registered; and ever since, each new extension – gTLD: generic Top Level Domain – publicized by the media adds fuel to the fire of covetousness. However, of the approximately 32 million (domain) names registered at the time of writing, a mere quarter are actually in use. (It may also be noted that several million of these '.com' brands died when their registration came up for renewal between 2001 and 2002. Because their owners were not using them and/or had not found anyone to sell them on to, they became available once again, but ceased to appear in registrars' lists. The internet wave had passed, and had carried these creations of the digital era away with it.) The remaining three-quarters have been placed in reserve, or are simply dead of premature ageing. The internet was rapidly described as a meta-medium that shrinks distance, bringing together places and information often thousands of miles apart at the click of a button. Remember also that the internet contracts time too; for by nature, there is no real chronological cycle in cyberspace; and real-world brands are making their way online in increasing numbers. At the same time, the brand manager – the custodian of the brand and the equity it represents – realizes that for this reason he or she must be far more vigilant in order to track down any early signs of ageing. In such cases, the permitted timescale for reaction is now much too short to allow the brand manager enough time for a detailed study and/or to allow him or her to improvise.

No brand is immune to ageing, especially considering the fact that we have all entered a digital information age in which everything is speeding up. There is no absolute anti-ageing remedy, but it is permissible to build a genuine anti-ageing strategy with the intention of protecting the brand against ageing. Reworking a logo or modifying a signature are potentially profitable techniques, provided they are not considered merely as one-off actions divorced from any coherent overall picture. The perceived image of the brand is the entire promise of that brand, conveyed, suggested and transferred. It is the reflection of precisely what constitutes the brand; its positioning, its values, its target market; and if any one of its aspects is undesirable, the reflection will be clouded and the image altered. Only a strategic approach can allow all of these components to be integrated and, more importantly, arranged in a logical and coherent way.

This strategy is not an end in itself, but it does allow the brand manager to work in advance on the characteristics of the brand and on some key components of its environment in order to energize the brand on a lasting basis. Every marketer knows just how costly and difficult the launch of a new brand can be, especially if there is significant competition in the sector in question. However, rejuvenating a brand is even more difficult than launching a new one. Products and services need to be re-examined, retail partners must be convinced at all costs to keep faith with the brand during its rejuvenation, the tide of consumer attitudes towards the brand must be turned around, new customers must be won over while doing everything possible to retain those who still have confidence in the brand, attacks must be dodged from competitors who will generally seize upon the opportunity of this weakness to advance their own positions. And all of this is happening at a time when the affected brand's human, technical and financial resources are generally limited. Most of the time, unfortunately, brand managers are so absorbed in managing the everyday realities of the brand that they overlook, or pay little attention to, the strategic choices they should have been making to prevent the brand from declining.

The anti-ageing strategy is a constant alert mechanism that allows the manager to remain vigilant to the potential factors of ageing and to be able to react effectively and in accordance with the chosen strategy as soon as the first sign of ageing is detected. Of course, the deployment of such a strategy presupposes that the brand equity is being managed on a *day-to-day* basis. The brand is precious. It can allow itself to grow older, and can even sometimes take advantage of this age. Its past, its achievements, its experience and all of its history may provide very positive opportunities for promotion, as well as valuation factors, provided this age capital is strategically managed and presented in an attractive way. By contrast, it cannot allow itself to age – or, to put it another way, to be perceived as an old brand – for to do so is to run the risk of creating a gradual or sudden loss of interest among an increasing share of its clients.

In theory, the consumer has no reason not to like the brand – but the trick is to give him or her something to love about it. Only by applying itself daily to the task will the brand be able to continue meeting the consumer's needs precisely in terms of innovation, product range, retail method, price and, of course, advertising. The consumer likes 'his' or 'her' brands primarily because he or she likes their identity and everything they represent. They correspond to his or her values (conscious or subconscious), expectations (secret or expressed), needs (actual or redundant) and priorities (current and future). This identity forms the entire soul of the brand and everything it represents. It is up to the brand manager to do everything possible to ensure that time does not alter one or more of its components. The fact that Tesco overtook Sainsbury's in the UK in the late 1990s was not attributable to its projection of a 'better' image. The image of Tesco remained more downmarket than that of Sainsbury's. Instead, it was able to dominate the sector because of its attentiveness to meeting the needs of its consumers precisely and working hard to achieve their satisfaction.

Managing a brand's capital is an absolutely fundamental task. More important than just a name and/or a logo, a brand is a promise – a promise that, if it is constantly maintained, will gradually play its part in building the brand's equity. This gives an idea of the constantly renewed effort that will be called for each time an opportunity arises to promote the brand. This promise is a value chain linking the brand to its consumers, but also to its employees, suppliers, clients, partners, government contacts, etc. If just one link is weakened, the entire chain will become unable to fulfil its role; its function; its mission. Every opportunity for communication, regardless of level, between the brand and one of its points of contact must also be an opportunity for strengthening a win-win relationship that will ensure that the brand enjoys a high-quality image. Yes, the brand has to be profitable, because profit forms the very foundation of its economic activity in a market economy. However, it cannot ultimately be profitable if its contact does not win each time as well. The brand does not exist merely through the marketing intentions of its manager. In fact, it only exists at all because of its employees, consumers, clients, partners, etc. If they are ever disappointed or dissatisfied, the seeds are sown for an alteration of the brand's image and thus, by definition, of the brand itself.

Ultimately, then, perhaps, certain brands age simply because their managers have given up the unequal struggle when faced with the enormous job at hand and its need for constant renewal. For requiring the brand manager to reinvent, establish and impose his or her will on a daily basis is truly a Sisyphean task. However, it was clear from the outset that the battle was against Father Time himself. Anyone thinking that the task would be a simple, straightforward one will have been guilty of a level of naïvety as touching as it is ignorant. Given that the opposing parties are of such unequal strength, the initial strategic objective for the battle is to choose, as wisely as possible, the most favourable battlefield available, while at the same time turning each company contact into a valuable ally. The brand is, self-evidently, unable to exercise any form of control over its own chronological age and must therefore focus all its efforts on its perceived age, the contributory factors of which may be controlled and managed effectively on the brand's behalf. In this way, ageing stops being a handicap to the brand, and instead becomes a challenge as to how exactly to age. It may be a sizeable challenge, but it is not an impossible one; and it is likely to provide ample motivation for the thoughtful, courageous brand manager.

In the end, ageing could turn out to be rather a good thing!

References

Aaker, D A (1991) *Managing Brand Equity*, Free Press, Arial NY

Aaker, D A (1997) Should you take your brand to where the action is?, *Harvard Business Review*, **75** (5), September–October, pp 135–43

Aaker, D A and Joachimsthaler E (2000) *Brand Leadership*, Free Press, New York

Aaker, J L (1997) Dimensions of brand personality, *Journal of Marketing Research* **XXIV**, August, pp 347–56

Adaval, R (2003) How good gets better and bad gets worse: understanding the impact of affect on evaluations of known brands, *Journal of Consumer Research*, **30** (3), December, pp 252–67

Agres, S J (1990) Emotion in advertising: an agency's view, in *Emotion in Advertising*, S J Agres, J A Edell and T M Dubitsky, Quorum, New York

Anschuetz, N (1997) Point of view: Building Brand popularity: The myth of segmenting to brand success, *Journal of Advertising Research*, **37** (1), January–February, pp 63–66

Baldinger, A (1993) Measuring brand equity for enduring profitable growth: the research contribution, Actes du séminaire ARF, *Brand Equity Research, Advertising Research Foundation*, New York

Balmer, J M T and Greyser, S A (2003) *Revealing the Corporation: Perspectives on identity, image, reputation, corporate branding and corporate-level marketing*, Routledge, London

Barak, B (1987) Cognitive age: a new multi-dimensional approach to measuring age identity, *International Journal of Ageing and Human Development*, **25** (2), pp 109–25

Barak, B and Schiffman L G (1980) Cognitive Age: a non-chronological age variable, in *Advances in Consumer Research*, ed F J Olson, Association for Consumer Research, Ann Arbor MI

Barthes, R (1967) *Système de la Mode*, Seuil, Paris
Barwise, P (1993) Brand equity: snark or boojum, *International Journal of Research in Marketing*, **10**, March, pp 93–104
Barwise, P and Meehan, S (2004) *Simply Better: Winning and keeping customers by delivering what matters most*, Harvard Business School Press, Boston MA
Batra, R and Homer, P M (2004) The situational impact of brand image beliefs, *Journal of Consumer Psychology*, **14** (3), pp 318–30
Baumgarth, C (2004) Evaluations of co-brands and spill-over effects: further empirical results, *Journal of Marketing Communications*, **10** (2), June, pp 115–32
Bendapudi, N and Bendapudi, V (2005) Creating the living brand, *Harvard Business Review*, **83** (5), May, pp 124–32
Benezra, K (1996) Silver bullets & brass rings, *Brandweek*, **37** (19), 6 May
Bennett, R and Rundel-Thiele, S (2005) The brand loyalty cycle: implications for marketers, *Journal of Brand Management*, **12** (4), April, pp 250–63
Berens, G, Van Riel, C B M and Van Bruggen, G H (2005) Corporate associations and consumer product responses: the moderating role of corporate brand dominance, *Journal of Marketing*, **69** (3), July, pp 35–48
Berry, L L (2000) Cultivating service brand equity, *Journal of the Academy of Marketing Research*, **28** (1), Winter, pp 128–37
Berry, N C (1988) Revitalizing brands, *Journal of Consumer Marketing*, **5** (3), pp 15–21
Blichfeldt, B S (2005) On the development of brand and line extensions, *Journal of Brand Management*, **12** (3), February, pp 177–90
Brown, S, Kozinets, R V and Sherry, J F Jr (2003) Teaching old brands new tricks: retro branding and the revival of brand meaning, *Journal of Marketing*, **67** (3), July, pp 19–33
Carpenter, G S, Glazer, R and Nakamoto, K (1994) Meaningful brands from meaningless differentiation: the dependence on irrelevant attributes, *Journal of Marketing Research,* **31**, August, pp 339–50
Carrigan, M (1999) The representation of older people in advertisements, *Journal of the Market Research Society*, **41** (3), July, pp 311–26
Carrigan, M and Szmigin, I (1999) Targeting the cognitively young, *Marketing and Research Today*, **28** (1), pp 1–9
Cégarra, J-J and Michel, G (2001) Co-branding: clarification du concept, *Recherche et Applications en Marketing*, **16** (4), pp 57–69
Clancy, K J (2001) Save America's dying brands, *Marketing Management*, **10** (3), September– October, pp 36–41
Coulter, K S and Punj, G N (2004) The effects of cognitive resource requirements availability, and argument quality on brand attitudes, *Journal of Advertising*, **33** (4), Winter, pp 53–64
Dahlén, M and Lange, F (2005) Advertising weak and strong brands: Who gains?, *Psychology & Marketing*, **22** (6), June, pp 473–88

David, A (1998) in *Brands, the New Wealth Creators*, ed S Hart and J Murphy, Interbrand– New York University Press, New York

Davis, S M (2000) *Brand Asset Management: Driving profitable growth through your brands*, Jossey-Bass, San Francisco

De Chernatony, L (2001) An integrated approach to building and strengthening brands, *European Retail Digest*, **9** (1), pp 32–44

De Chernatony, L and McDonald, M H B (1994) *Creating Powerful Brands*, Butterworth-Heinemann, London

Delano, F (1998) *The Omnipowerful Brand*, AmaCom Publications, New York

Desai, K K and Keller, K L (2002) The effects of ingredient branding strategies on host brand extendibility, *Journal of Marketing*, **66** (1), January, pp 73–93

Deutsch, F M, Zalenski, C M and Clark, M E (1986) Is there a double standard of ageing?, *Journal of Applied Psychology*, **16** (9), pp 771–85

Docters, R G (1999) Branding: shotgun or rifle?, *The Journal of Business Strategy*, **20** (4), July– August, pp 9–14

Doods, W B, Monroe, K B and Grewal, D (1991) Effects of price, brand and store information on buyers' product evaluation, *Journal of Marketing Research*, **28**, August, pp 307–19

Duckler, M (2003) Testing your brand limits: How extendible is your brand? A four-step road map can help find the answer, *Marketing Management*, **12** (6), pp 28–33

Duffy, N and Hooper, J (2003) *Passion Branding: Harnessing the power of emotion to build strong brands*, Wiley, Hoboken NJ

Dyson, P, Farr, A and Hollis, N (1996) Understanding, measuring and using brand equity, *Journal of Advertising Research*, **36** (6), November–December, pp 9–21

Edwards, H and Day, D (2005) *Creating Passionbrands: Getting to the heart of branding*, Kogan Page, London

Ehrenberg, A, Barnard, N and Scriven, J (1997) Differentiation or salience, *Journal of Advertising Research*, **37** (6), November–December, pp 7–14

Eliott, R and Wattanasuwan, K (1998) Brands as symbolic resources for the construction of identity, *International Journal of Advertising*, **17** (2), pp 131–44

Eppler, M J and Will, M (2001) Branding knowledge: brand building beyond product and service brands, *Journal of Brand Management*, **8** (6), pp 445–57

Erdem, T and Swait, J (2004) Brand credibility, brand consideration, and choice, *Journal of Consumer Research*, **31** (1), June, pp 191–98

Ewing, T and Fowlds, D A (1995) Renaissance: A case study in brand revitalization and strategic realignment, *Journal of Product and Brand Management*, **4** (3), pp 19–27

Fombrun, C J (2005) Building corporate reputation through CSR initiatives: evolving standards, *Corporate Reputation Review*, **8** (1), Spring, pp 7–11

Fournier, S and Yao, J L (1997) Reviving brand loyalty: a reconceptualization within the framework of consumer–brand relationship, *International Journal of Research in Marketing*, **14**, pp 451–72

Fram, E H and McCarthy, M S (2004) What's not to like? If employees aren't buying your brand, it's important to find out why, *Marketing Management*, **13** (4), July–August, pp 36–40

Franzen, G, Goessens, C, Hoogerbrugge, M, Kappert, C, Schuring, R J and Vogel, M (1999) *Brands &Advertising: How effective advertising effectiveness influences brand equity*, Admap, Henley-on-Thames

Freeman, L (2000) Who are you? Saying a marketing message is part of a branding campaign doesn't make it so, *Marketing News*, 14 February

Gantz, W, Gartenberg, H M and Rainbow, C (1980) Approaching invisibility: the portrayal of the elderly in magazine advertisements, *Journal of Communication*, **30**, Winter, pp 56–60

Garner, R (2005) What's in a name? Persuasion perhaps, *Journal of Consumer Psychology*, **15** (2), pp 108–16

Graham, J R (2001) If there's no brand, there's no business, *Direct Marketing*, **64** (2), pp 58–60

Greco, A J (1989) Representation of the elderly in advertising: crisis or inconsequence?, *Journal of Consumer Marketing*, **6** (1), pp 37–44

Grove, A S (1999) *Only the paranoid survive: How to exploit the crisis points that challenge every company*, Currency, Random House, New York

Guiot, D (1996) *L'âge cognitif: un concept pour le marketing des seniors*, Proceedings of the XIIth AFM International Congress, Poitiers, pp 45–60

Haig, D and Knowles, J (2004) What's in a brand? How to define your brand and determine its value, *Marketing Management*, **13** (3), May–June, pp 22–28

Haig, M (2003) *Brand Failures: The truth about the 100 biggest branding mistakes of all time*, Kogan Page, London

Haig, M (2004) *Brand Royalties: How the world's top 100 brands thrive and survive*, Kogan Page, London

Hamel, G (2000) *Leading the revolution*, Harvard Business Press, Boston MA

Harris, F. and de Chernatony, L (2000) Corporate branding and corporate performance, *European Journal of Marketing*, **35** (3/4), pp 441–56

Hart, S and Murphy, J (eds) (1998) *Brands, the New Wealth Creators*, Interbrand–New York University Press, New York

Hatch, M J and Schultz, M (2001) Are the strategic stars aligned for your corporate brand?, *Harvard Business Review*, **79** (2), February, pp 128–34

Haxthausen, O (2004) Secrets of challenger brands, *Marketing Management*, **13** (3), May–June, pp 34–38

Henderson, P W and Cote, J A (1998) Guidelines for selecting or modifying logos, *Journal of Marketing*, **62**, April, pp 14–30

Holt, D B (2004) *How Brands Become Icons: The principles of cultural branding*, Harvard Business School Press, Boston MA

Humby, C, Hunt, T and Phillips, T (2004) *Scoring Points: How Tesco is winning customer loyalty*, Kogan Page, London

Hupp, O and Powaga, K (2004) Using consumer attitudes to value brands: evaluation of the financial value of brands, *Journal of Advertising Research*, **44** (3), September, pp 225–36

Ind, N (1997) *The Corporate Brand*, New York University Press, New York

James, D (1999) Rejuvenating mature brands can be a stimulating exercise, *Marketing News*, **33** (17), 16 August

Johansson, J K and Ronkainen, I A (2005) The esteem of global brands, *Journal of Brand Management*, **12** (5), June, pp 339–54

Jourdan, P (2001) Le capital marque: proposition d'une mesure individuelle et essai de validation, *Recherche et Applications en Marketing*, **16** (4), pp 3–23

Kapferer, J-N (1998) *Les Marques, Capital de l'Enteprise*, 3rd edn, Éditions d'Organisation, Paris

Kapferer, J-N (2001) *Reinventing the Brand: Can top brands survive the market realities?*, Kogan Page, London

Kapferer, J-N (2004) *The New Strategic Brand Management*, Kogan Page, London

Kapferer, J-N and Laurent, G (1992) *La sensibilité aux marques: Marchés sans marques, marchés à marques*, Éditions d'Organisation, Paris

Kastenholz, J, Kerr, G and Young, C (2004) Focus and fit: advertising and branding join forces to create a star, *Marketing Research*, **16** (1), Spring, pp 16–21

Kates, S M and Goh C (2003) Brand morphing: Implications for advertising theory and practice, *Journal of Advertising*, **32** (1), Spring, pp 59–68

Keiningham, T L, Aksoy, L, Perkins-Munn, T and Vavra, T G (2005) The brand–customer connection, *Marketing Management*, **14** (4), July–August, pp 33–37

Keller, K L (1999) Managing brands for the long run: brand reinforcement and revitalization strategies, *California Management Review*, **41** (3), Spring, pp 102–24

Keller, K L (2001) Brand research imperatives, *Journal of Brand Management*, **9** (1), pp 4–7

Keller, K L (2004) *Strategic Brand Management: Building, measuring and managing brand equity*, 2nd edition, Prentice Hall, Upper Saddle River NJ

Keller, K L (2005) Branding shortcuts, *Marketing Management*, **14** (5), September–October, pp 18–23

Keller, K L and Aaker, D A (1992) The effects of sequential introduction of brand extensions, *Journal of Marketing Research*, **XXIX**, February, pp 35–50

Kim, W C and Mauborgne, R (2004) Blue ocean strategy, *Harvard Business Review*, **82** (10), October, pp 76–84

Klein, N (2000) *No Logo: Taking aim at the brand bullies*, Alfred A. Knopf, Toronto

Kumar, N (2003) Kill a brand, keep a customer, *Harvard Business Review*, **81** (12), December, pp. 86–95

Kumar, P (2005) Brand counterexpositions: the impact of brand extension success versus failure, *Journal of Marketing Research*, **XVII**, May, pp 183–94

Kumar, V. and Ganesh, J (1995) State-of-the-Art in brand equity research: what we know and what needs to be known, *Australasian Journal of Market Research*, **3**, January, pp 4–21

Langmeyer, L (1983) Age role portrayals in magazine advertisements: a content analysis, in *Theories and Concepts in an Era of Change,* ed J H Summery et al, Southern Marketing Association Proceedings, Carbondale IL, pp 286–89

Leand, J (2000) The SGB interview: Angel Martinez, executive vice president & chief marketing officer, Reebok International Ltd., *Sporting Goods Business*, **33** (17), 8 December

Lederer, C and Hill, S (2001) See your brand through your customer's eyes, *Harvard Business Review*, **79** (6), June, pp 125–33

Lee, A Y and Labroo, A A (2004) The effect of conceptual and perceptual fluency on brand evaluation, *Journal of Marketing Research*, **XLI**, May, pp 151–65

Lehu, J-M (2001) *Strategiesdemarque.com*, Éditions d'Organisation, Paris

Lehu, J-M (2003) *Stratégie de Fidélisation*, Éditions d'Organisation, Paris

Lehu, J-M (2004) Back to life! Why do brands grow old and sometimes die and what managers then do: an exploratory qualitative research put into the French context, *Journal of Marketing Communications*, **10** (2), June, pp 133–52

Levine, R, Locke, C, Searls, D and Weinberger, D (2000) *The Cluetrain Manifesto:The end of business as usual*, Basic Books, Perseus Books, Philadelphia PA

Lewi, G (2003) *Les Manques, Mythologie du Quotidien,* Pearson, Paris

Lewi, G (2005) *Branding Management*, Pearson, Paris

Lindgreen, A and Swaen, V (2005) Corporate citizenship: Let not relationship marketing escape the management toolbox, *Corporate Reputation Review*, **7** (4), Winter, pp 346–63

Lindstrom, M (2005) *Brand Sense: How to build powerful brands through touch, taste, smell, sight and sound*, Kogan Page, London

Liu, S S and Johnson, K F (2005) The automatic country-of-origin effects on brand judgments, *Journal of Advertising*, **34** (1), Spring, pp 85–97

Loden D J (1991) *Megabrands: How to build them, how to beat them*, Irwin, Burr Ridge IL

Loken, B and John, D R (1993) Diluting brand beliefs: When do brand extensions have a negative impact?, *Journal of Marketing*, **57**, July, pp 71–84

Louro, M J and Cunha, P V (2001) Brand management paradigms, *Journal of Marketing Management*, **17** (7/8), pp 849–76

Maathuis, O, Rodenburg, J and Sikkel, D (2004) Credibility, emotion or reason?, *Corporate Reputation Review*, **6** (4), Winter, pp 333–45

Maklan, S and Knox, S (1998) *Competing on Value – Bridging the gap between brand and customer value*, Financial Times Management, Prentice Hall, Upper Saddle River NJ

Masson, D (2000) Ces marques victimes de leur succès, *Stratégies* (1153), 30 June

Mathur, A, Sherman, E and Schiffman, L G (1998) Opportunities for marketing travel services to new-age elderly, *Journal of Services Marketing*, **12** (4), pp 265–77

Mazis, M B, Ringold, D J, Perry, E D and Denman, D W (1992) Perceived age and attractiveness of models in cigarette advertisements, *Journal of Marketing*, **56** (1), pp 22–37

McAlexander J H, Schouten, J W and Koenig, H F (2002) Building brand community, *Journal of Marketing*, **66** (1), January, pp 38–54

Merunka, D, Changeur, S and Bourgeat, P (1999) Les limites de la concurrence entre les marques: pratiques et limites, *Recherche et Applications en Marketing*, **14** (4), pp 9–22

Michel, G (2004) *Au cœur de la marque: créer, gérer, développer et évaluer sa marque*, Dunod, Paris

Michon, C (2000) La marque: son röle stratégique au coeur du marketing, *Revue Française du Marketing*, **176**, pp 7–21

Montgomery, C A and Wernerfelt, B (1992) Risk reduction and umbrella branding, *Journal of Business*, **65** (1), pp 31–50

Muehling, D D and Sprott, D E (2004) The power of reflection: an empirical examination of nostalgia advertising effects, *Journal of Advertising*, **33** (3), Fall, pp 25–35

Netchine, S (1994) Les racines de la psychologie de l'enfant, in *Cours de psychologie*, vol 2, ed R Ghiglione and J-F Richard, Dunod, Paris

O'Cass, A and Grace, D (2004) Service brands and communication effects, *Journal of Marketing Communications*, **10** (4), December, pp 241–54

Oakenfull, G, Blair, E, Gelb, B and Dacin, P (2000) Measuring brand meaning, *Journal of Advertising Research*, **40** (5), September–October, pp 43–53

Peterson, R A and Ross, I (1972) How to name new brands, *Journal of Advertising*, **12**, pp 29–34

Phau, I and Lau, K C (2001) Brand personality and consumer self-expression: Single or dual carriageway?, *Journal of Brand Management*, **8** (6), pp 428–44

Plutchick, R (1980) *Emotion: A Psychoevolutionary Synthesis*, Harper & Row, New York

Porter, M E (1998) *Competitive Advantage: Creating sustaining superior performance*, Free Press, Arial NY

Posavac, S S, Sanbonmatsu, D M, Kardes, F R and Fitzsimons, G J (2004) The brand positivity effect: When evaluation confers preference, *Journal of Consumer Research*, **31** (3), December, pp 643–51

Pringle, H and Thompson, M (1999) *Brand Spirit*, Wiley–Saatchi & Saatchi, Chichester

Ragas, M W and Bolivar, J B (2002) *The Power of Cult Branding: How 9 magnetic brands turned customers into loyal followers (and yours can, too!)*, Crown Business, New York

Randazzo, S (1993) *Mythmaking on Madison Avenue*, Probus, Chicago IL

Rao, V R, Agarwal, M K and Dahlhoff, D (2004) How is manifest branding strategy related to the intangible value of the corporation?, *Journal of Marketing*, **68** (4), October, pp 126–41

Recker, J. and Kathman, J (2001) The role of consumer research in the brand design process, *Design Management Journal*, **12** (3), pp 70–75

Richins, M L (1997) Measuring emotions in the consumption experience, *Journal of Consumer Research*, **24** (2), September, pp 127–46

Ries, A and Ries, L (2004) *The Origin of Brands*, Harper, New York

Ries, A and Trout, J (2000) *Positioning: The battle for your mind*, McGraw-Hill, New York

Roberts, K (2004) *Lovemarks*, powerHouse Books, New York

Roberts, S D and Zhou, N (1997) The 50 and older characters in the advertisements of modern maturity: growing older, getting better?, *Journal of Applied Gerontology*, **16** (2), pp 208–17

Romaniuk, J and Sharp, B (2004) Conceptualizing and measuring brand salience, *Marketing Theory*, **4** (4), December, pp 327–42

Rust, R T, Zeithaml, V A and Lemon, K N (2004) Customer-centered brand management, *Harvard Business Review*, **82** (9), September, pp 110–18

Ruth, J A (2001) Promoting a brand's emotion benefits: the influence of emotion categorization processes on consumer evaluations, *Journal of Consumer Psychology*, **11** (2), pp 99–114

Ryder, I (2004) Anthropology and the brand, *Journal of Brand Management*, **11** (5), Special issue, May, pp 346–57

Saporito, B (1986) *Has-been brands go back to work, Fortune*, **113**, 9 April

Sawchuck K A (1995) From gloom to boom: age, identity and target marketing, in *Images of Ageing: Cultural representations of later life*, ed M Featherstone and A Wernick, Routledge, London, pp. 173–87

Schiffman, L G and Sherman, E (1991) Value orientations of new-age elderly: the coming of an ageless market, *Journal of Business Research*, **22**, pp 187–94

Schultz, D E (2001) Getting to the heart of the brand, *Marketing Management*, **10** (3), September–October, pp 8–9

Schultz, D E and Schultz, H F (2000) How to build a billion dollar business-to-business brand, *Marketing Management*, **9** (2), Summer, pp 22–28

Schultz, D E, Tannenbaum, S I and Lauterborn, R F (1993) *Integrated Marketing Communications: Putting it together & making it work*, NTC, Lincolnwood IL

Semans, D (2004) The brand you save: Improving the brand is cheaper than watching it suffer a slow death, *Marketing Management*, **13** (3), May–June, pp 29–32

Sengupta, J and Fitzsimons, G J (2000) The effects of analysing reasons for brand preferences: disruption or reinforcement?, *Journal of Marketing Research*, **XXXVII**, August, pp 318–30

Shipley, D, Hooley, G J and Wallace, S (1988) The brand name development process, *International Journal of Advertising*, **7**, pp 253–66

Simoes, C, Dibb, S and Fisk, R P (2005) Managing corporate identity: an internal perspective, *Journal of the Academy of Marketing Science*, **33** (2), Spring, pp 153–68

Smith, R B and Moschis, G P (1985) A socialisation perspective on selected consumer characteristics of the elderly, *Journal of Consumer Affairs*, **19**, Summer, pp 74–95

Sommier, E (2000) *Mode, le Monde en Mouvement*, Village Mondial, Paris

Sordet, C, Paysant, J and Brosselin, C (2002) *Les Marques de Distributeurs Jouent dans la Cour des Grands*, Editions d'Organisation, Paris

Spears, N and Singh, S N (2004) Measuring attitude toward the brand and purchase intentions, *Journal of Current Issues and Research in Advertising*, **XXVI** (2), Fall, pp 53–66

Srinivasan, S and Pauwels, K (2004) Who benefits from store brand entry?, *Marketing Science*, **23** (3), Summer, pp 364–90

Stephens, N (1991) Cognitive age: a useful concept for advertising?, *Journal of Advertising*, **20** (4), pp 37–49

Stuart, Helen and Jones, C (2004) Corporate branding in marketspace, *Corporate Reputation Review*, **7** (1), Spring, pp 84–93

Travis, D (2000) *Emotional Branding*, PrimaVenture, Roseville CA

Trout, J (2001) *Big Brands: Big trouble*, Wiley, New York

Upshaw, L B (1995) *Building Brand Identity*, Wiley, New York

Van Auken, B (2004) *The Brand Management Checklist: Proven tools and techniques for creating winning brands, 2nd edition*, Kogan Page, London

Van Auken, S and Barry, T E (1995) An assessment of the trait validity of cognitive age measures, *Journal of Consumer Psychology*, **4** (2), pp 107–32

Variot, J-F (2002) *La Marque Post-publicitaire*, Village Mondial, Paris

Villas-Boas J M (2004) Consumer learning, brand loyalty, and competition, *Marketing Science*, **23** (1), Winter, pp 134–45

Vincent, L (2002) *Legendary Brands: Unleashing the power of storytelling to create a winning market strategy*, Dearborn Trade/Kaplan, Chicago IL

Wansink B (1994) Developing and validating useful consumer prototypes, *Journal of Targeting, Measurement and Analysis for Marketing*, **3** (1), pp 18–30

Wansink, B (1997) Making old brands new, *American Demographics*, **19** (12), December, pp 53–58

Wansink, B (2000) Brand revitalization scorecard, *Brand Marketing*, August, p 78

Washburn, J H, Till, B D and Priluck, R (2004) Brand alliance and customer-based brand equity effects, *Psychology & Marketing*, **21** (7), July, pp 487–508

Wedel, M and Zhang, J (2004) Analysing brand competition across subcategories, *Journal of Marketing Research*, **XLI**, November, pp 448–56

Wernerfelt, B (1988) Umbrella branding as a signal of new product quality: an example of signaling by posting a bond, *Rand Journal of Economics*, **19** (3), pp 458–66

Wernerfelt, B and Montgomery, C A (1992) Risk reduction and umbrella branding, *Journal of Business*, **65** (1), January, pp 31–50

Wescott Alessandri, S and Alessandri, T (2004) Promoting and protecting corporate identity: the importance of organizational and industry context, *Corporate Reputation Review*, **7** (3), Fall, pp 252–68

Wetlaufer, S (2001) The perfect paradox of Star Brands: an interview with Bernard Arnault of LVMH, *Harvard Business Review*, **79** (9), October, pp 116–23

Whitlark, D B and Smith, S M (2004) Pick and choose: pick data holds promise for measuring brand performance, *Marketing Research*, **16** (4), Spring, pp 8–14

Woods, R (2004) Exploring the emotional territory for brands, *Journal of Consumer Behaviour*, **3** (4), June, pp 388–403

Ye, G and Van Raaij, W F (2004) Brand equity: extending brand awareness and liking with signal detection theory, *Journal of Marketing Communications*, **10** (2), June, pp 95–114

Zhou, N. and Chen, M Y T (1992) Marginal life after 49: a preliminary study of the portrayal of older people in Canadian consumer magazine advertising, *International Journal of Advertising*, **11**, pp 343–54

Index

ALSO AVAILABLE FROM KOGAN PAGE

"It is the tremendous variety and diversity of venues 'visited' that make this tour so exciting."
Brand Strategy

0 7494 4573 4 Paperback 2006

Sign up to receive regular email updates on Kogan Page books:
www.kogan-page.co.uk/signup.aspx and visit our website:

www.kogan-page.co.uk

KOGAN PAGE